Narrating European Society

Narrating European Society

Toward a Sociology of European Integration

Hans-Jörg Trenz

LEXINGTON BOOKS
Lanham • Boulder • New York • London

Published by Lexington Books
An imprint of The Rowman & Littlefield Publishing Group, Inc.
4501 Forbes Boulevard, Suite 200, Lanham, Maryland 20706
www.rowman.com

Unit A, Whitacre Mews, 26-34 Stannary Street, London SE11 4AB

Parts of this book were originally published as Trenz, Hans-Joerg, "The Saga of Euro-peanisation: On the Narrative Construction of a European Society," in Boerner, S., and Eigmueller, M. (eds), *European Integration, Processes of Change and the National Experience*, New York, NY: Palgrave Macmillan, 2015, 207–227.

British Library Cataloguing in Publication Information Available

Library of Congress Cataloging-in-Publication Data

Names: Trenz, Hans-Jörg, author.
Title: Narrating European society : toward a sociology of European integration / Hans-Jörg Trenz.
Description: Lanham : Lexington Books, [2016] | Includes bibliographical references and index.
Identifiers: LCCN 2015044091 (print) | LCCN 2015046012 (ebook) | ISBN 9781498527057 (cloth : alk. paper) | ISBN 9781498527064 (Electronic) | ISBN 9781498527071 (pbk:alk, paper)
Subjects: LCSH: European federation. | Regionalism—Europe. | Institution building—Europe. | Social integration—Europe. | Europe—Economic integration.
Classification: LCC JN15 .T746 2015 (print) | LCC JN15 (ebook) | DDC 341.242—dc23 LC record available at http://lccn.loc.gov/2015044091

∞™ The paper used in this publication meets the minimum requirements of American National Standard for Information Sciences Permanence of Paper for Printed Library Materials, ANSI/NISO Z39.48-1992.

Printed in the United States of America

Contents

Preface and Acknowledgments   vii

Introduction: The Uniqueness That Binds   xi

1   Integration of What?: Toward a European Society or the
    Europeanization of National Societies?   1
2   The Triumph of Europe: Europeanization as a Success Story   31
3   Banal Europeanization   55
4   From Triumph to Trauma: Resistance to Europeanization   79
5   The Crisis of Europeanization   113

Conclusion: An Overview of the Discursive Field of
    Europeanization: Unified, Fragmented, or Complementary?   149

References   159

Index   177

About the Author   187

Preface and Acknowledgments

This book has been written as a research synthesis. The overall aim is to re-discuss established EU scholarship from the perspective of European society. For that purpose, I outline a sociology of European integration along four main themes or narratives: first, the elite processes of identity construction and the framework of norms and ideas that carries such a construction (together with notions of European identity, EU citizenship, etc.); second, the socialization of European citizens, processes of banal Europeanism, and social transnationalism through everyday cross-border exchanges; third, the mobilization of resistance and Euroscepticism as a fundamental and collectively mobilized opposition to processes of Europeanization; and fourth, the political sociology of crisis, linked not only to financial turmoil but also, more fundamentally, to a legitimation crisis that affects Europe and the democratic nation-state. The European society perspective which I propose in this book is therefore not simply meant as a multi-disciplinary opening of the more narrowly confined EU studies agenda. The sociology of European integration is rather advanced in the form of a dialogue within the European Studies community and its main representatives from political science, law, cultural studies, history, media studies, or ethnology. Sociological theory is in this sense explored with the aim of integrating scientific disciplines and overcoming the fragmentation and increasing specialization within European Studies. What sociologists can offer is to draw attention to the distinctiveness of European society and contribute to our understanding of its dynamic unfolding.

In terms of content, the chapters draw on several research projects which I have been involved in over the last ten years. The book is not meant to report full data from these projects (which can be found elsewhere). Given the broad range of themes covered and also the time frame of research, the focus of this book is rather on a critical reflection of the recent history of European integration from euphoria with the constitutional project in early 2000 to the enduring trauma of crisis in the years since 2008. The chapters, in short, describe how the project of European integration was powerfully launched in postwar Europe as a normative venture that comprises polity and society building (chapter 2), how this project became engrained in everyday life histories and experiences of Europeans (chapter 3), how this project became contested and how it confronted resistances (chapter 4), and, ultimately, how it went through its most severe crisis (chapter 5). Even though there is a chronological order in these four narratives, my account of European integration is not meant as a history of decay. Sociology rather needs to account for the multiple structural configurations of European social and political space where the protagonists of European integration position themselves and relate to each other in a dynamic way and in response to diverse publics (or constituents). In confining the discursive field of Europeanization, I will therefore not decide about the instrinsic value of narration nor about success or failure of the project of European integration.

The book has profited enormously from collaboration with colleagues at several universities and within various research networks in Europe. In the first place, I wish to mention the institutional environments within which my research projects were developed. It is my privilege that I have been associated with two of the most excellent places of specialization for the intellectual interpretation of Europe: ARENA, the Centre for European Studies at the University of Oslo, where I have been employed as a research professor since 2005 and with an adjunct position since 2011, and CEMES, the Centre of Modern European Studies at the Faculty of Humanities of University of Copenhagen, where I have been employed since 2011 as a professor with 'special tasks in modern European Studies.' As a member of the EU studies community my ambition has always been to set the mark as the sociologist in these interdisciplinary research environments. The book is the outcome of this dialogue between scientific narratives and of their translation into accounts of a European society. Especially at ARENA, the Centre for European Studies of the University of Oslo, I have learned about different ways to relate an institutional perspective and a society perspective of Europeanization and about the importance of confronting the intrinsic normativity of the project of European integration. Among the scholary environments that have supported me over the last years, I ultimately wish to mention the European Political Sociology Research Network 32 within ESA (European Sociological Association) that was established as a self-organized and bottom-up initiative among scholars who made a collective effort to defend a genuinely sociological position within the European studies community. These European study environments are an intrinsic part of the story I am telling in this book as the life stories of Europeans reflect my own life as a mobile EU scholar who travels between these different locations.

A sociology of European integration could not be written without reference to the many people who populate these institutions and make the European Studies Centers lively places for intellectual debate and exchange. I have profited from close collaboration with the following colleagues and friends: At ARENA, I am most thankful to Erik O. Eriksen and John Erik Fossum for their constant wisdom and encouragement and for providing the most supportive research environment. Their appetite for critical thought is legendary, and there are only a few sentences in this book which have not been critically commented on by them in previous versions. Among the many at ARENA with whom I discussed the topics of this book and entered a very intensive and fruitful exchange about how to relate institutional and normative perspectives of European integration, I wish to mention Ian Cooper, Morten Egeberg, Cathrine Holst, Chris Lord, Agustín José Menéndez, Asimina Michailidou, Espen D. H. Olsen, Johan P. Olsen, Marianne Riddervold, Helene Sjursen, and Anne-Elizabeth Stie. At University of Copenhagen, I received support from my colleagues at EURECO, the trans-faculty European research group of University of Copenhagen, in particular, from my 'Eureco professor' colleagues Rebecca Adler-Nissen, Ben Rosamond, Mikael Rask Madsen, and Marlene Wind as well as Niklas Olsen and Morten Rasmussen at CEMES. Thirdly, my gratitude goes to the European Political Sociology Research Network of ESA (European Sociological Association) for connecting me with sociologists all over Europe who share my interest in European society. I wish to thank all members of the ESA board and their former chairs Carlo Ruzza and Virginie Guiraudon for their constructive collaboration. A special thanks goes to Carlo Ruzza for giving me refuge at the University of Trento in the final phase of writing this book.

As researchers involved in collaborative projects, we strongly depend on the support by our university administration and management. I wish to thank Marit Eldholm and Geir Kværk at ARENA, University of Oslo, and Majka Holm and Lene Raben-Levetzau at the University of Copenhagen for keeping our institutions running, organizing conferences, and helping us to expand our research networks.

I have also greatly enjoyed the highly creative collaborative writing experience with several colleagues across Europe. In particular, I have gained inspirations from my longtime cooperation with John Erik Fossum and Asimina Michailidou. My biggest thanks goes to them for their enthusiasm, encouragement, and friendship during these productive years. The long list of co-authors further include Nadine Bernhard, Maximilian Conrad, Pieter de Wilde, Deniz Duru, Klaus Eder, Irena Fiket, Magdalena Góra, Virginie Guiraudon, Erik Jentges, Ulrike Liebert, Agustín José Menéndez, Espen D. H. Olsen, Guri Rosén, Carlo Ruzza, Paul Statham, and Regina Vetters.

The final drafting of the manuscript took place at the University of Copenhagen and has been supported by Eurochallenge (Europe and New Global Challenges), a transfaculty research project that receives funding from the University of Copenhagen 2016 grants and runs from 2013 to 2017.

Some of the ideas developed in this volume have been tested out in a previous book chapter under the title "The Saga of Europeanisation: On the Narrative Construction of a European Society," published in Börner, S., and Eigmüller, M. (eds): *European Integration, Processes of Change and the National Experience* (Basingstoke: Palgrave Macmillan), 207–227. I wish to thank Palgrave Macmillan for permission to reproduce the text from this chapter. Last but not least, I am indebted to the anonymous reviewers at Lexington for their thorough remarks on the entire book manuscript.

Introduction

The Uniqueness That Binds

Tales about Europe differ, but in all such tales, Europe has been a site of adventure (Bauman 2004: 3). Such adventures—whether the kidnapping of princess Europe by Zeus, the conquests of ancient empires, the crusades, and the discoveries—are told as stories of movement and travel between distant places. Europe has, first and foremost, been linked to the imagination of a land stretching beyond the local and the activity of distinct peoples, who left their sedentary lives behind. Europe is not *heimat*; Europe is departure. Yet Europe is also associated with a new form of imagining the social beyond the private and the familiar life. The story of Europe is told as a collective adventure requiring cooperation and socialization among these distinct people, who are different in origins but united in collective endeavor. This is the founding myth of European civilization as a cooperative adventure of the pilgrims, the crusaders, and the missionaries, who were fellow travelers in foreign lands as well as individual heroes in their quest for the unique. The history of European civilization can be told then as a sequence of adventures of collective undertakings by Europeans.

The founding myth of Europe as departure and as collective adventure explains some of the difficulties associated with intellectual efforts to establish the core idea of what Europe stands for. There is no fixed schedule that coordinates the travel dates, and there is no travel guide. Neither is there a common point of departure, nor can there be agreement as to the destination of travel. This does not mean that the question of 'what Europe stands for' cannot be raised. To the contrary, and throughout history, we find continual effort to harmonize the schedule, to set rules for fellow travelers, and to envisage an ultimate destination (or a *finalité*, as this has been labeled in more recent EU parlance). Europeans are familiar with these contestations of their trajectories. They are experienced fellow travelers who know how to steer a boat on unknown seas. The metaphor for expressing this inconclusive contestation of the common itinerary was found in the formula of a *unity in diversity*.

In Greek and Roman mythology, the uniqueness that binds was incorporated into the plurality of gods, who were strong and diverse characters fighting against each other but also bound and constrained in numerous ways by their mythological unity and coexistence. Ancient Rome established a highly successful and long-lasting form of this cultural and political unity: the empire, which represented a vast diversity of populations, languages, and semi-autonomous regions or cities simultaneously. The Roman Empire's 'unity in diversity' form of political authority lasted for a record period (in European history) of five centuries. There is even a concrete date for the fall of the Roman Empire (AD 476), but despite the dramatic changes in Europe's territorial and political landscape, there is also continuity and even expansion of cultural and spiritual unity. Christianity, which stood for the new transcendental order, provided an even stronger (monotheistic) formula for spreading the core idea of a 'unity in diversity.' The Christian god himself was conceived as a 'unity in diversity,' as a 'holy trinity' of distinct persons, imbued with one essence. Building on this core symbolism, the new monotheistic order remained compatible with internal diversity while at the same time allowing for sharper external delimitation. The realm of believers could now be internally differentiated and externally demarcated. At the same time, the Christian faith was conceived as universal, represented by one church and its claim to truth. This included, most importantly, a spiritual and political program of expansion and conversion. Europeans could now take on a double role: They continued to embrace the world by being travelers and conquerors, but they also took a step back as defenders of a joint heritage, as successors of the empire, and as protectors from the danger of intrusion from the outside. The meaning of Europe could then alternate between inclusion and exclusion. The 'otherness' of Islam allowed for a clear demarcation against the outside while maintaining the possibility of 'reconquista' and inclusion of 'otherness' through expansion and conversion. 'Unity in diversity' proved politically powerful as a formula for universal inclusion while at the same time permitting various layers of internal and external delimitation.

Modern European history is mainly told as a story of fragmentation and diversification of Christian Europe's spiritual and political unity, a process introduced by the Reformation and accelerated by the transition from ancient to modern society. European modernity also knew, however, many ways of recombining the spiritual and the political mandate for unification, most powerfully in the idea of the French Revolution and the Enlightenment, which renewed the universal civilizing effort and the call for global expansion. As emphasized in a recent essay by Étienne Balibar, the French Revolution also entrenched a new tension between two different kinds of rights in the constitution of the modern nation-state: equality (the social rights and the guarantee of collective political representation) and liberty (the individual freedom of citizens). This modern proposition of *égaliberté* (Balibar 2014) adds to the premodern proposition of *unity in diversity* as a supplementary formula for the uniqueness that binds Europeans.

Égaliberté also introduced an unrelievable new tension that infused social conflicts and divisions in modern Europe. Modern European history can be written not only in terms of the institutionalization and constitutionalization of *égaliberté* in the system of rights and the welfare state but also in terms of the continuous contestation of the validity and enactment of these principles in particular sociohistorical constellations. In Europe's sociopolitical development, this institutionalization and constitutionalization of *égaliberté* followed different paths and established particular divisions, which allow for the demarcation of a European sociopolitical space that is different from structures and experiences in other parts of the world, especially the United States (Crouch 1999).

Unity and *égaliberté* became most powerfully implemented as the founding principles of the European nation-state, but they have always claimed validity beyond the nation-state framework. From this latter perspective, they kept alive the idea of Europe as *civilization,* which allowed a different interpretation of the nation-state solution as contingent and incomplete. The European nation-state has therefore always been the target of an internal critique of Europe as civilization because it left the project of modernity unfinished, did not allow it to fully unfold its emancipatory and rational potential, and ultimately resulted in the continent's political fragmentation.[1] The Europe of nation-states was a 'frozen' order that grouped a diversity of people into territorially confined political units and permitted relatively stable conflict constellations along clear-cut ideological, ethnic, and cultural dividing lines (Rokkan 1999). The "frozen Europe" of the nation-states nourished numerous rivalries and hostilities among the diverse peoples of Europe. For a long period, throughout much of the nineteenth and twentieth centuries, the memory of Europe's spiritual unity and common cultural heritage faded in light of the continent's political diversification. It was only with the launching of the project of European integration that explicit attempts were made to turn the spiritual once again into a political formula of unification. This is the moment for the imagination of a European political society. A postnational account of European unification could be envisaged as an attractive alternative to the Europe of nation-states. The European political and cultural realm 'thawed,' and its new contours opened up to contestation.

At the heart of the postwar imagination for the reshuffling of European societies lies the classic formula of unity/diversity as well as the more specific modern notion of *égaliberté*. The European integration project thus refers to both a premodern notion of political configuration and a genuinely modern concept of inclusion, relating the individual with the collective. Precisely because these principles could only be incompletely validated in the context of national unification, the unity in diversity and *égaliberté* needed to be renegotiated at the European level. European integration is in this sense meant as a response to the 'unfinished project of modernity.' By explicitly taking reference to these two ordering principles, the new project of European integration was, however, never clearly demarcated from the old project of a Europe of nation-states. It was a continuation of the project of European modernity and not a departure. It was also not explicitly postnational but in many respects instead a renewal of the promise of the European nation-state. The commitment to an "ever closer Union among the peoples of Europe," established in the Preamble and in Article 1 of the EU Treaty as the guiding principle for the functioning of the organs of the European Union, revokes the classic formula of the paradox of 'unity in diversity,' so deeply ingrained in European history and self-understanding (Luhmann 1997: 1061ff.). It requires the institutions of the EU to preserve the current constellation of a diversity of particular member states, the integrity and uniqueness of the national peoples, while at the same time committing them to transnational or even supranational unification. For the institutional and constitutional design of the EU, this calls for a solution that constantly shifts between intergovernmentalism and supranationalism. The two-headed (bicephalous) character of the EU political system has been confirmed by recent treaty changes (Crum and Fossum 2009) and will, in all likelihood, also continue affecting the imagination of political and societal unity.

Unsurprisingly, the application of a paradoxical formula to the problem of the (self) imagination of political and societal unity also resulted in a number of paradoxical effects: For one thing, European unification went hand in hand with national diversification. In 1914, the European territory was divided into twenty-one states. During the Cold War period, this number was fixed at twenty-eight. Since 1990, however, new states have proliferated, raising the number to forty-seven. The affirmation that the European Community was built to strengthen its member states was not just ideology but was confirmed on numerous occasions, most prominently in Germany's reacquisition of full national sovereignty following unification (Ash 1993) and in the resurgence of Middle and Eastern Europe after the fall of communism (Schimmelfennig and Sedelmeier 2005). European integration also went hand in hand with regionalization. Even powerful centralized states such as France went through several rounds of decentralization as part of a wider process of state and governance reform that received its impetus from Brussels rather than from Paris (Keating and Jones 1995; Telò 2007). Across

Europe, the new regionalism also gave rise to ethnonationalist movements striving for separation and regional autonomy.

The European integration project furthermore revived the *égaliberté* notion of the French Revolution but visibly failed to develop sufficient capacities to settle the *égaliberté* mandate within its own institutional and constitutional setting. Postwar European unification was linked early on to the promise of securing the liberty of the people of Europe (against the threat of communism). The program for unification was later extended to encompass the promotion of democracy and creation of equal living conditions across the continent. Nevertheless, instead of empowering the people of Europe in its own right, the European Union that became established with the Maastricht Treaty in 1992 accumulated its own democratic deficits. The Brussels-style governance of the EU, with its incomplete division of institutional powers and mechanisms of accountability and control, torpedoed the credibility of the European path toward a more democratic, equal, and just society. The paradoxical effect is that the more the European Union expanded its agenda for redistribution and justice, the more the national project again became attractive in the eyes of many citizens as the safe harbor for their democracy and well-being. In order to avoid conflicts with national regimes of rights and welfare provision, the EU institutions stepped forward as promoters of a new transnational rights and citizenship agenda, which opened up to immigrants and minorities, thereby endorsing new philosophies of integration that were not previously occupied by the nation-state (Favell 1998).

In all of these seemingly contradictory developments, it became evident that Europeanization processes are not linear. There are a plurality of ways of interpreting them, making collective sense of them, and translating them into 'stories' or 'tales' of the social. As the boundaries between the nation, Europe, and the world remain blurred, there are not only numerous ways of accounting for Europe, but there are also frequent contestations concerning the validity or accuracy of these accounts.

The paradoxization of the unity of political Europe and its inbuilt tension between liberty and equality is at the heart of the tales of Europe that will be traced back in the subsequent chapters of this book. As paradoxes cannot be resolved, they are unfolded through narration (Luhmann 1997: 91). The unity of society and the unity of Europe cannot be grounded in substance; it can only be sustained through communication. In modern society, such discourses are inevitably plural and conflictual. They are processed through practices of societal self-observation and narrative translation (self-description, in Luhmann's terminology). Accounts of societal unity unfold as collective reflections upon the insufficiencies and inherent contradictions of the available formula for societal self-description and the various practices of identification linked to it (Trenz 2006b). To the extent that reflection upon the paradoxical unity in diversity is even searched for and actively promoted, these accounts are translated into official identity narratives that guide the collective identification of society (for instance as a 'community of equals' or as a 'community of democratic self-determination').

The inherent contradictions of the accounts of unity, democracy, and equality are the basis for the inconclusive conflicts through which Europe unfolds—internally and externally. The following chapters thus seek to connect different 'tales of Europeanization' and highlight their inherent conflicts. In this sense, the book's scope differs from the normative undertaking of validating the encompassing unity of society in terms of its core values or contents. Its aim cannot be to assess validity claims raised by these plural accounts or to resolve or pacify them. Different accounts of Europe are made alive in their dynamic contestations, through which validity claims are raised, exchanged, and reflected. This is not the single and unitary narration as a closed universe of discourse or an 'ideology'; only this ongoing conflict between plural and partially incompatible narratives can serve as the driving force for reflections among Europeans about what they are and what Europe stands for as a common reference point. The 'tales of Europe' and the various ways in which such 'tales' are collectively made available (through narration, education, socialization, or mediation) can then be read as operational programs for the self-observation of European society as a 'unity in diversity.'

Against this backdrop, the political reordering of the European continent and the launching of a common integration project following the Second World War initiated a new phase in the long history of European self-description. The founding fathers of European integration reappropriated—rather than invented, as it is sometimes claimed—the formula of a Europe 'united in its diversity.' In the current context, Europe's 'unity in diversity' is celebrated by the protagonists of European integration (Petersson and Hellström 2003). It becomes an important reference point for intellectual discourse concerning Europe (Lacroix and Nicolaïdis 2010; Lord and Magnette 2004), and the European Studies community is encouraged in various ways to contribute to this reflection—for instance, by analyzing the optimal constitutional design for an EU polity that—following the Treaty's mandate—has a distinct institutional and legal personality yet nevertheless respects the autonomy of its constituent parts.[2] Besides this progressive account of 'unity in diversity' as a program for European society building, a critical and skeptical account of Europeanization has also gained prominence, an account that questions the benefits of integration and emphasizes its intrinsic deficits, crises, or failures.

The notion of European unification as an open-ended cooperative adventure of departure remains the most fundamental historical bond uniting the destiny of Europeans in their diversity. Such adventures, as Zygmunt Bauman (2004: 3) has reminded us, need to be told. The journey of European integration continues to rely on such tales of adventure, discovery, and conquest. At the same time, the project of European integration critically questions some of the impasses into which Europe's adventurous past has led us. European integration departs from the adventures of European nationalism or colonialism and the collective traumas linked to them. For many, European integration was primarily meant as a process of settlement and consolidation. The observation that Europe's adventurous past has been replaced by its ordinary presence is seen by some as progress. Others criticize Europeans' new complacency: If European integration has opted for settlement instead of adventure, it has also begun fencing itself off from the rest of the world. There are others again who experience the nonheroic Europe as dull and boring. The 'banal Europe' is accused of not really being capable of mobilizing people in support of the common integration project.

In the postwar context of European integration, is it still the adventurer, like the crusader or the conquistador, who captures the European spirit? Is the adventurer the archetype of the European, or is the settler becoming the new prototype for a post-national European, someone who sticks to her native soil and begins appreciating the peace and comfort of home (Bauman 2004: 3)? *European integration*, which was launched as a new project and adventure, is also accompanied by *Europeanization*, which is less purpose than destiny. The *tales of Europeanization* that result from these collective and institutionally channeled interpretations lie at the heart of this book. The following chapters will explore the *discursive universe* or *semantic field* of Europeanization. They will delve into diverse tales of origin, of purpose, of destiny, and of project that have accompanied the journey of postwar European unification. The textual material is organized so as to contrast heroic and nonheroic, extraordinary and banal accounts of Europeanization. The task for the sociologist is to identify the social groups behind these histories of success and failure, their modes of engaging with these stories, and the ways in which these stories bind them together or divide them.

NARRATING THE SOCIAL BONDS:
TALES OF EUROPEANIZATION

Europeanization has become a fashionable term used by scholars from various disciplines. It is also a useful term for boosting the relevance of scientific publications that are meant to look beyond the familiar context of the national or that claim to be interdisciplinary. Within the European Studies community, this interdisciplinarity has been socialized by a new generation of researchers and is promoted by numerous study and research programs. The notion of Europeanization is variously applied to investigate long-term historical transformation, changing political cultures and identities, or the impact of European policies and law. Apart from its analytical use, there is a narrative element to scientific accounts of Europeanization as a story of social change and integration. From this latter perspective, Europeanization research concerns ways of imagining the emergence of a transnational European society, demarcating its unity and diversity, and contesting its trajectory. To understand how the scientific and common sense uses of the notion of Europeanization are narratively embedded in accounts of the social integration of a European society, the particular story lines along which Europeanization research plays out must be unraveled. Narratives are used as collective imaginations of the social bonds that bind people together and tell how society constitutes itself (Eder 2006a; 2011; 2013). Narratives of European society-building compete with existing narratives that imagine the social bonds of national societies or that postulate the bonds of a global or world society. Accounts of Europeanization therefore typically navigate between the local, the national, the European, and the global. They interpret our diverse pasts; propose specific balances of a "unity in diversity" of contemporary culture, politics, and society; and design paths for our common future.

In the following, I develop a discursive approach to Europeanization, one that considers scientific accounts as intrinsically related to the narrative construction of Europe as a meaningful social entity: a European society. Instead of looking at Europeanization from a political science perspective in terms of shifting power relations and causal impact, I explore variants of Europeanization as a form of social imagination of the unity and diversity of a European society. Europeanization as social imagination relates to all kinds of processes of interpretation and justification that provide us with explanations as to how Europe came into being as a meaningful social entity, how it is sustained over time, how it is contested, and how it should look in the future.

Much in this book will concern the narrators as well as the functions of narrations. The promoters of such narratives are typically intellectuals, journalists, and scientists. In the European integration context, there is, however, also an important process by which such narration is institutionalized. Professional narrators are found within the EU institutions and the EU studies research community. Moreover, this role as social carriers of narratives must be related to the roles played by the various audiences. These include the citizens who are addressed in various ways as recipients of narration. The citizens of Europe are, however, not just passive recipients of the narration of European society; they also act—consciously or unconsciously—in many meaningful ways as the protagonists of this narration, as the subjects who are involved in processes of identity and collective will formation, as the voters in national or European elections, as the consumers of goods and services provided by the Common Market, or as clients or individual stakeholders who make use of their rights of free movement and citizenship, become engaged in European exchange programs, receive EU funding, or simply populate the Common Market through their various commercial activities. One question raised by Europeanization research is to what extent such diffuse groups of citizens or stakeholders also develop a collective consciousness as Europeans—that is, whether they step forward as collective actors whose voice becomes distinguishable or as "critical publics" who take a democratic control function vis-à-vis the EU. Accounts of Europeanization treat such publics not just as those being addressed (i.e., as a passive audience) but also as protagonists who themselves play a role in collective identification and in democratization. The publics of accounts of Europeanization are not passive echo chambers of elite discourse. They are conceived as constituted through critical speech, and they are projected as a "European public" that is part of European discourse (Habermas 1974; Splichal 2012).[3] 'Acts of Europeanization' are in this sense not simply performed in the presence of an audience; the performers must, as Alan Finlayson (2014: 1) puts it, "to some degree tailor their performance to the outlook and interests of the publics they come before." The audience is then no longer object but becomes subject. It becomes a public in the emphatic sense of the word as an intertextual environment for critical engagement in discourse and creating the conditions for its circulation (Warner 2002). Such an emphatic public as the resonator of discourse about Europe is assigned an active role in the unfolding drama of Europeanization and, in many respects, is even becoming the protagonist. There is thus a new role differentiation for the protagonists of accounts of Europeanization, distinguishing between the agents who defend the public interest of Europeans and the principals who authorize and authenticate the story line. This interlinkage between processes of Europeanization and democratization is important for the self-imagination of European society. Europeanized audiences are increasingly addressed as democratic subjects, and they might, in many instances, develop self-reflexive capacities as a democratic constituency (Trenz 2010). This directs our attention to narration's important function of providing a perspective for collective identification that unites the narrators and their audiences in a shared experience and involves them in a variety of practices or performances, through which they see themselves and reflect upon themselves in their roles as citizens.

Apart from the carriers and protagonists of narration, an important component of narrative analysis is obviously the reconstruction of the plot of the story. The content of the narration is closely linked with the function of the narration. The narration's most basic function is to provide collective orientation. It is a lens for interpreting social life; it bundles social experiences and focuses attention on common viewpoints, shared ideas, or perspectives, which can, from the narrator's perspective, claim objectivity and general validity and an ability to convince an audience. Another function of the narration is to construct temporality and provide collective orientation and identification.[4] Narrations are used to tell a story over time. For the *story* to become *history*, it must be located in space and time. Accounts of Europeanization therefore typically develop a chronological dimension of the evolution of Europe's social and political space. The story is, however, not only history that is confined in time and space; it is also a *project* that is open to the future. Typically, both the interpretation of the past and the way it links to the future are contested, and these contestations involve both the story's protagonists and its interpreters/recipients. The narration's function is ultimately also to establish an arena of debate and contestation. Narrations are about conflicting interpretations of the collective past and their consequences for present action or future mandates.

In dealing with processes of narrative construction and interpretation, this book perceives the narrators (scientists or public intellectuals), their protagonists (EU actors and institutions), and the various recipients of these narrations of Europeanization (the publics or the people of Europe) in a new and innovative way. The focus will be on the configuration of available narratives and possible shifts and ruptures between them. Narrative contestation stands for different ways of claiming social bonds and sustaining them in a national or transnational setting. Conflicting narratives can thus be indicative of the divisions of an emerging European society. Narration shifts between the European and the national, between affirmation and contestation, between triumph and trauma, or between drama and the banal. By tracing these narrative lines, I will depict the discursive field of Europeanization as a circuit diagram in which different switches control the timing, strength, and direction of energy flows. More specifically, I will consider four interrelated switches in the narrative construction of European society:

1. Triumphant Europeanism: affirmation of the extraordinary (sacralization)
2. Banal Europeanism: affirmation of everyday life (banalization)
3. Euroscepticism: disruption of the extraordinary (desacralization)
4. Political crisis: disruption of everyday life (crisis)

The first two variants are success stories based on the alleged integrative effects of Europeanization on the emergence of a European society. They replicate, reconcile, and (up to a point) claim to replace national narratives. The latter two variants are stories of decay, speaking to the disintegrative effects of Europeanization on society. They emphasize the mismatch or even the incompatibility between society-building at the national and at the European level. Narratives of Europeanization concern, then, how social bonds between Europeans are either corrupted or maintained. All four of the stories furthermore relate to social situations in which fiction is either highlighted (glorified or demystified) or remains unobserved. In the first case, narratives of Europeanization can be discussed in relation to "triumph" and "trauma"

(Giesen 2004): either affirmation of the value of European integration and the emphasis of the extraordinary achievements of Europe or profanation of the value of European integration, as manifested in Euroscepticism and crisis. In the second case, no explicit efforts are made to narrate the story of Europeanization, to make Europe salient, or to reflect upon its merits. Europeanization instead operates as a mechanism on the subconscious level. In this book, I will look for evidences of these processes of affirmation and contestation of Europeans' common travel itinerary, of its path dependency and future trajectory. I will reconstruct how the extraordinary of Europe is defended and contested, and I will collect evidence for how Europe is rooted in everyday life and how it can be put at risk in situations of crisis.

The sociology of European integration, as I understand it in this book, develops around a theory of society as a cognitive and normative construct. Society materializes through the generation and application of knowledge and norms, which provide a context for communicative understanding about the meaning of equality, identity, rights, and justice. This typically involves individuals in a process of socialization that reaches beyond the mere exchange of goods and production in a market. Society is, in Polanyi's terms, a corrective of the market and not just an extension of it (Polanyi 1957). It is through the lens of a theory of society that Europe is turned *meaningful* and not merely useful (Delanty and Rumford 2005: 3).

The agenda for a sociology of European integration is outlined in the first chapter along the lines of the various meanings attributed to *Europeanization*. The different 'tales' or discourses[5] of Europeanization that are applied by scientific disciplines (such history, political science, or various micro- and macrosociologies) can be used as metaphors for the attribution of meaning in the discursive construction of a European society. The 'unity and diversity' of Europe functions here as a *leitmotif* of a sociology of European integration.

The remainder of the book is divided into four main empirical chapters that explore triumph, affirmation, trauma, and disruption (crisis) in relation to Europeanization. This results in a reconstruction of four main themes of a sociology of European integration: first, the elite processes of identity construction and the constitutional-institutional framework that carries such a construction (together with notions of European identity, EU citizenship, etc.); second, the socialization of European citizens, processes of banal Europeanism, and social transnationalism through everyday cross-border exchanges; third, the mobilization of resistance and Euroscepticism as a fundamental and collectively mobilized opposition to processes of Europeanization; and fourth, the political sociology of crisis, linked not only to financial turmoil but also, more fundamentally, to a legitimation crisis that affects Europe and the democratic nation-state.

NOTES

1. The unfinished modernization of the nation-state is discussed by Eder (2000), Habermas (1990), and Passerin d'Entrèves and Benhabib (1997).

2. This is so in numerous calls for the Commission Framework Research prorgams as well as in national funding schemes, such as the programme 'Unity amidst Variety? Intellectual Foundations and Requirements for an Enlarged Europe,' funded by the Volkswagenstiftung in Germany. (See http://www.volkswagenstiftung.de/en/funding/completed-initiatives/unity-amidst-variety-intellectual-foundations-and-requirements-for-an-enlarged-europe.html, last accessed: June 30, 2014)

3. A public is constituted through critical discourse as Habermas reminds us (Habermas 1974). There is thus a critical difference between publics and audiences (Splichal 2012: 69). Both are often treated as identical by empirical media and communication research, but they draw upon different normativities ranging from passive receivers and resonance bodies of public discourse to active recipients, interpreters, and critical voice in democracy.

4. This is not the place to recapitulate the debate concerning the (many) narrative turns in the social sciences and humanities. I just wish to emphasize the usefulness of a 'functional approach to narratives,' which simply asks, "How does narrative work to accomplish meaning making?" See Schiff (2012: 35), who provides a useful state-of-the-art overview.

5. The term 'tales,' 'narratives,' or 'discourses' of Europeanization, as I use it in this book, is not meant as an analytical distinction. I will in the following talk interchangeably of 'tales,' 'accounts,' 'stories,' 'narratives,' or 'discourses' of Europeanization.

Chapter One

Integration of What?

Toward a European Society or the
Europeanization of National Societies?

Sociology has taught us to address the question of the *integration* of modern society in relation to the question of its *internal differentiation*. In the terminology that has been developed and applied by the European Studies community to describe the 'uniqueness' and social dynamics of the unification of Europe, we speak of 'Europeanization.' Europeanization is meant, first of all, as a term signifying the simultaneity of integration and differentiation. In legal-political terms, we speak of the relationship between the supranational delegation of authority and the differentiated impact of integration on national and subnational units. In sociocultural terms, we speak of the manifestations and expressions of 'European society' and 'European culture' against the persistence of national or local cultures. In sociological terms, we describe the variety of responses to European integration that compete in a field of social practices.

In order to approach 'Europeanization,' we require a reference point. The first question to be addressed is *Europeanization of what*? The usual answer refers to national or subnational units as objects (or subjects) of Europeanization. One must thus presuppose the existence of national societies to tell the story of Europeanization in a meaningful way. The process of Europeanization applies to national societies, which undergo a specific transformation, are made more modern, rational, or simply more dynamic. Europeanization accounts for accelerated social change. As such, it is linked to harmonizing processes through which national societies become more similar, but it is also manifested in new heterogeneous practices, which increase internal diversity.[1] The sociological challenge here is to conceive of social integration

1

at a new level of abstraction and differentiation (Münch 2001: 233). The European society *integrates* by enhancing organic solidarity—that is, the dependencies and functional links between the national societies. The national societies *differentiate* by lowering the threshold of mechanical solidarity—that is, the primordial bonds and commonalities within the nation-state (Münch 2001: 230ff.).

In this book, I will follow the path of Europeanization, not in the usual political science manner, in terms of impact measured at the level of the political system, but in the sociological manner of attributing social and structural change at the macrolevel of society. European integration research has long been the preserve of political scientists who specialize in internal institutional analysis (the study of bureaucracy) or intra-institutional relationships. But at the same time, European integration has expanded into fields in which political science approaches have little explanatory power. European integration is no longer only relevant for bureaucrats and students who wish to become bureaucrats. Within the social sciences, Europe has become relevant for sociologists, cultural studies, media studies, and anthropologists. All of these disciplines contribute from different angles to the tales of Europeanization, which are at the focus of this book. An upcoming research program will look at how European integration through institutions, programs, norms, and rules shapes the ways in which citizens experience their daily lives as well as their relationships with each other. The study of European integration as social integration inevitably involves *European society*, which is perceived as a new unitary form of the plurality of social practices. Europe is a new social context for common experiences, shared values, and dense interactions that enter the familiar context of the national. This is implied in the discussion of the Europeanization of national societies.

European society does not figure prominently in normative and political debates about European integration, nor has it been taken up by academia as an analytical lens for understanding European unification processes. There is a striking absence of discourse about the unity of a European society in the imagination of Europe. European society is rarely part of the discourses that account for Europe's 'unity in diversity.' It is part of neither scientific nor everyday parlance. One of the few references found for the use of the term 'European society' in the singular is the denomination of professional associations or academic clubs, especially in the field of medicine.[2] Social scientists instead seem frightened by the singular use of the term 'European society,' which is rarely employed in the titles of academic publications. The term is to a small extent used by historians to denote particular constellations like "early modern European society" (Kamen 2005). Descriptive or analytical accounts of contemporary society instead turn a blind eye to Europe. For most sociologists, Europe is a context for comparison but not a category of analysis. The official journal of the European Sociological Association is

European Societies (in the plural). Only in the field of geographic area studies is there less reluctance to use the singular term to denote special regions (as in the journal *South European Society and Politics*).

Despite this non-use of the term in official and academic parlance, I maintain in this book that the normative debate surrounding the affirmation or rejection of European integration is ultimately grounded in accounts of a European society. To explicate what I mean, I will continue the discussion by considering the mechanisms identified by political scientists to carry European integration forward and shape a novel configuration of the political in relation to the social and economic realm. When European integration was launched in the immediate postwar period, the so-called founding fathers of Europe were guided by just such a broad vision of a European society. Jean Monnet's and Robert Schuman's pragmatism was grounded in a belief in the binding forces of institutions, which provided the foundation for cooperation among people and not just states. By trusting in the synergy effects between modern capitalist economy and society, the founding fathers of Europe were Weberian sociologists. They implicitly re-established the link between the authority of institutions and the market activities of individuals within a new regulatory framework of incremental supranational integration and bureaucracy.[3] They thus applied an encompassing and sociologically informed notion of 'integration' in the sense of using the building of a common market as a catalyst for the unification of the people of Europe. 'System integration' would be followed by 'social integration.' The establishment of a common market would occur alongside the creation of state-like supranational political institutions, which—through a set of shared norms and values—would socialize individuals into Europeans without necessarily discarding their national or regional belongings.[4]

In line with this tradition of sociological theorizing, we can observe how societal accounts delivered by sociological thinkers shift between unity and diversity, social integration and differentiation. In distinguishing European from national societies, they apply the sociological scheme of distinguishing 'modern society' from other (traditional) forms of social entities. Best known is the distinction between the exclusive but egalitarian community (*Gemeinschaft*) and the inclusive but disparate society (*Gesellschaft*) (Tönnies 1988). While the former represents a consensus of values and forms of life, the latter is based upon plural interests and economic transactions. The emergence of modern society did not, however, simply replace *Gemeinschaft* with *Gesellschaft* but instead provided, in the form of the nation, an ambiguous amalgamation of processes of social opening and closure. The coexistence and balance between *Gemeinschaft* and *Gesellschaft* refer to two mechanisms for fabricating societal 'unity' either through cultural bonds of similarity (mechanical solidarity) or through a division of functional tasks (organic solidarity). Emile Durkheim (1964), who delivered the classic account of these two forms of integration, also emphasized that the stability of social order is based upon equilibrium between its collectivizing and differentiating forces.

Early integration theorists can be read as creatively playing with central sociological categories and perceiving European integration as shifting between community and society. When Ernst Haas (1958) theorized in the late 1950s about the dynamics of European integration, his expectation was that integration would occur through functional spillover. Neofunctionalism, as this early theoretical strand was labeled, is sociological in the sense that it assumes a link between political integration and social integration and describes the social forces that determine societal change. It thus postulates the existence of endogenous social laws that promote the unity of Europe. European integration is not only political; it is also consequential. It is not simply a political construction, depending on the good will and intentions of particular actors, but is instead objective destiny, dictated by the laws of the social.

If neofunctionalism was ideologically inspired by the federal thinking of Jean Monnet, it was intellectually inspired by the grand social theory of Talcott Parsons. In this sociological tradition, society is conceived as an internally differentiated and externally delimited social system. It is stabilized through the interchange between different subsystems, each contributing to the maintenance of social order: the economic system through adaptation to the environment, the political system through goal attainment, the societal community through membership, and the cultural system through value attachment (Parsons 1967: 3ff.). The European Union is a social system to the extent that it provides services with regard to each of these subsystems. Neofunctionalism could therefore postulate the emergence of a European society as a structured entity in line with the national society. The European society would evolve as a new layer in a federal model of social and political order.

In the classic definition by Ernst Haas, the concept of *integration* was used in this broad sense, comprising both political and social integration: "Political integration is the process whereby political actors in several distinct national settings are persuaded to shift their loyalties, expectations and political activities toward a new center, whose institutions possess or demand jurisdiction over the pre-existing national states." The optimism of early integration theorists referred to a societal perspective of European integration: "The end result of a process of political integration is a new political community, superimposing over the pre-existing ones" (Haas 1958: 16).

To trace back this unspoken sociological heritage of early European integration theory, it is useful to recall the basic categories introduced by Emile Durkheim to explain the integration of modern, differentiated society. Already in his classic work on the "division of social labor," Durkheim postulated a spontaneous movement toward a "European society, which has, at present, some idea of itself and the beginning of organization" (Durkheim

1984: 405). How could Durkheim in the booming years of European nationalism arrive at such a conclusion?

Translated into contemporary political vocabulary, Emile Durkheim was a federal thinker. Such a Durkheimian entity is based upon a delicate balance between the harmonization of regulations and practices enforced by supranational institutions and the mutual recognition of difference among national-level models and regimes. It is necessary to cope with mutual dependency and coordinate the division of work at the European level, and it is necessary to uphold pluralism, to protect or even experiment with diversity at the national level. At the same time, the Durkheimian entity is driven by the laws of the social toward internal differentiation and higher levels of division of labor, which are accompanied by new regulatory efforts to set the rules and standards for coexistence.[5] Durkheim stands at the beginning of a long tradition of conceiving European society in terms of a federation: a society that is held together by functional necessity and shared interests and that embraces several national communities under a common economic and political umbrella. This federal vision of a European society operates through the distinction between *society* represented by the heterogeneity of purposive and interest-based social relationships and *community* represented by the homogeneity of primary and more intimate social relationships (Tönnies 1988). For Durkheim, community and society are linked to two different mechanisms of social integration: one based on the primordial bonds of sameness between members of the traditional (national) community (mechanical solidarity); the other based on the functional ties of difference between members of a plural and multiethnic society (organic solidarity). The evolutionary process of modern society also includes the transition from traditional collectivism to modern individualism. The segmental differentiation of societies as territorially confined units will, in this view, slowly be replaced by functional differentiation of society as a unity made up of the mutual dependencies of its plural elements. The socially and culturally homogeneous nation-state is therefore only transitory to a higher level of unity in diversity. This is the background, why Durkheimian sociology was very attractive for American sociology, and in particular for Talcott Parsons, to explain the integration of the Unites States of America as a heterogeneous society based on plurality and difference. For the same reasons, I will make reference in the following to Durkheimian sociology as a highly relevant framework for thinking about the processes of unification of the European society as a 'unity in diversity.'

In the aftermath of Ernst Haas, early theorizing of European integration developed no further this federal sociological agenda of society's unity in diversity. This federal vision of European society as a long-term achievement of European integration stood out against the short-term concern with European cooperation as a practical arrangement of economic governance. In the original treaties that laid the foundations for the European Communities, the newly established supranational institutions' scope of activity was ultimately restricted to market building. Given this clear priority of economic integration over political and social integration, the European federation and European society were soon off of the agenda. In addition, political scientists remained firmly anchored in the paradigm of International Relations, with its focus on interaction between states and with societies locked up at the intra-state level. The dynamics of integration were thus located in the purposeful action of Member State governments seeking to maximize national interests (the so-called realistic school). Alternatively, emphasis was placed on the regulatory capacities of supranational institutions that developed in partial independence from the states (the so-called neofunctionalist school) but also autonomously from societal constraints.[6]

A clear turning point in theorizing European integration was finally marked with the Single European Act of 1986, which set the schedule for completing the Common Market with encompassing free trade arrangements, free movement of workers and capital, and a monetary union. Neofunctionalism was now applicable to explaining how substantial treaty revisions by the Maastricht and Amsterdam Treaties of 1992 and 1996 extended the body of supranational law and competences and included a range of new regulatory policies in the fields of environment, education, culture, welfare, social rights, immigration, security, defense, and foreign policy (Schmitter 2004). The newly established European Union turned into a new kind of legal and political order with a far-reaching impact on people's individual and collective life chances. More importantly, these accelerated dynamics of integration had a deep normative impact on perceptions of the European project's legitimacy. Legitimacy could no longer be derived from the permissive consent of citizens, who profited from the outputs of the common market in terms of welfare and security (so-called output legitimacy). Legitimacy also had to be generated by providing specific inputs in the form of aggregating citizens' preferences and engaging them in political will formation (so-called input legitimacy).[7]

It is thus important to note that society returned as a concern with the normative deficits of European integration. Elements of a normative order were outlined in the Treaties in the definition of European citizenship and extended rights of participation. At this point, it was all but inevitable for there to be attempts to consider a European social model that crystallized visions of the 'good life' and the 'good society' that are common to Europeans and that would guide their political project toward the future.

If post-Maastricht Europe can be described in terms of a transition from market building to polity building, it implicitly also becomes committed to a project of society building. Once again, European society was primarily perceived as a normative desiderate that was indispensable for coping with the deficits of legitimation of the European integration project. It was, first of all, a corollary of a legitimate political order and a necessary social horizon for any debate on rights, justice, citizenship, and identity (Delanty and Rumford 2005: 5). What mattered was not the diagnosis of the absence or incompleteness of such a European society but the prognosis of its possible emergence.

In applying a prognostic view on the future emergence of a European society (in the singular), EU studies has arguably lost sight of the transformations affecting contemporary European societies (in the plural). The research focus has mainly been on institutional and constitutional design rather than on the social dynamics and mechanisms that drive or place constraints on European integration. Society has been conceived merely as a contextual variable, not as an intervening variable of European integration. In its ambition to constitutionally design the *finalité* of the European integration project during the late 1990s and early 2000s, normative EU studies has, for instance, paid insufficient attention to the possibilities of popular contestation that have unexpectedly brought the constitutional process to a standstill.[8] Society thus remains the blind spot of European integration studies. While there has been considerable writing that has tested the normative validity of a European order, there remains a 'noticeable absence of any concern with an underlying theory of society' (Delanty and Rumford 2005: 3).

TOWARD A (POLITICAL) SOCIETY OF EUROPE

How can sociologists shed light on this 'blind spot' of European integration studies? Various attempts have been made to formulate the agenda of a sociology of European integration, but debate concerning the contours of 'European society' and its relationship to the (presumably existing) national societies remains controversial.[9] From the sociological angle, the difficulties related to such a formulation of a theory of European society are twofold. Firstly, many sociologists, demarcating themselves from constitutional lawyers or political scientists, would consider the question of the viability of European society and its democratic-institutional design as implicitly normative and thus not falling under their competence. In response to the often implicitly normative agenda of EU studies, many empirically trained sociologists have abstained from expressing any preferences about the desirable contours of a European society or forecasting its possible development. Secondly, sociology is accused of a lack of imagination with regard to the dynamics and contours of transnational integration of society, which is symptomatic of the institutionally ingrained 'methodological nationalism' of the discipline. Sociology has been institutionalized at our universities as the discipline for the study of national societies. Sociologists have developed professional competences and rely on rich databases, which allow them to describe social integration and differentiation at the national level. They take

it for granted that they can map the structure and change of European societies from a plural and comparative perspective, but they do not admit to
speaking of a European society in the singular (Mau and Verwiebe 2010).
Postulating the absence of European society as a distinguishable social entity,[10] comparative sociologists have pled instead for a sociology of the Europeanization of national societies (Eigmüller and Mau 2010; Immerfall and
Therborn 2009). As such, they can at best engage in cross-national comparison but lack conceptual tools for reflecting the fluidity of transnational
(world) society (Beck 2003; Wimmer and Glick Schiller 2002).

By replacing the 'prognostic and normative view' of a European society
in the singular with the 'analytical view' of European societies in the plural,
sociologists have applied the social structural perspective of classic comparative sociology. This has raised the question of "fusion" or "fissions" for
empirical analysis (see Boje et al. 1999) but has not yet come up with an
explanatory framework for the possible convergence of European societies
and conceptions of their 'unity in diversity.' The objective of turning European society in the singular into a new object of empirical observation would,
however, be equally problematic as it would project some of the deficits of
national society studies onto the study of Europe as a distinct social entity.
The shift from the study of national societies to the study of European society
would not shift the paradigm of 'methodological nationalism.' It would still
apply the container model of society as the conjunction of social, economic,
political, and cultural relationships and concomitant structures.

Are sociologists then to blame for replicating the container model of
national society in a largely unreflective manner when looking at Europe?
Does the discipline—as has been insinuated by some of its critics (Beck
2003)—suffer from epistemic myopia and a lack of fantasy in imagining the
transnational and the global? For Claus Offe (2003), the question of whether
there is or can be a "European society" must be raised in the context of the
"Western tradition" of thinking society as a unitary form. The focus on the
"European society" in the singular not only reflects a methodological choice
by the researcher; it also relates to certain cognitive frames and normative
standards, which are part of the Western repertoire of imagining the social. It
is true that *society* is comprised of a community of strangers, who cannot be
expected to interact directly with each other. However, the social force behind this modern notion lies in imagining an anonymous society as a membership community and believing in the possibility of building "relationships
of trust, common attachment, toleration, understanding, and solidarity, as
well as a sense of obligation to our 'strange' fellow citizens" (Offe 2003: 72).
For Offe, the notion of "European society" in the singular specifically reflects Western conceptions of society as the realm of collective will in relation to a state, which has the means of unifying a large and diverse population. Society (in the singular) is ultimately always a political society, which

is distinguished by its capacity for efficient rule and which acts as a unitary hegemon to which its diverse members are subjected (Nassehi 2002). This Western tradition might serve as a model for other parts of Europe and the world, but its validity and applicability is also strongly contested in the wider European context. Against this backdrop, the prospects for Europeanization as society building are particularly discouraging (Offe 2003: 74). There is a lack of imagination of a 'constituent society' of the EU, which also largely explains the EU's failure or impossibility to constitutionalize as a polity in its own right. Attempts to represent the political will of the multitude of Europeans (the vain endeavor of EU constitution-making) have not simply failed; they have also aggravated the frictions among the people of Europe and their unrelenting identity conflicts.

This contestedness of the notion of a European society also leads to the idea that society's normative template can be investigated as a social and political driving force behind modern European history and that such contestations might indeed demarcate a particular social space or location for Europe. Michael Mann speaks in this regard of European society as a "contentious troika" of the national, the European, and the global (Mann 1998: 185). Through these contestations, a "third space" or a "third society" is demarcated over time, continuously transcending the national but failing to reach the global (Mann 1998: 184). The idea of such a "contentious troika" is useful for tracing back the historical trajectory of the construction of Europe's internal and external borders, but it has not yet arrived at a theory of society. Michael Mann ultimately proposes to define "human society" negatively, emphasizing that there has never been society as a unitary system, nor has there ever been a prime mover (capitalism, democracy, etc.) driving societal development. Historians can trace back power and political contestation over time and space. With a perspective on Europe, they can establish the variable degree of internal coherence and external closure of European social networks (which, in terms of content, can be distinguished as ideological, economic, military, and political power networks) (Mann 1998: 186). The "European society" is here simply a different way of narrating Europe's social and political history beyond the particularity of national historiography (Kaelble 2013: 7–8). Comparative methods can then be applied to identify European similarities or distinctive European features of societal development (for instance, by comparing industrial development of family structures in Europe and in other parts of the world).[11]

What this long-term historical account disregards is the possibility of a qualitative shift in the development of European society toward what is called 'deeper integration.' With its primarily comparative focus, a "historical sociology of European society" differs from a "historical sociology of European integration," which considers processes of state or polity building, the formation of cross-border solidarities, and collective identities in Europe's more recent past (Börner and Eigmüller 2015: 6–8). The emerging EU society develops in symbiosis with particular institutions, which rapidly gain competences and expand their economic, political, and legislative activities. EU society is there to question the legitimacy of these institutions, to express support for or opposition to EU institutional developments, yet European society is also the major addressee of these developments, filling the EU institutional space with people, their ideas, and their exchanges. In other words, European society is again vested in normative terms. A normative account of European society can therefore not simply be dismissed as ideological and replaced by sociostructural comparative analysis. The normative core of modern European society, which Claus Offe (2003) has so eloquently evoked, turns back in the self-descriptions of the main actors and institutions that drive European societal development. This applies, on the one hand, to European institutions, which constantly deploy a society language that emphasizes integration, cohesion, solidarity, and harmony when justifying their expanding political authority. The normative account of a European society is, on the other hand, also present in the collective orientations and perceptions of legitimacy of the people of Europe and informs their various practices of political mobilization.

It is here that Chris Rumford discusses the usefulness of an account of European (civil) society to characterize the distinct character of the transnational social space of Europe (Rumford 2002: 98–103, 2003). The dominant understanding of European society as 'civil society' in part reflects the powerful idea of societal self-organization through bottom-up interactions of citizens who feel attached to Europe. A European civil society, however, also finds strong institutional anchorage through the establishment of European citizenship, 'good governance,' and democratic procedures of decision-making.[12] The application of civil society discourse to the EU context thus has the advantage of introducing a model for EU society building, which is simultaneously a benchmark for EU democracy. This 'modeling' of the European (civil) society is an experimental and open process that opens up a potential to break with the nation-state model of society but that is also characterized by a reluctance to renounce the idea of a unitary societal order.

One of the most comprehensive accounts of the nascent European society is presented by William Outhwaite (2013), for whom Europe should be seen as a particular region of the world that has been shaped over time by its dense internal and global interactions and networks. While this approach clearly draws upon insights from historical sociology, it is also original in its attempt to conceptualize the distinctiveness of 'European society' in the cultural, economic, and political sphere. This results in a list of themes for a sociology of Europe as a region, which occupies a particular location in the globalized world. A sociology of Europe is concerned with Europe's geographical and geopolitical positioning, with sociocultural distinctions, and with distinct economic formations that are putting 'Europe in its place' in the contemporary globalized world. Sociological responses to the question of a 'European society' thus point, for instance, to the European social model and its emphasis on solidarity and welfare, to the European political model and its emphasis on egalitarian democracy, or to the European economic model and its emphasis on sustainable development and 'flexicurity.' Although comparative history is useful for exploring these themes over time and emphasizing the origin of the distinctiveness of 'European society,' sociologists go well beyond this task of a comparative mapping of European diversity by analyzing whether Europe still serves as a model and how the normative foundations of these models are reinterpreted and renegotiated in contemporary European society(ies).

There are three main conclusions to draw from this state-of-the-art overview of a possible sociological research agenda for analyzing processes of Europeanization/European integration. First, it makes sense to treat Europe as a whole from a societal perspective and not just to apply a comparative perspective to the developments of European societies. A European society is historically anchored in the narrative of Europe's *unity in diversity*, and it solidifies through processes of socialization (*Vergesellschaftung*) among the Europeans. Contemporary Europe is in this sense shaped through processes of Europeanization as *society building*, which take place at many different levels and in close interaction with societal (trans)formation at regional, national, and global levels. Secondly, European society is a politically constructed postnational space. Processes of Europeanization unfold in symbiosis with political integration and are confined in their relationship to Europe's nascent political order, the various opportunities related to it (such as mobility, free movement, common market exchanges), and the collective experiences and interpretations of the Europeans who live under a shared authority. European levels of state (polity) and society (constituency) interact and reinforce one another (Fossum and Trenz 2006a). A sociology of Europeanization/European integration is thus in some sense always a political sociology and approaches the question of social order through the lens of the political.[13] Thirdly, a sociology of Europeanization/European integration is normatively grounded in the modern self-understanding of society as an entity of autonomous individuals and their capabilities for self-rule and self-organization. This normative self-understanding is used as the matrix for constituting society, organizing relationships among its members, and sustaining autonomy vis-à-vis the state and the market. Norms are in this sense not just counterfactuals, which tell us how a European society should be or should come into existence; they actually constitute European society and possess a creative force in its dynamic unfolding. Sociologists must account for this intrinsic normativity in how European society is addressed as a unitary form, suggesting that a sociology of Europeanization/European integration cannot simply be established as a science of 'social facts,' distinct from the normative agenda of political science and law. European society has been turned into an object of normative contestation by the actors who inhabit it, and these normative disputes must be taken into account by sociologists who choose it as an object of empirical research. Finally, a research program that takes this intrinsic normativity of European society seriously can be developed by relying on Europeans' self-accounts, shared practices, and collective interpretations. This research program is not at all intended as a departure from classical sociology but in fact relates to the tradition of interpretative sociology in important ways, seeking the beginning of society, as Georg Simmel (1908) has famously put it, in the awareness of forming a society. A political sociology of Europeanization/European integration thus builds upon the collective interpretations of the Europeans themselves: the stories told by the protagonists of European integration, their diffusion across the European space, and the many ways in which these stories find public resonance.

Along these lines of thinking about a nascent European society, the sociological approach to Europeanization/European integration that is applied in the following chapters is neither normative nor factual. My intention is not to propose a model for the societal integration of Europe or to assess its achievements in light, for instance, of the standards set by the nation-state. Nor do I intend to systematically collect data that could be used to measure the levels or degrees of social integration/disintegration in Europe, for instance, through the parameters of political culture, solidarity, trust, or density of social networks.

In line with my main argument that a sociology of Europeanization/European integration cannot dismiss the normative perspective of a European society, I will seek in the following chapters to understand how the normative horizon for social integration is currently renegotiated in the European context. How and by whom are such assumptions about the 'unity in diversity' of society upheld and validated? And how do such assumptions feed a process of critical thinking and practices of society building that unite or divide the people of Europe?

The observation that particular norms are held valid and applied in the context of European integration is the starting point for any reflection upon European society. Despite the constant criticism from a more empirically informed research perspective and its emphasis on existing diversity and structural or cultural divisions that divide European societies (in the plural), the prognostic view on European society (in the singular) as the normative horizon of integration is not entirely unfamiliar to sociologists. Within the normative framework of European modernity, the appeal to the idea of the 'unity' of society (the 'good society' or the 'great society') has always been a point of collective orientation. These normative ingredients in the form of inbuilt assumptions and expectations of social order are not only the basis for how society is collectively represented but also translate into critical practices, which engage the people as the subject of such collective representations (Cooke 2006).

To take up and develop the agenda of a 'theory of society' that can inform European integration studies, we must therefore go beyond the empirical criticism of sociology and its emphasis on the diversity of existing societal constellations (which, in the classic sociostructural account, is categorized and registered on maps of European diversity). Instead of rejecting the 'normative approach' of European Studies as being in conflict with the agenda of empirical sociology, we must empirically observe how the normative universe of European integration unfolds, claiming validity and relating back to the normative foundations of modern democratic society and its emphasis on equality, individual rights, and freedom. Society accounts are thus seen as part of the sociological discourse of modernity (Nassehi 2006). There is a sociological frame of reference that applies to European integration and that perceives societies as learning units and promotes critical discourse concerning the desirable forms of social and political order. From this perspective, the sociological discipline is part of this discourse and critique. Classic sociology has always assisted society in the practical unfolding of reasons and its endeavor for higher levels of rationality, unity, and internal differentiation. The normative foundations of European modernity have not only informed the traditional macrosociological account of society as a self-organized, internally differentiated, and externally delimited social entity. Sociology has itself played an important role in invigorating these norms, upholding their validity and formulating a critical agenda for social reform. In applying this sociological frame of reference to the process of European unification, we can discover European society in the ways in which the European project is supported and contested and in relation to the normative ideas that are held valid in this process of public contestation. European society need not be externally observed and categorized but contains its own self-descriptions. Accordingly, this book will contribute to disclosing these (plural) accounts of European society and the ways in which they are internally contested.

Europeanization refers to processes of both society building and community building. It incorporates the view of society in the singular and societies in the plural. Social relationships that are described in terms of Europeanization resemble modern sociology's accounts of *Vergesellschaftung* and *Vergemeinschaftung*.[14] The dynamics of social relationships that can be exterior and outward looking as well as interior and inward looking and shift between rational, affectual, and traditional orientations is meant here to replace the old dichotomy between *Gemeinschaft* and *Gesellschaft*. Strictly speaking, there is no *society* in Max Weber's sociology but only concomitant processes of institutionalizing social relationships. The European Union follows a Weberian program by experimenting with forms of market building that are intended to be related to community building and not detached from it. Like Early Modern society, the European Union seeks to expand and to consolidate (widening and deepening). It thus dislocates the dichotomy between community and society as two antithetical types of human collectivity. There is a dynamic concomitance between the emergence of European society and the persistence of national communities. As a result, communal transnational social relationships also transform national associative relationships (the national container societies). Europeanization is then observed by sociologists in the dynamic dislocation and relocation of concomitant processes of *Vergemeinschaftung* and *Vergesellschaftung* in the bounded institutional setting provided by the EU. Europeanization in terms of *Vergemeinschaftung* and *Vergesellschaftung* relates to both associational and communal relationships that are institutionally embedded, legally empowered, and collectively interpreted as continuations of the core narratives of European modernity.[15]

Europeanization will throughout this book be used as a key term for the sociology of European integration. Within political science, Europeanization is generally conceived of as a one-way process of domestic change that is *caused* by European integration. In sociological terms, Europeanization is not a one-way causal relationship. It instead proceeds in accordance with the same patterns of social integration and transformation already identified by Emile Durkheim, Max Weber, or Georg Simmel more than a century ago. When I speak of *Europeanization* in the following, I relate in broad terms to such processes of European *Vergemeinschaftung* and *Vergesellschaftung* and analyze the many ways in which these processes are carried and reflected upon by its own protagonists: the institutions and citizens that populate, experience, interpret, and contest Europe.

There is good reason to assume that a sociology of European integration will be a political sociology.[16] It will be a sociology that places political institutions center stage and analyzes vertical processes of Europeanization and their impact on society. Europeanization in terms of *Vergemeinschaftung* and *Vergesellschaftung* takes place in a bounded institutional setting. It can be open or closed to outsiders who wish to join the European associational and communal relationships. Europeanization not only distinguishes between internal and external relationships but also constitutes majority and minority relationships. Europeanization is thus constitutive of power as much as it transforms existing power relations. The political institutions of the EU are central to this dislocation and relocation of social relations in contemporary Europe.

It is hard to imagine alternatives to an account of Europeanization that is informed by the political. If it were still possible to reduce the European Communities to a common market, we could imagine an economic sociology that studied the integration of market economies or that looked at markets as social fields for the production and sale of goods and services (Fligstein 2002). This is not in line with most existing accounts of Europeanization, which describe the effects of European integration reaching far beyond the market. There is a putative normative impact of European integration that affects social cohesion and the way we draw the boundaries of our societies. At the same time, many analysts still claim that it is too early for sociology to step in because Europe still lacks the social foundations of an emerging society. Political institutions, power, and decision-making are, from this perspective, better described by political science, and sociologists need not bother as long as the social foundations of member states' national societies are not altered. The assumption of many EU scholars is thus that EU politics can be analyzed independently from the notion of a European political society. As I shall argue below, such a vision of EU politics without society has not only become increasingly obsolete; it is, in fact, an oxymoron.

This rejection of the political science agenda of the EU does not in turn mean that political sociology should fully embrace the agenda of classic sociostructural analysis of society as an internally differentiated and externally delimited social entity (the so-called national container society). The emerging European society cannot be simply narrowed down to variables of class, education, socialization, division of capital, or welfare as has been proposed by comparative sociologists. [17] An alternative research agenda has been developed in an attempt to relate analysis of the social foundations of European integration to the social practices and discourses that unfold in relation to institution building, the delegation of political authority, and the application of law in an EU context (Delanty and Rumford 2005). This is strongly reflected in the Europeanization research agenda I wish to promote in the following chapters. I apply and develop an understanding of 'Europeanization' as 'practice' and as 'discourse.' Neither an economic sociology of the European market nor a political sociology of European institutions are of primary interest to me. Nor am I interested in a microsociology in the sense of reconstructing Europeanization as socialization of citizens or as group formation. My program is, rather, to look at different accounts of *Europeanization as society building*. I refer to Europeanization as comprising processes of the social construction of a European society. Europeanization unfolds in ongoing practices and discourses through which social relationships among Europeans are redefined and re-embedded. Europeanization is a process of interpretation and the justification of such processes of re-allocating social relationships. It is measured in the production and exchange of meaning among the protagonists, interpreters, and recipients of these practices and discourses concerning distinctly European ways of structuring social relationships.

Sociology starts with the insufficiencies of explaining European integration merely with reference to efficiency and functionality of governance. For sociology, society is more than just wishful thinking. Sociology cannot be interested in the European society as the *telos* of integration. Sociology instead seeks to understand the distinctive way of structuring social relationships within European space (Favell 2006). It identifies regularities in how Europeans behave and enter into relationships with one another. Sociology focuses on society as a *constraining factor* of European integration that shapes the present choices and preferences of the actors involved. It also analyzes the conditions under which society becomes an *enabling factor* of European integration, accounting for accelerated change in Europeans' behavioral patterns and expectations (Trenz 2011).

What is the specific way of looking at European integration that distinguishes sociology from political science and normative accounts of European integration? In identifying the legal and political order of Europe, sociology is not limited to ad hoc explanations of decision-making processes. It does not ask how political authority is applied but rather how it is constituted. This implies a broad view of political institutions, which are analyzed not only as formal legal bodies with particular mandates but as patterns of social relationships. As such, institutions represent shared norms and expectations and thus lay the groundwork for trust and solidarity among the members of society. Sociology reconstructs the belief systems that shape the practices of legitimation and delegitimation as driving forces of European integration. In identifying the normative order of Europe, sociology does not ask: What is the adequate and legitimate way of shaping the European Union? It instead asks: What kinds of norms and ideas are held as valid, and how do they operate within the EU? It does not ask: What are the ideal contents of European citizenship? It asks: How and under what conditions can European citizenship as a formal legal category be transposed into citizenship practice? (Eder and Giesen 2001). Nor does it ask what kinds of procedures of participation ought to be enacted by the EU but instead asks how new opportunities for participation become salient and how they are occupied by the people of Europe (Ruzza 2004). Finally, with regard to the long-term EU constitutionalization process, the sociology of European integration is not interested in the legal contents of a written constitution but rather in the possible shape of a European society as a *constituent* of a particular kind of polity that bestows it with legitimacy (Fossum and Trenz 2006a).

The basic insight for any sociological theorizing is that European integration is not only useful, it is also meaningful (Delanty and Rumford 2005: 3). It produces and reproduces *social sense*, which according to Max Weber (1978) is to be deemed the basic category of sociological thinking. The search for the 'meaning' of European integration has transformed the European Union from a common market into a political and social entity. The European Union has become committed to a normative project of society building. There is, however, a huge discrepancy between concern about the normative deficits of European integration and the lack of a theory of society. European society is not simply an object of utopian thinking; it becomes, in the voice of another classic of the sociological discipline, a *social fact* (Durkheim 1982): European integration establishes stable patterns of behavior between state and non-state actors. It raises norms and expectations that bind these actors together into a unified whole that is independent from and constrains individual responses and preferences.

One problem for contemporary social theorizing is that most analytical categories of the social sciences were developed within the nation-state framework. As such, they account for the discipline's mainstream "methodological nationalism," which considers nation-states and nationally bounded societies as the basic units of analysis (Beck 2003). The nation-state model has also shaped sociological understanding of the stability of society and the possibility of social order. By relying on some basic commonalities, such as language, culture, and tradition, national society was able to accommodate internal diversity and appease redistributive conflicts. Its historical achievement consists of further recognizing its members as equals and thus laying the foundations for trust and solidarity among its citizens.

The European Union is a double challenge with regard to this traditional thinking of society as a hierarchically organized and culturally homogeneous space. First, the European Union has consolidated as a non-state entity. In contrast to traditional forms of *government* as the realm of states and authoritarian rule over a given territory, European integration unfolds as a new form of *governance*, which is advanced mainly by independent regulatory bodies and agencies. Governance is not located within one central authority but instead dispersed across a variety of state and non-state actors, administrators, and experts at the regional, national, and supranational levels of political aggregation.[18] From this new form of political organization as a complex system of multilevel and multicentered governance, it would be a mistake to assume that the EU is also a nonsociety entity (Rumford 2002: 46ff). The overcoming of the traditional state focus instead becomes a dynamic element for societal forces to leave the national container behind. The dispersion of rule-making is also linked to a new plurality of governance, including various societal stakeholders, affected parties, and social constituencies (Kohler-Koch 2007).

Second, the European Union is designed to accommodate enhanced social and cultural diversity within an open and still largely undefined societal space. It is committed to *positive integration*, with the aim of guaranteeing the continent's social cohesion and stability. The EU has, for instance, been particularly successful in promoting economic development in structurally weak regions. It has also defended the rights of workers, women, and minorities. European integration thus has direct and indirect redistributive effects, which reconfigure the space of solidarity among citizens. At the same time, the European Union's competences are increasingly expanding into areas that affect national society's autonomy and internal cohesion. These disintegrating effects are manifested in the opening of internal borders, the new mobility and competition in the labor market, the breaking of local traditions and solidarity, and a new heterogeneity of social practices and milieus.

We can summarize at this point the possible contributions of sociology for an understanding of European integration as a *social fact*. Sociological insights are needed to understand a) the 'meaning' of European integration beyond rational design and purposeful action; b) the constraining and/or enabling factors of integration as a teleological project that stretches from market building to polity building and society building; and c) the dynamics and mechanisms of integration and disintegration, of binding and unbinding, of internal differentiation and external adaptation, which demarcate the conflictual field of the emerging European society.

Sociological accounts of European integration focus upon this basic problem of the internal differentiation and external adaptation of an emerging European society. "Unity in diversity" is the phrase that perfectly captures these social dynamics of Europeanization (Olsen 2007; Delanty and Rumford 2005). The European Union today is caught in the contradictory situation of needing to define a European commonness that is universal but nevertheless distinct from the global. At the same time, the European Union is committed to protecting and even enhancing its internal diversity of cultures and social milieus (Delanty and Rumford 2005: 60). We can expect this process of coping with differences and striving toward unity to be highly conflictual. In the following, I will argue that it is precisely this conflictual situation of negotiating the unity and diversity of a new political order that makes European society thinkable.

In the following chapters, I will group sociological accounts of modern society along different lines by mapping the unity and diversity of Europe's social space. European society will then become visible from two angles. First, European society will become visible as a structured diversity of national societies and as a new heterogeneity of practices within the institutional space demarcated by the EU. Second, it will become visible as a unitary social order through specific integrating efforts and mechanisms, which are linked to new social imaginaries of Europe as a meaningful whole. Table 1.1 provides an overview of the various sociological perspectives for studying the diversity and unity of Europe.

EUROPEANIZATION: DIFFUSE BUT POPULAR

The meaning that is attributed to Europeanization is wide ranging, encompassing long-term historical transformations (Kaelble 2004; Conway and

Table 1.1. The Sociological Mapping of the Unity in Diversity of Europe

Unity in Diversity	*Market Europe*	*Political Union*
differentiation	*unification*	
territorial	structured diversity of national societies	common constitutional framework
functional	heterogeneity of practices within an institutionally demarcated space	common legal standards

Patel 2010); the dynamics of societal change and advance of modernity (De-lanty and Rumford 2005); the convergence of political cultures, the public sphere, and collective identities (Koopmans and Statham 2010; Risse 2010); and more confined political science analyses of adaptive processes of member state law, policies, and administration (Heritier 2007). Like modernization or globalization, Europeanization refers to large-scale processes of transformation of contemporary politics and society that are experienced by large groups of people and collectively interpreted. It affects not just economy or politics but also society, which is involved in its interpretation. There is furthermore often an implicit underlying normative assumption as to what Europeanization should aim for and achieve. It would enhance economic and social cohesion and integrate the Common Market. It would turn elite support into mass support. It would turn ordinary people into good Europeans. It is, of course, possible for bad Europeans to promote some form of Europeanization as well, and it is equally possible that Europeanization is correlated with enhanced conflicts and the emergence of new divisions among Europeans.

In all of these uses, Europeanization is introduced as a generic concept of shared relevance for researchers who look for commonalities beyond their particular cases. As a concept for interdisciplinary research, the term invites dialogue and broader understanding in the social sciences and humanities. Some scholars explore causalities in terms of the European Union's policy impact on nation-state law and administration. Others are primarily interested in multiple structural configurations of European social and political space. Europeanization is an important bridge concept for these different schools of European studies. Even though these scholars do not necessarily share the same epistemic presuppositions, reference to Europeanization enables them to put away from their disputes and agree on a joint research agenda.[19]

As part of such routine references to Europeanization, the research community is also united in its complaints concerning the term's deficiencies and its imprecise or ambivalent theoretical and empirical focus. Johan Olsen, in an article on the "many faces of Europeanization," asked already in 2002: "Europeanization: A fashionable term, but is it useful?" To approach the term's usefulness, he distinguishes between five different uses, from the generic to the more specific: 1) Changes in external territorial boundaries; 2) the development of governance institutions at the supranational level; 3) implementation and impact of EU policy and regulation at the subnational and national levels; 4) exporting EU policies and standards beyond EU borders (widening); and 5) long-term institutionalization and constitutionalization of the EU (deepening).

At the most generic level, Europeanization is often regarded as a form of either *institutionalization* (in terms of the development of the market, the public sector, and government) or *socialization* (in terms of the development of individual life chances and orientations). Most researchers discuss Europeanization in relation to larger processes of cultural, social, and political embedding but also in terms of the commitment of smaller units to larger systems. There is a hidden Durkheimian agenda in Europeanization research, which is linked to the evolution of shared practices, routines, and rules of enduring cooperation and collective problem solving (Swedberg 1994). Europeanization research provides a wider framework for investigating the expected spillovers from market to polity and society. Functionalism and (new) institutionalism are the main intellectual inspirations of Europeanization scholars who occupy new and broader research agendas in the study of European culture, values, and identities. Europeanization is reinterpreted here as a social experience that includes the people of Europe and thus expands from institutions to society at large. The enthusiasm for the term Europeanization is partly related to the self-understanding of the European studies research community as explorers of a new polity, a new system, or even a new society (Eigmüller and Mau 2010).

More specifically, Europeanization can be related to processes of vertical integration and processes of horizontal integration of society (table 1.2). From the first perspective, Europeanization is about shifting power relations. It is about how Europeanization affects the exercise of political authority and control. The exercise of political power is a good element for building drama, but depending on the social situation, it can be also routinized and integrated into everyday life experiences. Both processes of dramatization and normalization are relevant to understanding how Europeanization occurs through vertical integration and impact. From the second perspective, Europeanization is about shifting loyalties. It is about how Europeanization affects people's lives, social networks, and forms of mobility. It constitutes horizontal relationships among the people of Europe, which again are collectively interpreted and used as elements of life histories. In common with the exercise of political power, identities may become salient, mobilized, or contested, or they may remain beneath the surface. In light of the difficulties in accounting

Table 1.2. Europeanization as Related to Vertical and Horizontal Integration of Society

Europeanization	Impact	Social Dynamics
Vertical: legal and institutional hierarchies	shift of political authority and control	• routine: compliance (permissive consensus) • drama: politicization (constraining dissensus)
Horizontal: social transnationalism: networks and mobilities	shift of loyalties	• routine: socialization (banal Europeanism) • drama: new identity politics

for the core content of what is called a 'strong' European identity, Europeanization research has focused on the emergence of a "European identity light" (Risse 2010). As such, Europeanization is seen as occurring through horizontal integration and the slow but steady socialization of European citizens. It is about living across the Øresund in Sweden and commuting to Copenhagen, about going for shopping tours from Denmark to Germany, about using cheap Ryanair flights for weekend trips, about paying with the same currency in several European countries, about studying abroad, about meeting a partner from another country, about entering a European association—all of these interesting new opportunities that people use to make profits, to expand their radius in professional work, to plan their leisure activities, or to spread their expenditures throughout the common market (Favell 2008; 2009).

Johan Olsen's tentative answer to the question of whether these different 'uses' of the term Europeanization also warrant its 'usefulness' was 'yes,' but less as an explanatory concept than as an "attention directing device" (Olsen 2002: 942). The challenge is thus not primarily to insist on conceptual clarity and agree on an analytically sharp definition of Europeanization. Many scholars, especially within the political sciences, start their books and articles with a note of caution concerning the poorly defined and diffuse use of Europeanization in the literature (and how this particular publication intends to make a difference). Yet this generic and differentiated use of the term succeeds in encompassing the complexity of the European integration processes and the mechanisms of change that are associated with it. It is thus perfectly possible that the strength of the term Europeanization lies precisely in its polysemic translations by various disciplines. The popularity and even the usefulness of the term Europeanization as part of interdisciplinary scientific writing and 'storytelling' is depending on some element of conceptual vagueness and confusion. References to Europeanization are meant to capture a complex process of societal, political, economic, and cultural transformation rather than to imply causal inferences between analytically confined variables. In the following, I will further explore this theme and suggest that Europeanization can be approached as part of interdisciplinary scientific storytelling. I will first outline core elements of the scientific story informing the self-understanding of the European studies community. Against this template, it will be possible to distinguish four narratives for the social imagination of Europe, which contain elements of triumph and success but also of drama, failure, and trauma.

EUROPEANIZATION AS INTERDISCIPLINARY SCIENTIFIC STORYTELLING

European integration studies has applied discourse-analytical approaches to emphasize how meaning is attributed to political processes and how the interests and identities of participating actors are derived from an ideational context (Diez 2001a; 2001b). Europeanization has come to "provide a cognitive filter, frame or conceptual lens or paradigm through which social, political and economic developments might be ordered, narrated and rendered intelligible" (Hay and Rosamond 2002: 151). To identify 'stories of Europeanization' from a multidisciplinary perspective is then to reconstruct the discursive repertoire of ideas, knowledge, narratives, and understandings at the disposal of Europeans. Such an approach could ultimately be elaborated upon in the form of a sociology of knowledge of European integration that accounts for the interwoven nature of academic and politico-bureaucratic knowledge production in the case of the EU (Adler-Nissen and Kropp 2015).

From such a sociology of knowledge perspective, we can say that an important element of the scientific story is its attribution of causal relationships. One relevant data source for discourse analysis of Europeanization is found in texts that are used and produced by the European studies research community. For legal and public administration scholars, Europeanization is about the implementation of EU regulations and the direct and indirect effects of European policymaking in the domestic realm (Börzel 1999: 574; Vink 2003). Yet the attribution of causalities is not just an analytical operation of empirical science; it is also used as a defining element of the underlying concept. Goetz and Hix (2001: 27), for instance, define Europeanization as "a process of change in national institutional and policy practices that can be attributed to European integration." The notion of Europeanization operates through underlying causalities, which are simultaneously social attributes. Sociology speaks of attributions of causality as part of the semantic structure of modern society, not only in the sense that people willingly attribute meaning and actively interpret the social world but also in the sense that these attributes are inscribed in our social world and form part of the semantic structures through which we interpret society (Luhmann 1997). Europeanization suggests continuity and 'ordered' change. It synchronizes and historicizes contingent processes that could equally be perceived as asynchronous and disordered. It is the concept itself that allows the ordered view of society and its transformation. This is precisely the function of a narrative, which in this case is developed by the rather heterogeneous European studies scholarly community for the purpose of interdisciplinary scientific storytelling.

THE NARRATIVE CONSTRUCTION OF EUROPE: A RESEARCH PROGRAM

Europeanization relates to stories or narratives through which we can describe the contours of European societies in the plural and European society in the singular. Europeanization confronts us with societal differentiation and unification. It is no coincidence that the European Union appeals to the ancient symbolic formula of 'unity in diversity.' *United in diversity*, which was proposed by the Constitutional Treaty of the European Union as the motto of the EU, can be considered the meta-narrative from which various scientific and popular story lines departed to enter a new imagination of society. Cornelius Castoriadis regards this as a social instituting imaginary (Castoriadis 1975). Europe elaborates a particular imaginary, in this case the motto of unity in diversity, through which it can be experienced as a unitary social form even though its meaning remains internally contested and differentiated. Europeanization as social imagination relates to all kind of processes of interpretation and justification that provide us with explanations as to how Europe came into being as a meaningful social entity, how it is sustained over time, and how it should look in the future.

This book follows the path toward a sociology of Europeanization/European integration by approaching European society through its narrations. The author takes a participatory perspective on the various efforts of modelling European society that have been promoted over time by European institutions, public intellectuals, academics, journalists, and citizens. The empirical focus is on the field of discursive contestation of the meaning of Europe as 'society.' This includes, on the one hand, a focus on the intellectual history of Europe: the official story lines promoted by institutions, intellectuals, and academics in an explicit, reflexive, and often purposeful way. In the tradition of modern political thought, this intellectual endeavor unfolds through rational argumentation and justification, with the aim of delivering authoritative accounts of European integration and society. On the other hand, focus will rest on the various resonances of narration present in the practices of interpretation by various audiences and critical publics, which experience Europeanization through narration and which have experiences that in turn become objects of further contestation. As we shall see, narrative shifts (e.g., between the official, authoritative account of European integration as a 'success story' and the alternative accounts promoted by Eurosceptics) are often shifts of the protagonists of narration, when audiences become active interpreters who enter the stage of Europeanization (the 'people of Europe').

The problem is that Europe has over time accumulated an immense repertoire of stories, narrative threads, symbols, and images of its unity in diversity and that these stories are told differently in different locations of Europe. This renders arbitrary any attempt to establish the generalized validity of these stories. The aim cannot be to test the plausibility of the narration of European society but instead to collect evidence for the cognitive structures and norms that underlie the narration and allow its dynamic contestation (Eder 2006b, 2011). The project of a sociology of European integration goes beyond the application of a comparative method, which simply documents the differential emphases given to these stories in different parts of Europe. In order to reconstruct how Europe as a "cognitive project" is turned into a "narrative project" (Eder 2006b: 262), we must highlight the existence of a shared identitarian space that can be explored through text and discourse analytical methods. A basic distinction in text interpretation is the underlying genre. The genre that best applies to tell the story of Europeanization is the ancient form of the *saga*. A *saga* refers to 'what is said' in common. This is not so much explicitly in the form of officially approved and valid stories but rather implicitly in the everyday use of language. There is thus an inbuilt ambivalence in the tale, which makes it difficult to distinguish what is real from what is fiction. The accuracy of the saga is often hotly disputed among those who share it. There is a dispute about the fictional and the real elements of the story of Europeanization, which not only drives the 'science' of European studies but is a defining element of and driving force for Europe's narrative construction.

From this last perspective, Europeanization research could be used to program a cultural sociology of European integration that analyzes precisely these processes of constructing and diffusing Europe's meanings and interpretations. The object of analysis could, on the one hand, be the so-called 'high culture' of Europe. European studies scholars within the humanities look, for instance, at various cultural products, at processes of articulating culture, and at the media institutions at disposition for the diffusion of culture. The more detailed focus could be on the role of producers of culture or the role of receivers, for instance, of European film production and the audiovisual policies that are implemented for transnational film promotion and diffusion (de Smaele 2009). The common market as a space for 'cultural Europeanization' operates through the products of 'high culture' as potential vehicles "to spread norms, ideas and identities; and the European Union clearly has the ambition to foster a 'sense of Europeanness' and a 'European identity,' as well as an awareness and appreciation of Europe's national cultures" via the Europe-wide distribution of its cultural products (de Smaele 2009: 17). On the other hand, a cultural sociology of European integration could be programmed so as to analyze the changing social practices through which people experience and ascribe meaning to transnationalism. We would then not primarily be interested in the active production of culture and its interpretation but instead in the effects of Europeanization on people's everyday lives. The former is contained in what I will reconstruct as 'triumphant Europeanism' while the latter relates to what I will call 'affirmation of everyday life' or 'banal Europeanism.'

The saga of Europeanization can thus embrace the extraordinary and emphasize 'high culture,' but it can also tell popular stories, reflect routines and common practices. The validity of the underlying stories can furthermore be emphatically confirmed or rejected. Europeanization can be supported, or it can meet resistance. Along these two axes of extraordinary/routine and affirmation/disruption, we arrive at the following matrix of genre distinction for narrating the social bonds in Europe (table 1.3):

Following the first and the third variants in table 1.3, Europeanization affects the world of ideas and collective identities. The first genre narrative relates Europeanization to affirmation of the extraordinary of Europe. Europeanization is value driven and goal oriented. The negative template of this optimistic narrative is found in the third variant of Europeanization, which is interpreted as unsettling or negating the extraordinary of the national. The triumph of Europe is turned into the trauma of Europe, which is feared and perceived as a threat to traditional values and identity. Following the second and fourth variants, Europeanization affects material life chances. The second variant is linked to Europeans' concrete life experiences and ordinary coexistence. The negative template of this second narrative is the crisis narrative, in which the routine is disrupted, and material life is threatened. The social basis of the carriers of the stories shifts from the elites as narrators of triumph to the subversive challengers of Europe (the Eurosceptics) and eventually also includes the 'ordinary people' as those who either profit from the opportunities brought about by European integration or suffer from the crisis attributed to Europe.

Table 1.3. Narratives of Europeanization

Europeanization	*Affirmation*	*Disruption*
The extraordinary (heroic)	1) triumph	3) trauma
The ordinary (banal)	2) routine	4) crisis

Throughout this book, the four narratives of Europeanization will be treated as 'life stories' of the Europeans themselves, that is, as collective interpretations of their shared experiences of living in Europe. We will encounter various practices of European citizens and their representatives, who discursively share and interpret collective socialization experiences. They generate stories about what it means to be part of the common market, to take profit from it, or to suffer from its provisions; to be a European citizen and, as such, to cross borders, enjoy rights, and make claims for their extension; to be governed or to claim greater autonomy and self-governance. The form these narratives of Europeanization take is to a large extent determined by existing media outlets through which knowledge and information are channeled, collective interpretations are promoted, and their validity contested. A European public sphere forms the infrastructure for societal communication concerning the meaning and relevance of shared European experiences. This has its roots in the traditional offline media outlets such as quality newspapers, tabloids, and public broadcasting, but it is quickly expanding and transnationally diffusing online, including through social media networks. [20] The common narrations of Europe become, so to speak, reference points for processes of collective identification if they meet the condition of public resonance. This introduces an audience perspective into the narrative construction of a European society. In the literature on EU identity and legitimacy, the audience is made measurable through opinion and attitudinal research, which tests the plausibility of the narration of Europe through parameters such as support, trust, and conviction. [21] This book, however, goes significantly beyond the audience perspective on European narrations and their passive reception. In the citizens of Europe, European narrations encounter a general audience of resonance but also a critical public with its own interpretative performance. It is thus important to consider how the stories, tales, or narrations of Europe constitute social relations among the Europeans. "Telling stories implies a social relationship and implies a space within which such stories circulate" (Eder 2006b: 257). The sociological perspective on Europe's symbolic space, which is bordered by shared stories (Eder 2006b), implies an analysis of the public performance of narration through the eyes of the narrators, their interpreters, the critical publics, and the receptive audiences.

When reconstructing the public performance of European narrations in the following chapters, I will thus draw upon manifold sources. In methodological terms, the chapters will focus on political and cultural elites who propose narrative constructions of Europe that differ from the narrations of the national. In the first empirical chapters, this is the intellectual discourse that constructs Europe as a distinct symbolic space drawing open-cosmopolitan borders. In the second chapter, this perspective changes to the one of the 'ordinary citizens,' whose border constructions are often implicit, banal, and everyday. In the third chapter, we will encounter a narration of opposition in which the symbolic space of cosmopolitan Europe is contested and boundaries are re-appropriated. In the last crisis narration, we encounter a symbolic space of deconstruction in which boundaries are dissolved. Those who speak and will be quoted from in the chapters are therefore rarely 'ordinary citizens.' Those who amplify the public voice are institutional actors, intellectuals, academics, and journalists. A central role is played, for instance, by EU scholars themselves, who, as shall be seen in the chapter on Europe's triumph, play an important pro-integrationist role and have lately reappeared on the scene as interpreters of crisis (see chapter 5). This does not turn these four narratives into purely academic discourses but simply testifies to their strong interlinkage.

The methodological choices made in this book are informed by this narrative approach toward the reconstruction of contested meanings of European society. Narrations of Europe's triumph and trauma, of routine and crisis, will be extracted through text and discourse analytical methods. Those who speak are the carriers and the protagonists of Europeanization, but they are observed at different points in history, at extraordinary turning points in European integration and in everyday routine interactions. We zoom in on them through several lenses: through the accounts given by EU scholars and their professional observations of Europeanization, through institutional self-descriptions and texts delivered by EU actors and institutions, through critical accounts of public intellectuals, and through public accounts filtered and framed by the media.

This book has been written with the intention of delivering a research synthesis and not in order to provide full documentation of single project findings. The different accounts of Europeanization that are elaborated upon in the individual chapters all result to different degrees from the author's previous involvement in several European cooperative research projects, yet they also make a broad use of secondary literature, which, in fact, is used as an important intellectual source of narrative reconstruction. This method has the advantage of delivering comprehensive state-of-the-art reconstructions of the historical sociology of Europeanization (chapter 2), of the sociology of everyday Europeanization and social transnationalism (chapter 3), of the field of EU contestation and Euroscepticism (chapter 4), and of the growing literature on European crisis and forms of social resilience (chapter 5). Bringing these different strands of sociological research on Europe together requires me to draw upon different methodologies, to be conceptually open, and to constantly shift between academic and public discourse/media narratives. In terms of the methodologies used for the interpretative reconstruction of these narratives, I have employed the following discourse and text analytical tools: In chapter 2, I approach the 'cosmopolitan Europe' mainly through the 'authoritative account' of science, which is delivered by academic texts and normative political theory writings on the distinctiveness of the European political order and its relationship to global justice and democracy. I further draw upon findings from two large comparative research projects on EU constitutional debates in the media in the period of 2002–2008.[22] Chapter 3 mainly builds upon secondary readings of the sociological literature on social transnationalism, which is reinterpreted by making use of Laura Cram's (2001, 2012) conceptualization of "banal Europeanism" and Charles Taylor's (1989) notion of the "affirmation of everyday life." The usefulness of this perspective is further tested with reference to selected findings from comparative media studies and their emphasis on the role of journalism, film, television, and more recently social media as promoters of shared lifeworlds for the Europeans. In chapter 4, I build upon comparative research on Euroscepticism, which has been developed together with Asimina Michailidou and Pieter de Wilde and documented in a couple of publications that map Euroscepticism during 2009 European Parliament election campaigns.[23] Finally, chapter 5 returns to dispersed writings and project designs for collaborative research on the current crisis, among which I draw, in particular, on a large comparative online media survey, designed together with Asimina Michailidou and Pieter de Wilde, concerning the contestation of EU legitimacy in the context of crisis (Michailidou et al. 2014). I further rely on important ideas and insights developed for the purpose of an edited book project on the political sociology of crisis in Europe, carried forward together with my colleagues Carlo Ruzza and Virginie Guiraudon (Trenz et al. 2015). The contributions in this volume were discussed at several workshops and conferences in the framework of the ESA (European Sociological Association) European Political Sociology Research Network 32.[24] They provide important material for the discussion of social resilience and resistance practices in chapter 5.

NOTES

1. It is for this reason that many sociologists prefer the more dynamic concept of Europeanization over the conventional and normatively loaded term of European integration (Delanty and Rumford 2005: 6).

2. A quick Google search for the term 'European society' in March 2015 ends with the following first-ranked entries: "European Society of Urogenital Radiology," "European Society of Aneastisiology," "European Society of Medical Oncology."

3. The Weberian historical context is also decisive for the years in which people like Robert Schuman and Konrad Adenauer received their university educations. Both Schuman and Adenauer were educated at the University of Bonn as constitutional lawyers, or in *Staatswissenschaften*, as this was called in Germany.

4. The most powerful testimony of this trust of the 'founding fathers' in the power of supranational integration can be found in Jean Monnet's autobiography (Monnet 1974). For the historical account of the "lives and teachings of European saints," see Milward (2000).

5. This reflects the inbuilt tensions of the EU regulatory regime and the question of whether harmonization (integration) is preferable over diverse and flexible arrangements (Bronk and Jacoby 2013).

6. For the range of political science theories on European integration, see the volumes of Rosamond (2000) and Wiener and Diez (2003).

7. The debate on input versus output legitimacy in EU governance is an attempt to set standards for the legitimation of the European integration project but also to agree on its limits. The hidden agenda of this legitimacy debate is controversy concerning the character of the EU and its novelty as a political entity. The new institutional and constitutional identity of the newly established European Union was heavily contested within the EU studies community after the reforms of the Maastricht and Amsterdam Treaties. By insisting on the difference between "output" and "input" legitimacy, European integration theorists could more clearly demarcate the European Union from the existing nation-states and exclusively allocate particular competences and policy areas as belonging either to the EU (thus open to supranational regulation) or to the member state (thus grounded in the solidarity community of the national community). For the latter, see, in particular, the work of Fritz Scharpf (1999) and Giandomenico Majone (1998).

8. See my own work on the politicization of the EU constitutional project (Fossum and Trenz 2006b; Statham and Trenz 2012). Most prominently, Hooghe and Marks (2009) reflect on the constitutional referenda experience to formulate a 'postfunctionalist' theory of integration, which brings societal contention back into focus. See also chapter 5 for a further elaboration of the need to once again make conflict an element of theorizing about Europe.

9. This controversy concerning how to frame a sociological approach to European integration is also reflected in the titles of the most important recent publications on the topic: Favell and Guiraudon (2011) propose a "sociology of the European Union," Eigmüller and Mau (2010) a "sociology of Europeanization," and Kauppi (2014) a "political sociology of transnational Europe."

10. Most explicitly Maurizio Bach, who claims that a political sociology of European integration does not need to be based on a theory of society but instead on an institutional theory of governance: "Europe without Society: Political Sociology of European Integration" (Bach 2008).

11. For an elaboration of the social history of 'European Society,' see the work of Hartmut Kaelble (1997, 2004, 2013).

12. For the institutional entrenchment of EU civil society see the two highly informed comparative case studies by Sanchez Salgado 2014; Bouza Garcia 2015; and the earlier work by Ruzza (2004).

13. A political sociology of Europeanization is outlined by Guiraudon et al. (2015); Kauppi (2014); and Zimmermann and Favell (2011).

14. Vergesellschaftung: "A social relationship will be called 'rational' if the orientation of social action rests on value- or end-rational comparison of obligation and interests. It is especially common, though by no means inevitable, for the rational relationship to rest on a mutual agreement. In that case the corresponding action is, at the pole of rationality, oriented either to a value-rational belief in specific obligation, or to an end-rational expectation of the loyalty of the partner."

Vergemeinschaftung: "A social relationship, on the other hand, will be called 'communal' if the orientation of social action—whether in the individual case, on the average, or in the pure type—is based on subjective sentiment of the parties, whether affectual or traditional, that they belong together" (Weber 1978: 40–41, emphasis in the original).

15. For the empirical research program of a sociology of Europeanization see the contributions in Eigmüller and Mau (2010) and Mau and Verwiebe (2010). In Germany, even a funding scheme for individual and collective research projects has been launched by the German Research Council (DFG) under the heading "horizontal Europeanization": http://www.horizontal-europeanization.eu (last accessed on August 3, 2015).

16. The theoretical alternatives in the political sociology of the EU are discussed in Chandler 2014; Kauppi 2014; Zimmermann and Favell 2011; Bach 2008; and Rumford 2002.

17. This is the tradition of comparative sociostructural analysis of societies, relying mainly on statistical data sources to demonstrate that European societies have developed structural similarities that group them together into one distinctive cluster of societies (Bettin and Recchi 2005; Crouch 1999; Lane and Ersson 1999; Therborn 1995).

18. EU scholars speak here of the EU's 'multilevel governance.' See Jachtenfuchs (2003) and Marks et al. (1996).

19. These bridge-building qualities might also explain the popularity of the concept of Europeanization for the formulation of research policies and the building of interdisciplinary programmes. A prominent example is ARENA at University of Oslo: "Advanced Research on the Europeanization of the Nation State." Research programs and centers also frequently propose to explore the link between 'Europeanization' and 'globalization' and thus successfully exploit two generic terms.

20. The European public sphere is defined by content that has a European dimension, by the *possibility* of transnational diffusion of this content, and by its reception by transnational publics. This does not imply that media organizations are genuinely European nor that their content is also *factually* distributed to a substantial degree in order to reach a genuinely European audience (or public). The public sphere defines the potentiality of societal self-communication, while its institutional shape remains incomplete and its principles only insufficiently implemented (Trenz 2005a, 2006b).

21. For an overview on EU identity research and its different variables of measurement see Lucarelli et al. (2011) and Risse (2010).

22. This research has been developed with my colleagues Paul Statham, John Erik Fossum, and Ulrike Liebert in the framework of two research grants under the ECRP scheme of the European Science Foundation (ESF) 2005–2009 for the project "Building the EU's Social Constituency: Exploring the Dynamics of Public Claims-Making and Collective Representation in Europe" and under the EU Framework Programme 6 for the RECON ("Reconstituting Democracy in Europe") project 2006–2011. The detailed findings are documented in Statham and Trenz 2011; Eriksen and Fossum 2011; and Liebert and Trenz 2008a, 2008b.

23. This survey on Euroscepticism was part of WP5 of the RECON ("Reconstituting Democracy in Europe") project funded by the Framework Programme 6 of the European Commission. For the full documentation of project findings see de Wilde et al. (2013); Michailidou et al. (2014).

24. For more information, please visit: http://www.europeansociology.org/research-networks/rn32-political-sociology.html (last accessed on September 9, 2015).

Chapter Two

The Triumph of Europe

Europeanization as a Success Story

The original plot of the saga of Europeanization is a success story. This is what I will call the heroic account of Europeanization as a triumph of history. Europeanization is not only anchored in shared history; history is also progressively interpreted as evolution toward a better future. European modernity in particular became the driving force for Europe's rise and continual expansion. Europeanization is thus synonymous with social progress that combines individual and societal learning and leads to higher aggregate levels of social integration. In the following, I will refer to this 'success story' as the authoritative account of Europeanization. For the reconstruction of the intellectual history of European integration, I mainly rely on official sources in which the protagonists of European integration engage in "rational argumentation" or seek justification for their pro-integrationist choices. The focus is, in other words, on the search for EU legitimacy through the promotional activities of EU actors and institutions. I have not, however, engaged in archival research, nor do I draw systematically upon primary sources such as institutional self-accounts, governmental statements, or politicians' speeches.[1] An important intellectual source for the reconstruction of this authoritative account of European integration is found instead in the academic discourse itself. I refer here to the important work by Schrag Sternberg (2013), who found direct resonance between the academic and the wider public debates, for instance, in the ways the democratic deficit of the European Union is identified and contested. From a sociology of knowledge perspective, we can also say that I seek in this chapter to trace the "co-production of social science research and European integration" (Adler-Nissen and Kropp 2015: 157).[2]

The prototype, which these stories of European triumph implicitly or explicitly follow, is the nineteenth century success story of nation-building and its inclusive and expansive drive. This is more applicable for a country like France, where the triumph of Europe can be interpreted as a continuation of the triumph of the French Revolution, than for a country like Germany, where the triumph of Europe instead substitutes the lost national narrative. The postwar history of European integration provides, however, a common denominator of positive identification for all Western societies, which have various reasons for distancing themselves from their national pasts. The triumph of Europe is found in the overcoming of the trauma of fascism, colonialism, or authoritarianism (Giesen 2004). At the same time, European integration is meant to renew national history. Europe is seen as more than just a feeble substitute for the national past: it releases the nation from its aberrations and more eccentric developments to authenticate again the 'real values' and 'common heritage' of our 'European civilization.' As such, the account of the triumph of Europe has been associated with the heroic epos of the founding fathers, their rescue of the shared heritage of European Enlightenment, their true beliefs and firm convictions—the lives and teachings of the European saints, as Alan Milward (2000) famously puts it.

The triumphal Europe reflects classic optimistic thinking that was prevalent at the time of industrialization as a generator of progress and civilization:

> The mood was triumphalist and optimistic: change was taken to be synonymous with betterment, improvement, amelioration of human condition. It was grasped by the concepts of evolution, growth and development: inevitable and irreversible unravelling of inherent potentialities of society. Change was raised to the level of autotelic value, it was seen as always good, sought and cherished for its own sake (Sztompka 2000: 5).

In this spirit, the promoters of a pan-European union in the interwar and immediate post-war period developed a vision of a united Europe of civilization and peace that would triumph over the divided Europe of nationalism and violence (Klausen and Tilly 1997). This "triumph of Europe" was endorsed as an intellectual project that was given expression mainly by poets, philosophers, and artists (Giesen 1999). As such, it continues to inspire intellectual discourse, typically appealing to the higher moral and aesthetic values of universalism and cosmopolitanism and rejecting the utilitarian play of power and particular interests. Turned into a credo, the vision of the triumph of Europe contains an element of holiness, representing the sacred realm of Europe as distinguished from the profane realm of national politics (Swedberg 1994: 383).

The triumph of Europe did not, however, remain abstract and limited to intellectual discourse. On the contrary, it was very much in line with the life experiences of ordinary Europeans. Individual life histories could be told as triumphant recoveries. The *Wirtschaftswunder* of the postwar period facilitated unprecedented wealth, social security, and technological innovation. Europeanization stood for the continuation of the historical process of industrialization and a guarantee of urban, industrial, and individual-liberal forms of life, for which most Europeans gave their approval as private citizens and as voters.

This emphasis on the main postwar achievements of European integration—the overcoming of Europe's historical divisions, the banning of fascism and aggressive nationalism, the guarantee of peace, and the facilitation of economic growth—become the main reference point for promoters of European integration. The central credo of peace, prosperity, and progress is also reflected in the accounts delivered by the EU studies community (Schrag Sternberg 2013: 14–44). The plot is based on the parallel story of deepening and widening and the *telos* of an ever-closer integrated union as inscribed in the Treaties. European studies scholars are connected through funding programs that closely associate them with this *telos* of integration. Protagonists of European integration were driven by the idea of the possibility of 'enlightened social engineering': "The motif that the foundation of the European Communities was a manifestation of voluntaristic action upon the world, of deliberative social engineering, was common in discourses celebrating their foundation" (Schrag Sternberg 2013: 31). The EU-funded Jean Monnet Programme, for instance, is devoted to spreading and enhancing knowledge about European integration.[3] They often join the chorus of public intellectuals to promote European integration as a vehicle for wealth, peace, justice, and democracy. Historians also build on them for pedagogical purposes to draft a European historiography, which according to Knudsen and Gram-Skjoldager is schematized in accordance with a dominant narrative template of progress and victory of values that originated in (Western) Europe and thus have a strong Eurocentric bias (Knudsen and Gram-Skjoldager 2014: 160). EU scholars form a rather closed and homogeneous community, held together by a strong belief in transnationality as a value and life project (ibid.). In an explicit and exemplary manner, museums also select and promote such narratives with a pedagogical purpose that often engages historians. Following this tradition, European historians have recently begun reflecting upon their mandate as educators and reformulating the idea of the museum as a possible place for the transnational deliberation of shared European history. As proposed by Wolfram Kaiser, the new professional group of European historians should help Europeans engage in an open-ended exchange concerning history and their common future (Kaiser et al. 2014). A 'teaching of history' perspective would thus contribute to the reunification of national histories, to the proclaiming European days of commemoration of Europe's liberation and victory over the nationalist and totalitarian past (such as Europe Day on May 9, which commemorates the Schuman declaration from 1950; or August, 23 which commemorates the date of the signature of the 1939 Ribbentrop-Molotov agreement between Nazi Germany and the Soviet Union; or January 27, which commemorates victims of the Holocaust) (Leggewie 2008; Closa 2010).

Part of the story of the triumph of Europe is its understatement. In distinction to nationalism, triumphant Europeanism is neither celebrated nor exposed to the world. In further distinction to nationalism, triumphant Europeanism does not rely on mass mobilization but instead proceeds through the top-down diffusion of values and symbols, through education, cultural policies, or the media (Sassatelli 2009; Shore 2000). It thus builds on forms of subtle communication through which progressive European elites address the as-yet 'immature' citizens. This understatement in the European integration project's teleology might also account for the rather low salience of culture and identity, which have been considered by-products of market integration. According to the functionalist belief, European integration is not something that needs to be promoted; it happens regardless. Similarly, there are only limited ways in which European culture and identity can (or should) be propagated. According to integrationalists such as Ernst Haas, socialization into a European identity will follow automatically from the material benefits received through European integration (Risse 2005). There is therefore no need to actively propagate European identity or even play it off against existing national identities. The federal dream of the founding fathers, based on the idea of a European rescue of the nation-state, was less tangible in the lives of the many bureaucrats who became established in Brussels (Milward 2000). It also contrasted with de Gaulle's vision of a Europe of nations, which was primarily intended as a French venture to promote the glory of *La Grande Nation* in the form of a Grande (Napoleonic) Europe, but with the exclusion of Britain (Schulz-Forberg and Stråth 2010: 35). There was thus also a strong political incentive for European elites to understate the truth they sought to propagate, the only truth they believed imaginable: the triumph of Europe.

A more explicit agenda for a European identity project was only set in the context of the enlarged Europe of the nine, that is, after the first round of accessions in 1974, when the heads of state and government felt the need to consolidate the institutional structures and secure support for the agreed-upon long-term plans for deepened integration. The Copenhagen summit of 1973 agreed for the first time on the declaration of a European identity, which was meant to sustain the idea of a united people of Europe but which, remarkably, required no immediate action (Schulz-Forberg and Stråth 2010: 40–42). With the priorities set for market integration and building institutional capacities, the issues of democracy, rights, and identities were sidelined in the 1970s and 1980s, but they were never completely off of the agenda. If anything, these years confirmed Europeanists' belief in incremental integration. Europeanization progressed through the intrinsic relationship between the market Europe and the social Europe as well as the slow socialization (and in some cases democratic re-education) of European citizens.

It was only after the fall of the Iron Curtain that the idea of the triumph of Europe was powerfully reasserted and the project for a Europe closer to its citizens was launched (Schrag Sternberg 2013: 76–100). The collapse of the communist regimes in the East of Europe was, however, mainly interpreted as an affirmation of Western values and the inevitability of liberal democracy rather than as a departure toward more inclusive, participatory, and cosmopolitan models of democratic order (Blokker 2009). The fall of the Wall was, in the words of Niall Ferguson, a moment of revelation, not of revolution.[4] Fukuyama's famous notion of the 'end of history' was meant as a diagnosis and not, as interpreted in some of the Feuilletons, as an expression of American-Western superiority over the world. In a way, this diagnosis of the "the universalization of Western liberal democracy as the final form of human government" (Fukuyama 1992: 3) was again formulated as an (under)statement of facts since it also disclosed the utopia of global justice and cosmopolitan democracy. The 'victory' of the West was thus not triumphantly celebrated, and even German unification simply 'happened' as a natural event instead of as a new turning point of national (or European) history. The long decades of incremental integration taught European elites to avoid open expressions of triumph. Similar to German unification implemented by ministerial bureaucracies, the whole post–Cold War settlement of Europe was left to bureaucrats in Brussels and the national capitals while the people of Europe, who were the heroes of the first hours, soon stepped back off the stage of European politics.

From a long-term perspective of global history, the Eastern transformations could be classified as the third wave of democratization in the late twnetieth century (Huntington 1991) and thus as confirmation of a historical trend and not as a departure. From a more radical tradition of democratic thinking, the post-communist settlement of Europe nonetheless raised important doubts concerning liberal representative democracy's claim to superiority and set the agenda for democratic innovation in both the post-communist societies of the East and at the heart of Western democracy. One important line of thought was the interpretation of the peoples' revolutions of 1989 in light of the idea of the self-democratizing civil society (Blokker 2009). This idea was trendsetting for a newly decentralized and participatory approach of local government. At the European level, this tradition was used to blame the 'democratic deficits' of the European Union and to call for more participatory designs of governance through citizen involvement. The status of European civil society was often discussed in analogy to the role played by civil society in the East of Europe (Arato 2011). Alternatives to liberal representative democracy were furthermore discussed in relation to deliberative designs and the notion of citizens' assemblies that could inform, if not replace, representative government (Bohman and Rehg 1997; Fishkin 2009; Gutmann and Thompson 2009).

The second—and related—line of thought was the dissatisfaction of many intellectuals and associated movements with national democracy, which was seen as insufficient for dealing with global problems. Justice, peace, and environmental sustainability had been high on the agenda in Western democracies since the mid-1970s, producing a global agenda in search of new models and solutions. Processes of denationalization, as manifested in the supranational delegation of power and competencies, left national democracies as empty shells and required catch-up democratization of the institutions built for European and global governance (Zürn 1998). The European Union was the most obvious candidate for the projection of such a new utopia of postnational democracy (Habermas 2001). As such, it would integrate through a form of deliberative supranationalism and detach itself from the need for coercion and centralized authority that was associated with the nation-state.[5]

It initially seemed that the newly established European Union would enter upon this path of postnational unification. The most explicit attempt to collect this narrative in the history of European integration was the more or less explicit constitution-making venture. The European institutions and the heads of state and governments entered the new millennium with a firm determination to settle the *finalité* of the European Union and to constitutionalize a European democracy that would be perceived as complying with higher standards and higher normative value than nationally confined democracy. The speeches that were delivered by European leaders around that time reflected a sense of euphoria over the unity and identity of Europe. The constitutional moment was thus meant as a revival of the credo of 'enlightened social engineering,' which drove the founding fathers of European integration (Schrag Sternberg 2013: 30). The deliberative drafting of a European constitution became for this class of European leaders the embodiment of their successful agency and their higher rationality, which triumphed over the irrational national past (Trenz 2007a). This was symbolized in new EU achievements and competences, such as the common currency and the emergence of the EU as a foreign policy actor. Very importantly, this new optimism for Europe's triumph was also conveyed by the media, and many influential journalists supported the idea of an EU constitutional settlement (Trenz 2007a). In this framework, a constitution was seen as the new *Zauberwort,* the new buzzword, for unification of a better and more democratic Europe (Schulz-Forberg and Stråth 2011: 57).

As I will explain in chapter 5 on the crisis of Europeanization, this constitutional hype of the early millennium cannot be detached from the catharsis that followed it at the end of the decade. In the EU context, postnational constitutionalism was primarily designed to introduce a new discussion concerning the norms and values that should guide European unification. As such, it was not simply about drafting a constitutional document; it was about reconceptualizing and contesting the key principles and processes on which a political constitution must reside (Shaw 1999: 579). By assessing the "constitution's gift" and merits of the postnational democratic settlement of the European Union (Fossum and Menéndez 2010), the EU scholarly debate has contributed to processes of value production and normative contestations at the core as well as informed the public and media debates related to them (Statham and Trenz 2012; Schrag Sternberg 2013: 153–186).

From the discursive-sociological understanding of Europeanization that I seek to develop in this volume, I depart from the existing literature by assessing the EU constitutional project not in terms of substance and product but rather in terms of process. The emphasis is here on the many competing claims about how to draft a genuine constitution for what type of polity and how to establish the *finalité* of integration and resolve the European Union's democratic deficits. These different and often competing accounts must be considered as part of the public contestations raising the 'type of polity question' in terms of defining what the EU is and how it should be reformed. The processes of public communication and mediation from the center to the peripheries of European value production is then crucial for explaining the socially integrative (or disintegrative) dynamics of European integration and the effects of enhanced Europeanization on the transformation of political order and society at large.[6]

The "process of value production at the European center" (Schulz-Forberg and Stråth 2010: 132–137) is, of course, plural and multifaceted since elites themselves possess different visions of Europe's path of integration and *finalité*. While it seems plausible to assume that Europe is formed by a broad consensus on the values of democracy in the égaliberté tradition that has informed European modernity (see the introductory chapter), there are important differences with regards to how the 'triumph of Europe' is anchored in history. In broad terms, a secular and a religious variant of triumphant Europeanization can be distinguished, which, as I will argue, delivers complementary rather than competing accounts of the success story of European integration.

COSMOPOLITAN EUROPE

The secular variant of the account of Europe's triumph takes as its main reference point the shared history of European Enlightenment. It combines the ideals of the French Revolution with an account of modern civilization and democracy that has been passed on to the European communities as a joint commitment and mission of European leaders. At the heart of this project is the idea of a need to overcome the nation-state, which is rejected on normative grounds as incomplete and increasingly at odds with the agenda of global justice and cosmopolitan democracy (Beck 2005; Held 2010). Cosmopolitan Europe is thus seen as a radical departure from the nation-state and its inappropriate and normatively deficient responses to global challenges (Beck and Grande 2007). Processes of Europeanization instead take the form of reflexive modernization, which "forces us to view Europe with the eyes of the others too, and hence to confront and overcome the provincialization of Europe simultaneously" (114). Cosmopolitan Europe is in this sense part of the "epochal perspectival shift of globalized modernity" (113) and can be traced empirically in the "simultaneity of unity and disintegration" of "boundary transcending practices," which go hand in hand with the establishment of new legal norms and institutions of transnational governance (114).

What kind of political restructuring does the cosmopolitan narrative envisage? The drafting of a European constitution was embraced by the cosmopolitans on the premise that it would be based on universalistic norms, defend an agenda of global justice, and at the same time become a positive reference point for the identification of the people of Europe. Constitution-making would have a catalytic effect on the emergence of a European civic demos, as Jürgen Habermas (1995) maintained in an influential essay in the mid-1990s. A constitution for Europe was thus closely linked to the democratization of Europe, not only as a legal and institutional form but as a practice that was expected to evolve over time. Constitutionalization, Europeanization, and democratization were seen as interrelated and occurring simultaneously, even interchangeably. In this way, the European constitution would symbolize the ultimate triumph of Europe over national particularities. European democracy would be grounded in a politically strong but culturally weak identity of constitutional patriotism, expressing the will of unity of a new political entity rooted in citizenship rights and practice as well as establishing bonds of mutual recognition between its plural cultural expressions (Eriksen and Fossum 2008; Magnette 2007: 17).

From the cosmopolitan perspective, a constitutionalized EU would be a kind of postnational arrangement with a global justice vocation that could be transposed upon the universal and inclusive community of democracy (Eriksen 2006). Part of this cosmopolitan storytelling is also Europe's collective learning from the past, reflecting over the deficits of Europe's first modernity and entering upon the path of "reflexive modernization" (Beck and Grande 2007). Cosmopolitanism as a 'higher reflexivity' of society over the particularism of national belonging is not simply a normative choice but follows the rules of the social. At the same time, social scientists translate cosmopolitanism into a political project for a Europe that strives for higher levels of 'civicness,' inclusion, and democracy. The cosmopolitan vision of Europe reinterprets society as open civil society rather than as a nationally confined community of citizens. Instead of a communitarian notion of European civil society, the cosmopolitan account embraces civic forms of interaction within and across Europe (the latter also allowing for clear demarcation of "uncivil society," see Rucht (2005) and Ruzza (2009). The embedding of civil society in world society is turned into a political program by Beck and Grande (2007: 195), who wish to reactivate the cosmopolitan component of the idea of civil society to open new societal spaces in which human and civil rights, legal status, and identity are interconnected and new transnational forms of life and political-democratic participation can proliferate.

This account of world (civil) society as a cosmopolitan project of rights is enacted by citizens who 'act locally and think globally' to engage in global justice and human rights activism. In challenging, for instance, liberal capitalism, the European market or the restrictive regime of border and migration control, they ask for justice beyond contextualized belonging and define a common good for "another Europe" that is not represented by the states and governments (Della Porta 2009). The question remains: Why should global civil society embrace European integration as a political project? Advocates of such an alliance point to the possibility of an institutional anchorage of claims for global justice endorsed by EU institutions. The European Commission in particular is committed to 'reflexive governance' and promotes global public goods through its policy programs and long-term strategies of sustainable development.[7] Involvement in such networks of governance is beneficial for civil society organizations for several reasons: strategically, to influence decision-making, as well as, from a more normative perspective, to be part of collective learning and agenda-setting, helping to overcome national particularism and engage European citizens in shared projects and experiences. Through the implementation of such policies, civil society is often bound in as a 'partner' at several levels, not only at the European level also in national and local government.[8] Another element of cosmopolitanization is the involvement of 'ordinary citizens' as addressees or stakeholders of such programs. Through rights and the recognition of difference, a new citizens' practice unfolds within the European Union (Saward 2013; Wiener 1998). As remains to be shown in the next chapter on the development of 'banal Europeanism,' citizens of the EU are to various degrees involved in unobtrusive everyday transnational social exchanges. Through such networks of "social transnationalism" (Mau 2011), European citizens experience diversity as "cosmopolitan conviviality" (Duru 2015). "Cosmopolitan conviviality" not only emphasizes the differences between people and groups but also the ability of people from different backgrounds to interact in daily life in a shared space, to socially produce a collective culture, collective identity, and sense of belonging in place (Duru 2015). In metropolitan areas like London, Paris, Berlin, and Copenhagen, people with different places of origin, nationalities, religions, and ethnicities share public space, interact, socialize, and develop postnational allegiances.

Such attempts to provide a sociological explanation for cosmopolitanism as a new ordering mechanism of postnational society continue to formulate social theory in the tradition of European modernity. The sociology of the "second age of modernity" (Beck et al. 1994) is built upon the old ordering principle of differentiated social order as 'unity in diversity,' the validity and applicability of which is reconsidered and adapted to the "postnational constellation" (Habermas 2001). Cosmopolitanism is thus meant to reference the higher reflexivity to which Europe has always been invited. The cosmopolitan imagination enables Europeans to look beyond their taken-for-granted identities and the membership categories derived from them (Delanty 2009). In practice, cosmopolitanism always works through the self's critical confrontation with the other and the world (14). In this sense, cosmopolitanism is not only a lived practice of transnationalism (as analyzed in chapter 3) but is also an evaluative standpoint (16) through which membership and belonging are challenged from the perspective of an applied ethics of global justice.

From this critical perspective, Europeanization can be seen as a form of cosmopolitanization to the extent that it is related to the building of such reflexive institutions and procedures (Delanty and Rumford 2005: 195). The ethical demand here is not so much that reflexive institutions and reflexive citizens would build a community of belonging based on the core value of peoplehood. The demand is rather that Europeanization should support a wider sphere of justice and solidarity (Delanty 2009: 202–203). The emerging European (civil) society is thus not based on a particular ethnos but is instead of a principally communicative nature (219). If the higher reflexivity of institutions or citizens proceeds in the form of a deconstruction of collective identities and membership, the arrival point cannot be a European notion of belonging. European cosmopolitanism cannot be fixed in a specific cultural form but only as an expanding horizon for existing cultural identities.

As I have argued previously, the idea that the higher reflexivity promoted by discursive understanding leads to a notion of cosmopolitanism is a sociological re-elaboration of the old European ordering problem of the unity and diversity of social and political order. In sociological parlance, cosmopolitanism is the organic solidarity that holds differentiated societies together. In the Durkheimian tradition, contemporary sociologists like Beck or Delanty deliver an account of cosmopolitanism as a mechanism of integration of modern differentiated society.

Cosmopolitanism is then, however, not simply politically desired; it is dictated by the laws of the social. Cosmopolitanism simply 'occurs,' but there are only limited ways of designing it. Cosmopolitanism is in this sense reinterpreted as a social condition and not as a political project. Similar to Durkheim, who argues that organic solidarity evolves in the transition from traditional to modern societies, cosmopolitanism evolves in the transition from the first to the second modernity. It results from functional differentiation, individualization, and globalization, which dissolve traditional solidarities and membership communities. Societies are forced into learning and reflexivity on how to organize diversity and the fluidity of boundaries and membership. They need to learn to accept difference, not strive to overcome it. Beck and Grande (2007: 509) consequently speak of cosmopolitan realism, meaning that cosmopolitanism is not targeting a higher morality but simply accepts the *indispensable* universal norms that impose themselves upon the postnational constellation.

In this last sense, the sociology of cosmopolitanism has been accused of an unintended naturalization of what was originally intended as a political project. According to Armin Nassehi (2006: 53–64), the "cosmopolitan realism" defended by authors such as Ulrich Beck risks being turned into a "cosmopolitan naturalism."[9] While the constructivist paradigm has been generally accepted to explain the emergence and political persistence of nation-states and national societies (constructed either through national interests or through the ideology of nationalism), the laws of cosmopolitanism are found in nature. They are, so to speak, prepolitical and presocial. The cosmopolitan principle of world society is not constructed through politics and as such attributable to particular social actors who enact it. Cosmopolitanism as something that 'simply happens' is instead formulated as a social law fundamentally underlying modern politics and becomes its 'asocial' driving factor. The implicit danger is that cosmopolitanism is employed as a device for overcoming not only social science methodological nationalism but also social science constructivism, which is meant as a critical tool for recognizing the contingency of any type of political order. For cosmopolitans, the universal (e.g., the defense of the global human rights agenda) is often given preference over the particular (e.g., the promotion of democracy in particular contexts). This implies a depoliticization of human rights, which are taken away from the collective and assigned to the individual in need of protection by global law and institutions against arbitrary state power. Rights are seen as preconditional whereas democracy remains contingent. As Beck and Grande (2007: 510) put it: "The basic principle of cosmopolitanism may be discovered and applied everywhere, at every level, and in every sphere of social and political activity—in international organizations as well as in families and neighbourhoods."

This epistemic critique of cosmopolitanism is also taken up by Delanty and Rumford (2005: 177), who have noted that the concept of cosmopolitan civil society draws upon a premodern and prepolitical understanding of the constitution of society. According to them, there is a tendency in the social sciences to replace methodological nationalism with a new essentialism. The idea that society is politically constructed and imagined through the nation-state as a political project that is made and promoted by humans is replaced by the idea that there is a different, more natural way of conceiving of society beyond the particularity of nationalism. Society is perceived as the unconstructed realm of nature, which paves the way for a new political thinking (and not a new political thinking that paves the way to a new concept of society). Accordingly, cosmopolitan (civil) society is composed of individuals who are subject to natural law, not state law. The universal validity of human rights is dissociated from state law. Whereas traditional civil society thinkingd regards rights as made by society against nature, cosmopolitan civil society is based on a natural law conception of human rights to preserve human nature against the arbitrariness of states (Delanty and Rumford 2005: 177). Thus, while national civil society is a contractual agreement to protect humans from nature, cosmopolitan civil society is perceived as the natural realm that liberates society from the unnatural, artificial, and arbitrary nation-state.

This indefiniteness of the kind of political order that is constituted and sustained by cosmopolitanism is also reflected in the diagnosis of Ulrich Beck, who on the one hand postulates the dissolution of nation-states as contained social spaces but on the other hand presupposes social laws of reflexive modernization that apply within existing political and institutional spaces and account for their transformation ('cosmopolitan Europe'). Beck can claim that cosmopolitanism automatically emerges whenever societies leave behind the national constellation and are confronted by the fundamental changes linked to globalization and reflexive modernization (the transition from first to second modernity). Cosmopolitanism that is grounded in the social laws of reflexive modernization is therefore meant as a smooth transition and not as a radical rupture or revolution. There is no need to base cosmopolitanism on reflexive learning or in the collective will for designing global law and governance. Cosmopolitanism simply imposes itself as indispensable, just as human rights and democracy are seen as indispensable ordering mechanisms, as "the sole remaining legitimation principle of political domination" as Eriksen and Fossum (2008: 16) put it. The cosmopolitan project in this sense perpetuates the image of a progressive and imperative modernization, which always starts from and always arrives at democracy and human rights—two co-original principles, which are mutually presupposing and supportive of one another (Habermas 1996: chapters 3 and 4).

There is, however, an inbuilt ambivalence in the cosmopolitan account when it comes to the definition of citizen membership and rights. Cosmopolitan civil society is all-inclusive, basing its ultimate legitimacy principle upon the force of universal human rights and not of particular membership categories. Members of this cosmopolitan (civil) society have little in common apart from their shared humanity (Eriksen and Fossum 2008; Eriksen and Weigård 2003: 244). All-inclusive cosmopolitan society thus constrains the ability of all other existing membership communities to justify constitutive distinctions between members and nonmembers. Membership is always suspected as incompatible with global justice and universal law and is, in fact, constantly thrown into doubt whenever and wherever the universal principle of rights applies. This incompatibility of membership categories with universal rights also applies to the EU citizenship project, explaining many of its inherent tensions and contradictions (Bauböck 2007).

The EU's attempts to construct a European (civil) society as a membership community can therefore be accused of relying upon a legitimation discourse that differs from the inbuilt cosmopolitanism of the European integration project. Instead of reference to cosmopolitanism and universal rights, EU institutions enhance citizenship and democracy through a focus on contextualized values of European citizens who develop a distinct identity based on a combination of civic and cultural components (Bruter 2004). The social science diagnosis of the cosmopolitan reality of Europe is in this sense not reflected in the particular identity projects of the EU and its citizens. "The EU is much happier to think of European citizens as national/European rather than cosmopolitan" (Delanty and Rumford 2005: 195). The lingering doubt, of course, is whether, in the event that European solidarity and the European demos came into existence, it would find that it was cosmopolitan rather than European.

The difficulties in translating cosmopolitanism into an institutional account of integration are also reflected in public and media discourse, where justifications of European integration approach the familiar models of civic and cultural community instead of cosmopolis. In our own comparative survey of EU legitimation discourse, references to the EU as a cosmopolis were nearly absent in media debates among political parties and journalists (Liebert and Trenz 2008a; 2008b; Vetters et al. 2009). Media tend to reinterpret the EU constitution as a political project designed to strengthen Europe's role in the world and to defend Europe's particular interest in a globally competitive market (Trenz et al. 2009). Accordingly, the emerging EU polity was conceived of either as a problem-solving entity or as a community based on fate and common values rather than as an inclusive cosmopolis based on universal rights. The EU's democratic deficit figures prominently in public and media discourse, but its proposed solution does not embrace the academic and intellectual discourse of postnational citizenship and the reflection of a multidimensional conception of sovereignty.

A normative critique of cosmopolitanism has primarily emphasized the possible elite bias of its intellectual defenders, who are often identical with those few who have the chance to engage in cosmopolitan lifestyles. "Cosmopolitanism of the few" is seen as a prerogative of Western elite groups (Brunkhorst 2006; Calhoun 2002). As Calhoun nicely characterizes this habitus of the new cosmopolitan elite: "We could say of cosmopolitanism that it requires too much travel, too many dinners out at ethnic restaurants, too much volunteering with *Médecins Sans Frontières*. Perhaps not too much or too many for academics (though I wouldn't leap to that presumption) but too much and too many to base a political order on the expectation that everyone will choose to participate" (Calhoun 2003: 100). Favell (2008: 32) provides an equally strong critique by typifying the new elite as the *Eurostars* (frequent travelers between Brussels, London, and Paris) "at the vanguard of European free movement," whose "lifestyles, consumer profile and cosmopolitan attitudes can be read off from the editorial content and advertisements found in the glossy on-board magazines."

From this critical perspective, one possible outcome of cosmopolitan projects like European constitution making could be an intensification of the struggles between what Bauman (1998) calls "globals vs. locals," "inside vs. outside," "here vs. there," "near vs. far away," and "margin vs. center." In the European sphere, this could lead to the reification of a new class bias between an elitist, highly educated, mobile, Europeanized (or cosmopolitan) new bourgeoisie and a nationalist, immobile, and traditional proletariat with a low educational profile. Universalist/European attitudes and particularist/nationalist attitudes would thus increasingly become indicators for class. On the one hand, this possible class bias in patterns of support and opposition to European integration has been partly verified by attitudinal research, where working-class people are found to display only low levels of Europhilia (Duchesne et al. 2013: 77). On the other hand, cosmopolitan attitudes are insufficiently measured in support of European integration but instead correlate with newly acquired lifestyles. As emphasized by sociological research on social transnationalism, rather than being limited to a small elite of Europhiles, Europeanization has become a middle-class phenomenon, with a new generation of mobile Europeans adopting cosmopolitan lifestyles (Favell 2014; for more details, see chapter 3).

CHRISTIAN EUROPE

Another path that has been chosen to promote the narrative of a triumphant Europe has been the call for a value-loaded Christian Europe. The turn toward Europe is part of the shared postwar orientation of Christian Democratic parties, mainly in the Catholic tradition in countries like Western Germany, Belgium, and Italy. In fact, major promoters of European integration were members of Catholic Christian Democratic parties.[10] Reference to a shared Christian heritage was less popular in the Protestant North, which combined benevolent welfare states with state churches and monarchies. The Swedish Social Democratic Prime Minister Tage Erlander suspected as early as 1950 that the driving force behind European integration was the consolidation of an underground Catholic political movement (Judt 2005: 158). The idea that the European Union should identify with the core values and historical traditions of Christianity was predictably promoted by the churches and by Christian Democratic parties, but across Europe, their defense of Christianity sought reconciliation with the secular values of the French Revolution, recognizing the primacy of popular sovereignty. In some parts of Europe, the twentieth century historical compromise of Christianity with democracy took longer to establish, yet these regions were frequently punished with marginalization or exclusion (like Portugal and Spain).

In many ways, European integration can be interpreted as a reconciliation of the historical confrontation between the premodern Christian Europe and the modern secular Europe. This is certainly explained by the postwar political constellation of firmly established secular democracies within which the churches had to contain their political ambitions. Western Europe's unique secularization is, however, misunderstood if one fails to take into account how the churches continued to play a key role as a moral and political agenda setter. Secularization may have marginalized religious politics, but Christian Democratic parties retained a power hold, and the role of the churches in education and socialization of a new generation of Europeans was substantial (religious education continues to be standard in many parts of Europe). Religion was therefore not simply reintroduced after Eastern enlargement (e.g., the strong role of the Catholic Church in countries like Poland) (Zielinska 2011); it was probably never absent in Western Europe, where the churches provided important impulses to the supranational integration movement. The churches were certainly active behind the scenes as powerful lobbyists with easy access to Western leaders in Brussels and the national capitals. Yet the churches were also campaigning out in the open for a united Europe as a moral and political project, often in opposition to reluctant national politicians (Foret and Schlesinger 2007).

The full embracing of the European unification agenda by Christian churches has also been driven by the churches' own efforts to overcome ecclesiastical division and reconcile the denominations. The path toward ecumenical communion allowed a redefining of the churches' relationship to plural (secular) society. In postwar Western Europe, churches could more easily position themselves as allies of the secular state in their defense of (Western) principles of freedom and democracy against the common enemy of communism. At the same time, the churches contributed to pluralism in Western societies, frequently opposing the state in defense of religious values and promoting a common good that was defined in opposition to nationalist particularism.

The reconciliation promoted by the churches did not remain abstract but crystallized into a genuinely European movement of moral and civilizational reconciliation among the formerly hostile populations of Europe (not least in an attempt to overcome internal divisions in pillarized multidenominational societies like the Netherlands and Germany). This movement became an important identifier for the postwar generation of young European citizens, including for instance the young Helmut Kohl. Under the broad umbrella of the churches, hundreds of thousands of (often young) people mobilized in Western Europe, campaigning for peace, reconciliation with former enemies, and international understanding. Offshoots of the post-1968 grassroots movements were also sheltered by the churches, expanding their agendas to embrace topics such as solidarity with migrants and the Third World or environmental protection. For these young generations, ecumenical communion was experienced as an opportunity for transnational encounters and routinized exchange with youngsters from other countries, for instance, through the legendary backpack pilgrimages and campground stays at almost mythical places such as the ecumenical Taizé community in France or the gatherings of young people in Assisi. For this generation of young Europeans, cosmopolitanism became a vocation, with religion constituting a shared reference point for overcoming one's own nationalist past.

Last but not least, the universal vocation of the churches is also reflected in their own organizational structures. The world church oscillates between an international organization and a NGO. As an international organization, it relies on a forceful institutional infrastructure that mediates in foreign relations among states. As a NGO, it builds upon the grassroots ecumenical movement as a powerful promoter of social transnationalism, promoting universal values such as peace and international solidarity (Byrnes and Katzenstein 2006; Mudrov 2011). At the EU institutional level, the churches—in their role as non-state transnational actors—became a natural ally of European institutions, committed to solidarity and supranational forms of allegiance. Church organizations such as Caritas assist, for instance, the European Commission in formulating and implementing the social policy agenda.

As an intellectual project, the defenders of a Christian Europe sought to distance themselves from the authoritarian and nationalist legacy of pre-war Europe and approached modernity through the back door of Western culture and civilization. The West could be fully embraced by the Catholic and Protestant churches in terms of its distinct value foundations and its inextricable allegiance with the United States (and Latin America). Apart from a cultural alliance between secular and religious forces, the West was also a political and military alliance against the threat of Eastern communism. The moral imperatives of Christian Europe were not, however, simply invoked to stabilize the authority of the Western regime. They could also be used to formulate a critical agenda with regard to what was perceived as excessive liberalization, industrialization, and individualization. The critique of the excesses of Western modernity as formulated by the churches matched the postwar European *Zeitgeist*, especially after 1968, with a new generation of

Europeans seeking moral and political renewal. Emphasis on the value foundations of Christian Europe embraced universalism in the message of community inclusiveness, solidarity, and peace. Christian intellectuals no longer supported a political resistance movement against secularization but instead sought common ground with other critical forces to defend the distinct value foundations and identity of Europe against communism and American-style excessive capitalism (Foret and Schlesinger 2007). Such a critical agenda was formulated by many ecumenical initiatives at the European level. The 'Together for Europe' initiative calls for a "relationship of communion," "a culture of reciprocity" through which different peoples and individuals can welcome, get to know, be reconciled with, and learn to respect and support one another.[11] Christianity here fully embraces the agenda of cosmopolitanism, promoting a multicultural and open Europe that respects diversity and is committed to global solidarity.

Through such programmatic writings, the churches made an important contribution to expanding the political agenda of cosmopolitanism and European integration. Christian Europe remained low profile, however, when it came to defining a moral and ethical agenda that differed from the Western project of enlightened universalism. The indeterminacy of the notion of a Christian Europe is reflected in the churches' own positioning between progressive supranationalism and deep conservatism. Outside of the church communities and their political adherents, the concept of a Christian Europe was rarely embraced by public intellectuals. Christian Europe remained not only intellectually indeterminate but also politically contested. The (rather unassertive) attempts of Christian politicians to promote an agenda of Christianity as part of Europe's political identity encountered the fierce resistance from people always alert to the churches' reactionary drive to impose the Christian faith upon secular society.

In the eyes of the progressive secular forces, the resurgence of a Christian Europe was necessarily antagonistic, not because their Christian counterparts occupied a radically different agenda in defense of European integration and cosmopolitanism but because the secularists regarded European integration as synonymous with secularization and thus interpreted it as a progressive historical force from which the decline of the old religious Europe would automatically follow. This view of religious decline as a "quasi-normative consequence of being a 'modern' and 'enlightened' European" (Casanova 2006: 89) explains the uncompromising refusal of many secular people to accept the resurgence of religion as part of public life. For them, the agreement that religion should not interfere in public life and should instead be a private matter had been the result of a decades' long political struggle, and the European Union should not be allowed to reverse this historic victory.

The fact that the balance between secular and Christian Europe was far from settled became evident in the struggle over the preamble to the European draft Constitution. The project of promoting cosmopolitanism through the drafting of a European constitution was meant as a consolidation of the civic European identity in the spirit of the European Enlightenment. The new 'civic religion' of a post-Christian Europe could not, however, simply ignore its own internal religious diversity. Religion was still strongly represented, not only by Christian Democratic parties in Western Europe but also by member states such as Catholic Poland and Ireland. The post-Christian Europe was furthermore inconsistent in its definition of internal and external boundaries against non-European immigrants, who happened to be nonsecular and non-Christian, as well as against Turkey as a secular country, which was still perceived as culturally different.

When the draft Constitution of Europe was negotiated in early 2000, the proposal to base the moral foundations of European integration on explicit references to Christianity remained heavily contested and was ultimately rejected by secular France, Belgium, and some of the Scandinavian countries. The question is whether this rejection of a Christian Europe was also reflected in the secular self-understanding of a civic community of Europeans or whether it merely reflected the political will and veto power of some member state governments. This relates to the quality of the constitutional debate and its capacity to become the driving force in the debate concerning the ethnic self-understanding of the political community of Europeans. Public debates about the moral and ethical grounds of a united and constitutionalized Europe would facilitate the self-constitution of a European demos, as was expected by adherents of constitutional patriotism such as Jürgen Habermas (1995). Such a form of "deliberative constitutional politics" has thus been regarded as a core condition for the capacity of a European constitutional project to generate public legitimacy.[12] In a large comparative project on constitutional debates in the media, the author and collaborators have tested these assumptions of the self-constituting dynamics of normative debates.[13]

Three waves of debate concerning the preamble and its (lack of) reference to God can be distinguished. The topic was first raised by Members of the Convention in 2002, who also sought to mobilize their respective parties within the national and European Parliaments. The European Peoples' Party (EPP) was the strongest proponent of a reference to the European religious heritage in the preamble, while other parties within the European Parliament were divided on the issue. In a second wave, the topic was raised by member state governments at the Intergovernmental Conferences (IGC) in 2003 and 2004. The proposal to include a reference to Christianity in the preamble was backed by a majority of member states but was categorically rejected by France, which threatened vetoes at the IGC. Church and civil society actors launched their lobbying campaign mainly during this phase, and the topic became most salient in the media. Thirdly, and with much less frequency, the call for a Christian Europe was used as part of the ratification campaigns of

2005 to demarcate pro-European or anti-European divisions. In our own comparative survey of ratification debates in the media, we find that public debates were divided on the issue.[14] In Germany, the ratification debate was rather consensual, and only a small number of MPs from the regional Christian Socialist Union (CSU) found reason to reject the Constitutional Treaty due to its lack of reference to Christianity. In France, the referendum debate was highly controversial, but public contestation led to a domestication of the debate in which self-understanding of the French *république* was at stake and common European frames of reference were set apart (Statham and Trenz 2012). Accordingly, nonreference to religious symbols in the final draft of the Constitutional Treaty was praised as a victory for French secularism. Claims in favor of a reference to God were typically promoted by foreign actors and the Vatican and as such perceived as an illegitimate intrusion into domestic debates. The external voice for a Christian Europe was perceived as a threat to republican French identity and its opposing vision of a Europe based on the values of the French Revolution.

The French referendum debate of 2005 cast doubt on the application of the notion of a Christian Europe, which in public debates is rarely associated with its universalist and inclusive mission but instead turned into a marker of European particularism and exclusivity. Appeals for a Christian Europe can be perceived as a threat to both the exclusivity and to the potential inclusivity of national identity. French republicans can rely upon a strong formula for establishing the criteria for political inclusiveness at the domestic level: Whoever adheres to the ideals of the French Revolution can adhere to the French republic, independently of ethnic or religious background. This differs when referencing the notion of Christian Europe, which remains culturally exclusive: While national citizenship is granted according to legal rules and guarantees, the recognition of being European remains purely cultural. Since European identity cannot be acquired, it is deployed negatively to demarcate the ethnic Europeans from the nonethnic European French. With reference to Europe, the national community can uphold its political inclusiveness while simultaneously insisting upon a new primordial distinction in the delimitation of collective identity: You can be included in the national community as a French Muslim, but you remain excluded from the community of Europeans as an ethnic Arab. Christian Europe is the most visible (and in contrast to racism, also more legitimate) signifier of this communitarian heritage of an ethnic community that demarcates a higher level of distinctiveness than the plural, republican community of citizens.

The prominence of Christianity thus points once more to the ambivalence of European cosmopolitanism, of which Christian identity claims to be a part. Yet it should also be noted that the limited range of debate over a Christian Europe rendered dubious its status as a hegemonic identitarian counter-discourse against the official variant of an inclusive political community based on equal citizenship. For most of its proponents, the idea of a reference to Europe's religious heritage was not introduced as a new particularism but was defended in inclusive and universalistic terms, allowing for different religious faiths to be identified with the European political project.

What kind of political configuration could be envisaged by this account of unification in the tradition of Christian heritage? One of the few initiatives by a well-known EU scholar to shape the agenda for a Christian Europe was promoted by the constitutional lawyer Joseph Weiler, who published his "explorative essay" in Italian (distributed by Catholic publishers in other languages but not available in English) (Weiler 2003). For Weiler, religion matters not only for the Christian faith's "mantra" of solidarity and 'unity in diversity.' The church also matters as a matrix of political organization, especially with regard to the principle of subsidiarity, according to which the higher authority should not interfere in the autonomy of subordinate life-worlds but should instead support them and help them coordinate their activities with a view to the common good (Cooper 2008). To the extent that this 'taming of pluralism' is specifically European, it contains an ethical order that is derived from religion yet remains applicable as a model of constitutional pluralism and tolerance in a transnational entity such as the EU.

The plea for a Christian Europe remained fairly unpopular among EU scholars and intellectuals. [15] In contrast to the cosmopolitan vision of a post-national Union that would replace the existing nation-state order, the idea of a Christian Europe is closer to federal thinking, according to which the existing national units would be subordinated but maintain a degree of autonomy. From the religious-federal perspective of subsidiarity, the constitutionalized political Union would be sufficiently strong to generate trust and solidarity among European citizens as members of a sovereign political community to which persisting cultural particularities could be clearly subordinated (Góra et al. 2011). From the secular-postnational perspective, however, Europe's triumph would consist in overcoming the particularity of 'identity constructs.' The European "cosmopolis" would rely on discourse and "shared humanity," not on collective identity (Eriksen 2006).

Whether the European integration project as proposed by the founding fathers is to be reinterpreted as a triumph of European universalism and Enlightenment is thus debatable from both secular and religious perspectives. While the secular and religious accounts of progressive Europeanization approach each other, the target of these accounts—namely, a united, constitutionalized, and democratic Europe—becomes increasingly blurred. This new uncertainty in Europe's political order is reflected in the post-constitutional debates since 2005, which accompany us to this day.

FROM IDENTITARIAN TO POLITICAL UNCERTAINTY

The secular and the Christian-religious accounts of progressive Europeanization reveal important affinities in the ways in which European integration is
interpreted as an inclusive project of polity building and society building. By
embracing cosmopolitanism and insisting on value universalism, they point
to the principled ambivalence of telling the story of Europeanization as
something different from globalization. Both promote the European legacy
of embracing the global. European secular Enlightenment is a continuation of
this tradition of European universalism. Its shared value foundations were
also recognized by religious movements in the postwar period, seeking an
alliance with democracy as the 'only game in town.' European Christianity is
reinterpreted as a non-bellic religion of peace and equality among humans.
Leaving behind the old battles, postwar Christian democrats seek reconciliation with European modernity and secular forces (e.g., in the sector of education) (Foret and Itçaina 2013; Foret and Schlesinger 2007). Last but not least,
religious forces could use references to the achievements of European modernity and Enlightenment to distinguish themselves from religions in other
parts of the world or from non-European minorities within Europe, which
were perceived as 'less modern' and 'less enlightened.' Christian Europe as a
cultural and identitarian project has in this sense been decoupled from the
community of faith of Christian believers. By emphasizing a new clash of
civilizations, secular and Christian forces frequently find themselves united
in a crusade against antimodern and anti-European forces. This is most evident in the recent rise of islamophobia, which has led to an alliance of ultra-
liberal and religious forces (as found in the rhetoric of populist, anti-immigrant political parties like Lega Nord, Danish People's Party, Austrian Freedom Party, and the Hungarian Jobbik) (Wodak et al. 2013). As a civilizational project that is ready to impose itself and its values upon the world, Christian Europe thus continues in many forms, mostly without the direct involvement of the churches but still with a high potential for mobilizing (often
predominantly secular) electorates.

As I have noted elsewhere (Góra et al. 2011), the triumph of Europe in
both the secular and religious variants stands in an ambivalent relationship to
expressions of collective political identity. Consensus and reconciliation seek
to overcome and invalidate the plurality of existing identities and their agonistic expression. Triumphant Europeanism is built upon an attempt to reconcile national identities, but it at the same time blocks attempts to formulate a
European identity that could substitute existing national identities. In the
secular variant, the notion of constitutional patriotism as a substitute identity
expresses this principled ambivalence. The Europe of constitutional patriotism is meant to be a 'thin identity' in the sense of being constituted by an
attachment to abstract universal norms and principles, thereby giving expres-

sion to a cosmopolitan vocation. At the same time, it is meant to be a 'thick identity' in the sense of being anchored in a historically specific culture and a particular institutional setting.[16] By emphasizing shared humanity, the cosmopolitan Europe of constitutional patriots would delineate an undifferentiated and thus basically identitarian free world. It would be asocial and, in this sense, would also be detached from democracy. Only by bringing social differentiation back in can the principled need for demarcating an identitarian space emerge (Eder 2011). In the religious variant as well, the claim for a Christian Europe can be read as an attempt to overcome the divides of national identity. For most of its intellectual (in contrast to its political) defenders, Christian Europe is not mobilized primarily to establish a European particularism but is instead within the tradition of European universalism. The reference to God is meant to create an identitarian-free space, in which borders and membership are replaced by the transcendental notion of the universally valid or true. As with regard to the story of secular cosmopolitanism, it is difficult to tell the story of Europe as distinct from the story of the global. Christian Europe opens out toward the world and the all-inclusive community of humans as equals; it does not constitute a membership community.

As a consequence of this identitarian indeterminacy, both the secular and the Christian Europe remain politically undetermined. As the European discursive space is unmarked and open, it can easily be occupied by anti-Enlightenment or religious-fundamentalist counter forces. The story of Christian Europe, just as that of the European cosmopolis, is incomplete in political terms precisely because it cannot establish membership criteria and rules for inclusion and exclusion. As with regard to the notion of EU citizenship, it is ultimately up to the member states to determine political belonging. The criteria for inclusiveness are then established within the domain of the national membership community while the notion of Europe remains elusive in both the religious and the secular variants. What is more, it is only the national membership community that can give guarantees for the inclusion and 'nationalization' of non-nationals. The indeterminacy of the European membership community can in turn be more easily transformed into a mechanism of exclusion: According to common parlance, you can be identified as a French Muslim but not as a European Arab. As a Muslim (and possibly an African or Asian) immigrant, you can—admittedly with some effort but according to legal guarantees—become French and German. There are no such guarantees and rules of inclusion, however, to be recognized as a European in cultural-political terms. European identity is, then, not something that can be acquired. It remains destiny: the fate of being born either in Sicily or 150 kilometers across the Mediterranean in Tunisia. By referencing Europe, the national community can again withdraw from its inclusive gesture toward immigrants who have become nationalized in accordance with constitutional rights and guarantees but who still do not fit under the common European cultural umbrella.

NOTES

1. I am referring here to the important body of literature by scholars who have reconstructed the history of European integration with reference to primary sources either from governments and EU protagonists (Moravcsik 1998; Milward 2000) or from institutional self-accounts (Morgan 2005; Schulz-Forberg and Stråth 2010, and Schrag Sternberg 2013).

2. My sources used in this chapter are partly drawn from a large comparative survey of EU constitutional debates in the period of 2002–2008. For the full documentation of these findings see Vetters et al. (2009) and Statham and Trenz (2012).

3. See Schulz-Forberg and Stråth (2010: 138–151) on the role of the academic value producers and the 'eloquence of optimism' of the European studies community.

4. See his blog entry at http://www.niallferguson.com/journalism/history/the-year-the-world-really-changed (last accessed on June 19, 2014).

5. For the deliberative turn in integration theory, see Eriksen and Fossum (2000) and Neyer (2006).

6. The question of 'Who are the people?' is the leitmotif of constitutional debates. For the constellation of competing discourses in EU constitutional debates and their different ways to imagine the people of Europe, see Risse 2010; Trenz 2010; Schrag Sternberg 2013: 153–185.

7. For the link between EU governance and civil society see, among many, Eising and Kohler-Koch (1999); Kohler-Koch (2010); Ruzza and della Sala (2007); Sanchez Salgado (2014); and Bouza Garcia (2015).

8. The key term used here by EU institutions is 'partnership governance.' See Hurrelmann (2007) and Ruzza and della Sala (2007).

9. The defence of "cosmopolitan realism" in the form of "cosmopolitan naturalism" is also part of political struggles, when a cosmopolitan position is imposed as a "no alternative option." This is sustained by the defenders of "radical democracy," who accuse "cosmopolitan realists" of being "cosmopolitan imperialists." Against the normative universalism, the so-called realistic critique of cosmopolitanism by Mouffe (2008) aims to 'rescue' the political. Mouffe challenges the idea of moral progress as expressed in the universalization of Western liberal democracy with its specific understanding of human rights and democracy (455). Her argument in favor of a pluralism of 'good political regimes' is, however, somehow contradictory, as it remains unclear from where the morality stems that is needed to define the 'good quality' of these regimes.

10. Schuman and Adenauer were even reported to have aligned with the same Catholic student association during their university years in Bonn. The students' association carried the revealing name UNITAS and was basically an oppositional movement to Prussian centralism and German nationalism.

11. "Movements and Christian Communites '*Together for Europe*,'" *Together for Europe*, http://together4europe.org/stuttgart/_en/home.html (last accessed February 15, 2015).

12. A deliberative constitutional politics for the EU has been outlined by normative political theorists in the early millennium. See the contributions by Brunkhorst (2004); Closa (2004); Eriksen et al. (2004); and Fossum (2000).

13. For the full documentation of the findings of our comparative EU constitutional debates project see Jentges et al. (2007); Vetters et al. (2009); Statham and Trenz (2012).

14. See Jentges et al. (2007) and Vetters et al. (2009) for details.

15. Up until the present day, no English translation of this work by Joseph Weiler is available. The work's reception is limited and mainly restricted to publications in Italian and German. See, however, Menéndez (2005), who argues that the proposal is counterproductive and not a sufficient guarantee for ensuring the civic integration of all Europeans.

16. The ambivalence of constitutional patriotism as applied to the EU is discussed by Fossum (2003) and Kumm (2005).

Chapter Three

Banal Europeanization

The heroic start to and unfolding drama of Europe is also the template for telling the story of postwar normalization and institutional settlement. The statement that Europe has become part of our everyday lives and has facilitated close interaction between Europeans has been told up to the present day as Europe's greatest success story. European integration has been successful because it has become ordinary. The treaty settlement of the European communities and the everyday functioning of the European institutions have facilitated a normalization of relationships between Europeans, who engage in peaceful exchanges in a common market. Europe provides services for market citizens and consumers. It is a new horizon for business and profit-making, and it increases the panoply of goods and products that are on offer in the marketplace. For governments, local authorities, private companies, and citizens too, Europeanization is experienced as both institutionalization and socialization. The European reality of rights, opportunities, and interactions has become an everyday experience through which successive generations of Europeans have grown up and with which they have had the opportunity to become familiar. This, in short, is the banal tale of Europeanization. The relationship between European nations is no longer played out as an endless power game but instead unfolds through learning, socialization, and institutional adaptation.

In the scientific EU studies narratives, this transition is marked by the slow replacement of the realist accounts of European integration as a power game between governments by the functionalist or institutionalist accounts of European integration as a regulatory regime of governance.[1] The focus in many recent studies is on administrative routines or processes of adapting domestic political systems.[2] EU-related domestic change is analyzed as a dependent variable, which is not only brought about directly by EU regulation but also through broader processes of the diffusion of ideas and practices.[3] As such, Europeanization has consequences for the organization of interest representation, the formation of political culture and identities, and the kinds of norms and values promoted by state and civil society actors. Civil society and social movement scholars, for instance, have analyzed how civil society actors, trade unions, and political parties have strategically adapted to the new opportunity structure provided by the EU. The involvement of civic actors in transnational networks correlates at the same time with attitudinal changes of domestic actors and activists, who often embrace European perspectives and opportunities.[4] These effects of the politics of Europeanization on society's cognitive and normative structures (Featherstone and Radelli 2003) can be witnessed at the level of public attitudes and discourse. First of all, Europeanization has had an impact on citizens' beliefs and identities (Díez Medrano 2003; Trenz 2008). In general, there is a positive relationship between becoming involved in the EU, becoming socialized, and consequently also supporting supranational integration and transfers of authority to the EU. Second, Europeanization affects the public at large and shapes patterns of opposition to and support for the European integration process or specific policies promoted by the EU. These socializing dynamics of European integration are addressed by numerous case studies that have inquired how Europeanization correlates with the institutionalization of common values and shared beliefs concerning what is 'good governance' and what concerns good governance ought to address.[5]

In all of these variants, European integration generates new routine manners of coexistence. It results in a distinct mode of life experiences and in a new taken-for-grantedness of the boundary constructions of European integration and its relevance for the delineation of social belonging. Charles Taylor's notion of the "affirmation of ordinary life" is useful here to situate these processes of routinization in a broader historical context and to interpret them as indicative of distinct value foundations for post-industrial societies that are constructing new modes of allegiance and conceptions of community (Taylor 1989: 289). From this perspective, the idea of the anti-heroic reflects the general decline of hierarchies of order and meaning, strengthening the notion of society as collectively made and as obeying social laws and norms that are subject to change. Emotive and cognitive aspects remain important and morally significant in Taylor's notion of the 'affirmation of ordinary life,' but the emphasis is placed on societal self-interpretations and self-steering capacities, not on hierarchies or forms of leadership. In terms of values, this affirmation of ordinary life is thus a rejection of other and more elitist, heroic, passionate, and 'glorious' traits that marked earlier conceptions of identity as highlighted, for instance, in various triumphant, romantic, and ethnic versions of national identity.

An essential element of the plot of the story of Europeanization is that it affects people's loyalties and identities, not necessarily through the formation of a new 'high culture' as an elite identity but instead through a collective experience that is open to everyone. The traditional focus on Eurobarometer data, which measures the shifting attitudes of individuals, is insufficient for gaining an understanding of Europe's impact on day-to-day lives (Bruter 2005). Opinion surveys and attitudinal research cannot explain how resocialized European citizens are involved in changing everyday practices and experiences. Here, the work of Laura Cram is useful.[6] Drawing upon the distinction between "hot" or "heroic" versus "banal" identifications (Billig 1995), Cram proposes that European identity be analyzed not in terms of the triumphant story of the great achievements of European integration but in terms of changing everyday practices. Cram (2012: 72) argues that European Union identity is underpinned by a process that is banal, contingent, and contextual. The saga of Europeanization would in this case not be based on deliberate choices by the individual to identify as a European citizen and support integration. Europeanization of social practices and identities would instead be driven by citizens' daily experiences (either positive or negative) with the reality of Europe that is imposed upon them. Europeanization is not choice; it is destiny. It is a form of the socialization of citizens who implicitly accept the changing European reality more than they explicitly consent to it.

Banal Europeanism provides a different interpretation of the so-called permissive consensus of citizens in support of European integration. This permissive consensus is usually seen as negative and undesirable. Passive and uninformed citizens do not correspond to the ideal of democracy. For this reason, the narrators of the tale of 'heroic' or 'triumphal' Europeanization have insisted on the necessity of overcoming the permissive consensus and grounding EU legitimacy in citizens' explicit consent. Citizens should not passively support but actively make their choices and raise their voices for Europe (or against it). Europeanization should proceed through deliberation, a process of reason-giving and justification that enhances citizens' knowledge and makes their individual and collective choices more rational. However, as we can learn from Cram, identity is not always passionate or heroic but may also be mundane, even banal. In line with the account of a banal nationalism by Michael Billig (1995), we might speak here of a form of banal Europeanism. Banal Europeanism draws attention to the subconscious processes that lead to the normalization of the EU as a legitimate political authority (Cram 2012: 76–78). The intuition is that there must be some level at which the EU as a political entity and reference point is taken for granted, and citizens accommodate with the status quo of European integration. The authority of a political entity such as the EU cannot be constantly contested; there are more than just great constitutional moments that transform Europe. European integration cannot always be extraordinary or special but instead needs to become a meaningful presence for citizens. So, the story goes, we must distinguish conscious or appreciated Europeanism from subconscious or banal Europeanism.

BOTTOM-UP EUROPEANIZATION

What kind of sociological research program can be formulated with reference to everyday processes of Europeanization? The new emphasis on everyday Europeanization has opened European studies up to other disciplines within the broader humanities and social sciences. The impact of Europeanization on the transformation of culture and society requires the formulation of a broader European studies agenda, beyond the traditional focus on market building and polity building but also beyond the historiography of the heroic deeds of the founding fathers and the tales of success that were the focus of the last chapter. To investigate processes of banal Europeanization, we would need to rely upon the contributions from other disciplines within the humanities and social sciences, combining cultural studies, microsociological, and ethnological approaches. Major funding institutions have over the past years begun formulating such a broader European studies agenda. The 2010 call for project cooperation within the Framework 7 Research Programme, for instance, was entitled the "Anthropology of European Integration," and the research community was called upon to "look from different disciplinary perspectives at cultural, social, behavioral formations and transformations of everyday life and perceptions in the context of European integration."[7]

One prominent account circulating within the wider European studies community is that top-down and bottom-up Europeanization are complementary. Banal processes of Europeanization would add a citizens' perspective to the elite-driven integration promoted by EU institutions and governments. Bottom-up and horizontal Europeanization would thus round out European integration. It would not undermine the hierarchies underlying the EU's representative architecture but would instead provide it with a social substrate. Ideally, these processes would build a solid foundation for bearing the European integration project forward with the implicit support of its citizens. The everyday realities of ordinary European life histories and the exemplary lives of the heroes of European integration would thus be seen as intertwined. Europeanization of everyday life is not opposed to cosmopolitanization but contributes to it from a bottom-up perspective. The cosmopolitan heroic tale is not contradicted by but is instead grounded in the cognitions of ordinary European citizens.

Bottom-up Europeanization would thus add an important dimension to the development of a methodological cosmopolitanism as envisaged by Beck (2005). It turns the focus back from the macrolevel to the microlevel. The official tale of triumphant Europeanization tends to address cosmopolitanism in terms of a normative innovation promoted by macrochanges of an institutional and constitutional order: a cosmopolitanism of law and human rights that must be backed up by international courts and institutions strong enough to break local resistance. While the existing literature has mainly focused on the consolidation of the international system and the world of states according to principles of a cosmopolitan global order (Held 2010), little attention has been paid to the growing cosmopolitanism from below. For many people in Europe, cosmopolitanism is not a new life project reflected in or solidified by new narrations of collective identity; it is instead an unintended consequence of shared cross-border practices and communications. The global and the European are neither emphatically embraced nor opposed but simply silently integrated into everyday practices and as such constitute an integral part of people's widened horizons. Cosmopolitanism is not taken up by such people as a new normative project fighting for recognition in the world of nation-states. It undermines the nationalistic mind-sets from below, affecting the cognitive and cultural horizons that make normative innovation feasible in the first place.

Instead of enforcing cosmopolitanism against the world of nation-states, Ulrich Beck (2005: 72–73) proposes investigating cosmopolitanization as a "non-linear, dialectic process in which the universal and particular, the similar and the dissimilar, the global and the local are to be conceived, not as cultural polarities but as interconnected and reciprocally interpenetrating principles." Everyday Europeanization points in this sense to important changes at the microcognitive level of societal transformation. As O'Mahony (2013: 456) argues, the cognitive-cultural foundations of European societies are far from antithetical to the prospects for transnational democracy. The national habitus has Europeanized in at least three directions: "partly for reasons connected to long run historical memory and collective learning about the destructive potential of partisan national identities, partly because of a common continental European culture of everyday life, partly because of the formation of transnational networks and contexts of experience" (456). In the remainder of this chapter, I will follow these tracks of banal Europeanization by considering first the culture of everyday life that shapes the knowledge and cognitions of Europeans and then by considering the expanding practices of social transnationalism, which involve an increasing number of Europeans in everyday exchanges and experiences.

AN EMERGING EUROPEAN CULTURE OF EVERYDAY LIFE

A European culture of everyday life emerging from below would develop independently and largely detached from the grand identity narratives of nationalism and cosmopolitanism. The emphasis is here on the cognitive learning of individuals who are exposed to transnational experiences, knowledge, and information. Everyday culture would influence cognitions in such a way that people who are continuously exposed to transnationalism would find themselves in increasing dissonance with the macronormative order of the nation-state. This could lead to a situation in which people not only develop more cosmopolitan orientations and lifestyles but also begin reflecting upon the preferred institutional and constitutional arrangements to support such a transnational culture and help it develop. We start our investigation into the contours of such a microcognitive transnational culture, however, at the constitutive level of people's basic involvement. Then we proceed to analyze in the following chapter how this is reflected or even contested by the participants.

Where can we find traces of such banal Europeanization at the level of sociocultural involvement? Cram (2012: 79) mentions a number of low-level engagements through which EU citizens identify with the EU in unremarkable ways: carrying passports or driver's licenses, conforming with legislation, walking past EU flags, not waving national flags. There is an everyday presence of Europe that reminds citizens of 'being involved in the larger EU system whether for good or ill' (79). There are many daily reminders of the presence of Europe: We automatically walk through the EU nationals' lane at customs; we watch a movie in the theater that is supported by the EU media program; we drive on a road that has been financed by EU infrastructure network funds; we eat Italian ham that has a EU guarantee of origin; we have an awareness, however vague, of EU rights in relation to equal pay or access to health care. The EU becomes normalized as individuals stop noticing the presence of these daily reminders.

The EU has in the past consciously used such banal references and unobtrusive symbols as markers of a European collective identity. A narrative perspective on European identity is, for instance, applied in the formulation of EU cultural policies. While institutional narratives may be quite formalistic, a European identity narrative can be performed through decentralized cultural initiatives, such as the European Capitals of Culture.[8] A more covert strategy of identity building was also implied in the common currency project. The creators of the common currency, who launched the Euro in 1999, remained inspired by the functionalist idea of spillover from market building to polity building and identity building. The idea of one currency for one Europe was based on the idea that identification would result from the creation of instrumental values of clear benefit to Europeans. The introduction of Euro bills and coins would create a familiar environment for ordinary people's daily exchanges and thus enhance trust with and loyalty to the EU, which were seen as essential for citizens' long-term changes of identification (Risse 2003). The Euro was meant to make Europe real and to reify it as a political order since it provided a visible link from EU rule to citizens' daily lives. The common currency was also conceived in such a way as to make it compatible with the hybrid nature of European identity: member states were allowed to use national iconographies in the individual designs of the Euro coins while bridges on the notes would signify the process of uniting in diversity (Karolewski 2010: 66). Most importantly, however, the Euro remained an ambiguous identity signifier because it has over the years provoked continuous resistance: early on and expectedly in countries like Denmark and Sweden but also later and rather unexpectedly in countries like Italy, where the introduction of the new currency triggered unanticipated price inflation. The instrumental value of Europe also proved to be the value that the population could most easily refute, and citizens still await the expected benefits and are perturbed in their daily habits. This is a point at which there could occur a politicization nourished by distress over experiences of broken habits (such as the accustomed use of national currencies) and dysfunctionalities that affect everyday interactions.[9] The narrative of the Euro thus proved to be not entirely innocuous and cannot be expected to function as a smooth identity signifier. It might equally be interpreted as standing for the victory of the unwanted neoliberal market forces and be experienced as a regime of oppression. Strategies of banal Europeanization might fail at this point and precisely the experienced perturbations of everyday life risk provoking the strongest resistance.

Another strand of research investigates how the big narrations of European integration are given meaning and inform practices of citizens' exchanges in local contexts. White (2010) involves taxi-drivers in everyday political talk to study the patterned ways in which citizens perceive and interpret the EU. His findings suggest that citizens often lack the tools of imagination to perceive the EU as an actor in defense of the public good. While the official symbols and rights of EU citizenship are often neglected, citizens tend to rely on tacit assumptions, instinctive answers, and routine interpretations, which undermine the EU's political credibility. Loosely structured discussions as analyzed by White are, however, also institutionally embedded. The role of institutional intermediaries for the imagination of the EU is emphasized by Scalise (2015), who assesses how different meanings of Europe shape opportunities and networking relationships of school children and their institutions in Italy (Florence and Prato). Schools and other educational institutions provide an important infrastructure for what Scalise calls the local everyday embedding of narrative constructions of European identity. Through participation in such institutional settings, school children transcend the local and take part (either indirectly through school curricula or directly through various exchange programs) in transnational practices and experiences. An agenda for what could be termed 'transnational citizenship education' is also actively promoted by new educational programs and textbook curricula that substantially deviate from the previous nation-state focus on education (Soysal and Schissler 2004).

Such a bottom-up approach to the collective identification of the Europeans is also chosen by Anamaria Dutceac Segesten who traces banal Europeanization in her work on Eurosymbols in metropolitan areas. In a project hosted at Lund University, she collects samples of graphic displays of references to Europe and/or the EU in three European capitals: Paris, Copenhagen, and Bucharest.[10] The idea behind this project is that there is a ubiquitous and often unconscious iconic presence of Europe (such as the stars of the European flag on a blue background in an advertisement banner). Eurosymbols are used by private entrepreneurs, shop owners, associations, and many others for branding products or places where people meet and offer services. Advertising slogans or mottos make frequent reference to Europe, often with a positive connotation. The impact of such banal processes of symbolization is also emphasized by Ian Manners for whom Europe is not only a heroic project but also a Union of everyday signs and symbols. According to Manners (2011: 244), lack of enthusiasm for recognizing official symbols of the EU during negotiations over the Constitutional Treaty itself has symbolic force and renders Europe meaningful as a space of nonheroic symbols.

Self-restriction in the use of symbols is also reflected in what Manners analyzes as "symbolic taboos," that is, phrases or slogans that represent the limits of integration and explain what is permissible in the EU and what is not. Such symbolic taboos are recognizable in the discourse that is applied to interpret the European integration process as "distinct" but "innocuous." As such, they are often manifested in a "series of inviolable and sacrosanct understandings about what the EU is and what the EU does" (Manners 2011: 258). Most commonly, these are phrases that explain what the EU does differently than other political entities, like "Europe will not be made all at once, or according to a single plan" (258). Such expressions function to reassure the general public of the virtues of the EU, which consist not only of being different but also more generally of being harmless and innocent. Symbolic taboos can be used by political representatives in public declarations or speeches. Through the filtering process of public discourse, they can also enter the Treaty text itself as part of the EU's official self-representation. Agreeing on such formulas as part of an official declaration and Treaty text can be sometimes quite arduous and implies long negotiations among government representatives involving EU institutions and other relevant actors. Emblematic of this is the transformation of the motto of integration over the years from the "ever closer Union" of the post-Maastricht period to "unity in diversity" as the formula to launch a Constitutional project on "united in diversity" as the compromise formula that should ultimately be established in the Treaty (Manners 2011: 259–60). The taboo of thinking of the EU in terms of 'unity' is ultimately reinforced as none of these mottos have found recognition by member-state governments, leaving the Treaty text in its current form of symbolic content. The void is rendered significant, however, by a new spirit of renouncing ornamentation and operating in a discreet and unobtrusive manner. The backstage might be more comfortable for routine operations that are not emotional but simply banal and require no further decoration.

Spectacles of popular culture in Europe have become important marketing events staged by public and private broadcasting companies, often in the form of a European coproduction. They are spectacles of collectively celebrating the trivial and as such create a collective memory of shared everyday popular culture events. One oft-cited example of such collective celebrations of the trivial is the Eurovision Song Contest (Raykoff and Tobin 2007). As Jones and Subic argue, "public events such as Eurovision are sites of identity creation precisely because they are so silly, everyday, prevalent, popular and ubiquitous in Europe" (Jones and Subotic 2011: 543). The "everyday ordinariness" of an event such as the Eurovision Song Contest as "a spectacle of kitsch and bad taste" (543) can, however, also be linked back to political struggles and acts of resistance. Popular culture as represented by Conchita Wurst, the 2014 Austrian winner of the Eurovision Song Contest, can become a powerful and politically significant symbolization. For younger and future generations, it might signify the playful and nonheroic queer world of a secular Europe mobilized against the heroic masculinity represented by the religious or nationalist Europe of the past. A repoliticization occurs through popular culture with geopolitical (East-West) and culturalist (secular-religious) connotations. Popular culture represents the powerful imaginary of the ordinary people over the authority of states and religions. In a similar vein, the European football scene has been analyzed as a symbolic domain within which practices of collective identification develop through the staging of sports contests among the nations and cities of Europe. As a key dimension of popular culture, football has become strongly Europeanized over the years, building a powerful market for the merchandising of brands and products as well as collective memories that are collected and shared by transnational fan communities (Sonntag 2012).[11]

Other powerful examples of the banal presence of Europe are given by media and communication researchers. On the one hand, qualitative content analysis of European news coverage points to reproduction of the great sagas as an important element of journalistic storytelling. Foreign news coverage in general and EU news coverage in particular focus on the 'big players' and the 'makers' of history. They provide neat distinctions between 'heroes' and 'villains,' 'friends' and 'foes,' and thus facilitate reception of foreign policy events and acknowledgment of their relevance.[12] Media scholars have thus mainly focused on the construction of 'drama' and the media strategies of priming and framing to amplify the theater of history and politics—for instance, EU constitutional debate, the membership of Turkey, the corruption scandal that shattered the European Union, or the failed referendum as moments of popular resistance. All of these were significant debates in which values and identities were deeply contested by calling attention to transnational publics. On the other hand, media scholars have recently begun paying attention to the unobtrusive presence of Europe in political and media talk. This points to an important function of media discourse, which provides not only a stage for power politics but also a backstage on which basic cognitions take shape and consciousness is shaped through language (O'Mahony 2013).

Rhetorical references to banal Europeanism are a constant and implicit element of political news coverage, where Europe is familiarized and rendered meaningful instead of being openly debated. To study these substrata of public and media talk, the author has surveyed residual categories of low-level 'banal' references to Europe within the following categories (Trenz 2006a): 1) Europe as a generalized reference that is used to raise problem awareness ("terrorism a threat to Europe"), to broaden the meaning and interpretation of particular concepts ("the European welfare state," "the European nation-state"), and to emotionally load particular contexts of action ("the European family"); 2) routine reference to European events that structure the daily activities of national politicians ("The secretary of state employment, Andrea Nahles, on her way to the EU Council meeting in Brussels, declared that she will strongly support a minimum wage in Germany"); 3) Europe as a comparative reference ("French milk production is the largest in Europe," "Europeans are less obese than Americans"); 4) references to European law and regulations ("In accordance with EU regulations, traffic rules in Bavaria need to be adapted"); and 5) references to European actors and institutions ("the Eurocountries," "with support from the European Commission," "the powerless European Parliament," the "Eurocrats").[13] The very term 'member state' provides an unremarkable but constant reminder of belonging to the European Union.

Such rhetorical references remain diffuse, but they are also common and frequent. In his comparative survey of political news coverage in six countries (France, Germany, Austria, Italy, Spain, and the UK), the author found such generic references in every fifth news article.[14] In addition, these references are quite distinct from the more explicit debates in which European elites engage over European choices and future directions. They cannot easily be categorized along pro-European or anti-European story lines but are simply pieces of the jigsaw puzzle tale of Europeanization, which remind us of Europe's daily presence in the form of routines in our everyday lives.

Another powerful example of banal Europeanism in media and communication is the integrating force of everyday cultural community, which television has enhanced since the early 1950s. Public broadcasting companies are undoubtedly key nation builders and in fact define their mandate in terms of promoting national culture and community. Public broadcasting companies are, however, also important transnational communicators, sharing popular formats, and developing joint programs. As Jostein Gripsrud (2007) highlights, many of the traits of this "everyday cultural community" of television are, in fact, transnational in character and engage audiences that are neither geographically nor linguistically confined. Europeans can easily communicate concerning television shows and series that are broadcasted in parallel and often use similar or identical formats. As audience studies have shown, some of these series might be American, but they nonetheless enable a thematization of distinctive Europeanness. TV has, in the words of Gripsrud, produced much of the everyday reality of being European, not by promoting a thick European identity but by Europeanizing our habits and life expectations as well as by sharing cultural contents. It contributes to the practical everyday sense of being European, even if you watch mainly (or exclusively) national TV (Gripsrud 2007). In addition to these historically developed habits of watching Europeanized television, there are also the Eurovision-produced TV shows, most prominently the Eurovision Song Contest, which promote cultural content mainly in the form of entertainment that is banal but still significant, in the sense that it builds shared experiences and memories (Raykoff and Tobin 2007). TV shows, TV dramas (like the highly successful Danish TV series), but also European cinema in this sense constitute a common cultural heritage and a feeling of cultural identity among Europeans, while at the same time facilitating new and dynamic cultural encounters in the everyday life of Europeans (Bondebjerg et al. 2015).

Finally, social media have become an important playground for mediated 'banal Europeanism.' Social networking media allow Europeans to turn their casual acquaintances, whom they occasionally meet during travels or stays abroad, into networks of 'friends.' Social media furthermore allow Europeans to train their language capacities, often communicating in English or other languages. For many Europeans, social media have also become an important reference point for shared information and everyday political talk. The social media activate audiences in daily routines of liking and sharing political content, thereby building common knowledge and sharing identities and experiences. Specific segments of the audience (like young people) who subscribe to specific news threads are often exposed to very similar agendas. In some cases, even EU institutions have developed successful formats in the form of specifically designed blogs or social media profiles that address large transnational communities of users in everyday political talk (Tarta 2014). It is interesting to observe how these formats are developed as distinct from the seriousness of political news sites, experimenting with formats that balance entertainment and engagement. Through these new formats, audiences related to the EU take part in what could be called "everyday-life politicization," which occurs from the bottom up by shifting boundaries between the private and the public and between the political and the nonpolitical (Graham and Hajru 2011). One of these sites for banal political talk is the Facebook profile of the European Parliament, with 1.7 million likes (as of May 2015) from people who receive daily updates about 'banal political themes' and information designed to motivate them to engage in political talk. Popular issues that attract various forms of social media activism include the sustainability of the Erasmus exchange program, the European Union receiving the Nobel Prize, International Women's Day, or campaigns against child labor. In these particular cases, the European Parliament Facebook page represents an easily accessible, shared European stage for topics and events with high European and international resonance, avoiding sharp polarization and controversies on these issues and instead engaging its users in a form of civic dialogue that facilitates the expression of political opinion without further commitment (Tarta 2014: 121).

EVERYDAY SOCIAL TRANSNATIONALISM

The trans-European cognitive-cultural lifeworlds are not just experienced passively but also involve individuals and publics that engage in transnational practices and are confronted by experiences of socialization in a trans-European context. The structural approach to everyday Europeanization—focusing on culture, new forms of solidarity, and belonging—must thus be supplemented by a microsociology of everyday practices as manifested, for instance, in networks of interactions, transnational experiences, and encounters or mobility. Such a focus on everyday social transnationalism is also reflected in Ulrich Beck's call for a methodological cosmopolitanism that investigates multipolar processes of interpenetration of the local and the global instead of bipolar confrontations in the world of nation-states. The manifold processes of interpenetration of the global (or the European) and the local can be studied, for example, in urban areas (Smith 2001). Focus here has often been on migrants, who bring the global into the local and are involved in various cross-border practices (Glick Schiller et al. 1992). In the European free movement area, such cross-border exchanges are, however, no longer exclusive to migrants but encompass various practices of mobility, such as educational exchange, intermarriage, and travel, which involve a growing number of ordinary citizens in everyday transborder activities (Mau et al. 2008).

All of these studies of everyday transnationalism find strong evidence that the degree to which ordinary people are involved in everyday transnational practices correlates with their adherence to more European and cosmopolitan values.[15] They thus help us shed light on the mutual interdependence of Europeanization from below and Europeanization from above. The sociological research agenda of Europeanization needs to focus precisely on this interrelationship between Europeanization as an 'impact' of institutional transformation on the microstructures of society (the political science approach) and Europeanization as an impact of the transformation of society on the institutionalization of the EU (see also Díez Medrano 2008).

Research on banal Europeanism is comprised of a microsociology of European integration, reconstructing Europeanization as a socializing experience among individuals that involves new processes of group formation. The idea that intensified economic, cultural, and social exchanges between countries entail the socialization of individuals goes back to Karl Deutsch (1966). This ultimately involves a Durkheimian structural-functionalist understanding of a European society that evolves like an organism. The differentiation of new macrostructures of political and legal institutions paves the way for the stabilization of social relations at a new level of aggregation. Based on this functionalist logic, early integration theory postulated an upward spiral of integration, according to which the building of a common market would automatically be followed by the political integration of states and the social integration of individuals (Haas 1958). Following the Durkheimian paradigm, a shift in individuals' loyalties can be expected as a result of intensified social transactions and communications between the differentiated parts. Integration is thus measured by the degree of horizontal transborder relationships and new opportunities for interaction that are stimulated by the vertical impact of EU rules and opportunities on member-state societies (Buttler et al. 2014: 6).

In many instances, however, social transnationalism is not restricted to Europe but also involves dense interchanges with other parts of the world. How can the European and the global be distinguished in social transnationalism, and does this distinction matter? To speak of Europeanization would, according to Delhey et al. (2014), imply that these networks of interactions are at least to some degree also geographically confined and distinguished from other (global) networks. From this perspective, Europeanization is a relational term that involves processes of external closure toward the world and processes of internal opening toward the national (Delhey et al. 2014). Defined as horizontal cross-border practices, Europeanization is taking place in a field in which geographical vicinity and distance play a greater role. This is distinct from other measurements of Europeanization through attitudinal indicators and values, which can more easily travel across time and space (see also Delhey et al. 2014: 369). Practices of place-bridging, as measured, for instance, through degrees of cross-border interactions, are in this sense simultaneously to be understood as practices of place-building. To capture this interwoven character of place-bridging and place-building practices, Europeanization, according to Delhey and collaborators, must be operationalized in relative rather than absolute terms. We must address not only Europe's salience vis-à-vis the national (the measure of 'absolute Europeaniza-tion') but also its salience vis-à-vis the rest of the world (the measure of 'relative Europeanization'). In order to develop such an understanding of 'relative Europeanization,' it is necessary to take systematic account of 'ex-ternal closure,' that is, how transnational practices consolidate within the European social space and how this European space becomes demarcated against the outside world as an effect of such practices. For this purpose, Delhey et al. (2014) develop a number of indices relating the absolute num-ber of trans-border practices and attitudes to degrees of internal (national) openness and external closure.

'Relative Europeanization,' as measured through such indices, allows us to demarcate spaces of intensified social interrelations, which still need to be rendered meaningful and related to shared cultural understandings in order to be identified as 'societal spaces' as well. The notion of 'relative European-ization' is useful for illustrating (and statistically ascertaining) that Euro-peans feel closer to Europe than to Africa, but its explanatory value remains unclear. In particular, it does not explain why, when, and for whom geo-graphical proximity matters in the making of Europe. The in-itself banal observation that Europeanization and not Africanization is occurring in con-temporary Europe less relevant as a scientific observation that needs to be underpinned with statistical data than it is as an indicator of a social artefact. As such, it relates to a taken-for-granted reality, which in most circumstances and for many Europeans apparently needs no explanation. 'Relative Euro-peanization' would, then, be more than simply a new technique for observing horizontal transborder activism. It would help explain how our taken-for-granted social reality is constructed over time through practices that confine social places, which are shared by Europeans in such a way that 'the obvious' is no longer in need of explanation.

For sociologists seeking to explain 'the obvious' of the spatial delimita-tion of Europe, it is thus not enough to relate to statistical indices. The added value of this approach to social transnationalism can only be fully developed by relating processes of internal opening and external closure back to deeply ingrained structures of knowledge, cognition, and culture that are shared by Europeans. Sociologists would need to relate the banality of Europeanization back to the historical structuration of Europe and to the institutionalization of shared lifeworlds and related opportunities within the context of the Euro-pean Union. It is only with reference to this historical and institutional setting that Europe's banal distinctiveness can be captured. Europeanization is dis-tinct from globalization or Africanization because it cannot be detached from these processes of historical structuration and institutionalization, not simply because individual attitudes converge or transborder activities intensify. It is, then, no longer a question of whether intensified transborder practices within Europe's confined geographical space will be followed by attitudinal change among Europeans. Neither is it a question of whether a European mind-set is needed in the first place to engage Europeans in new forms of transborder activism. Instead of the geographical confinement of attitudes and practices as well as assumptions about their causal relationships, an explanatory model of banal Europeanization would need to embrace more deeply engrained structures of meaning and interpretation that confine Europeans' collective experiences.

The interesting question here is thus why 'relative Europeanization' is needed as a distinct mode of defining values, ways of life, and opportunities to demarcate a European social space that simultaneously embraces the national and transnational/global levels. Because Europeanization is different from nationalization, the indicators of transnationalism that are applied by social research cannot be restricted to the measurement of how social practices are territorially confined. Europeanization research also needs to take into account the modes that these 'internal' and geographically confined practices develop within a particular institutional environment that constitutes Europeans' shared horizon. Transborder practices relate in this sense back to the use of specific European rights or participation by individuals beyond a horizon of shared expectations and norms, even if these people often express negative opinions about this institutional setting or are unwilling to consciously identify with it.

Looking further into the effects of banal social transnationalism helps explain the discrepancy between experienced life trajectories and meaningful interpretations of life history and identities. European citizens' changing life-worlds and experiences might result in *subjective Europeanization*, referring to "Europe's growing role in the cognitive, affective and normative perceptions and orientations of people and the weakening of the fixation on the nation-state" (Mau and Verwiebe 2010: 329). European studies scholars have put considerable effort into confirming the hypothesis that mobile citizens are becoming better Europeans in the sense of developing more pro-European attitudes.[16] More knowledge and experience often correlate with a more positive image of and attachment to European and cosmopolitan values. In the case of vulnerable groups affected by crisis, we would, however, expect that identity conflicts become more salient as the motivation for movement varies. In a migration context, movers (in contrast to stayers), who are forced to migrate by the negative effects of crisis, might develop more negative attitudes concerning their countries of origin but might at the same time also more readily cast doubt upon other categories of belonging (such as Europeanism). An example would be young Greeks or Italians moving to affluent Scandinavia out of discomfort over the life chances afforded to them at home. These young people have been socialized in a culture of complete mistrust with the performance of representative democracy in their home countries. Their migration is motivated by an outright negative attitude about the performance of the political system and complete skepticism about the possibilities of reform and future recovery. As we shall see in chapter 5, this negative identification with country of origin does not, however, turn these young people into future supporters of European integration. The European Union is identified not only as a causal factor of crisis, but its way of handling crisis through the imposition of austerity is seen as amplifying personal suffering. Indicators of subjective Europeanization in terms of transnational life orientations and use of opportunities offered by European integration might be high, but we are nevertheless confronted with a 'lost generation' for the cause of European integration.[17]

In turn, many Europeans can be deeply entrenched in transnational practices and lifestyles yet still hold predominantly nationalist attitudes (as measured through the Eurobarometer). Comparative research by Favell et al. (2014) suggests that Europeans' attitudes can indeed differ considerably from practices of everyday transnationalism. While support for the EU is in decline everywhere in Europe, ordinary people are at the same time deeply integrated into a network of transnational practices and relationships. Their banal reality of everyday transnational experiences does not translate into support for the European Union as a political project. This "apparent paradox of highly transnational yet supposedly Eurosceptic nations" like the UK and Denmark (3) can be dissolved by distinguishing more closely between cosmopolitan and European attitudes. In fact, these countries score highly when representing cosmopolitan values yet dislike the EU, which represents these values. Everyday life in Danish and British society is thus highly Europeanized, even if these populations often express negative opinions about it or are unlikely to explicitly identify with it (12).

Subjective Europeanization is therefore insufficiently measured by support for European integration. Patterns of participation in transnational practices are not translated into explicit life projects or identities that are given expression in support of or opposition to others. We must thus analyze 'ordinary Europeans' neither as winners of integration, who emphatically embrace the promise of a cosmopolitan life, nor as losers, who mobilize resistance against it (Favell et al. 2014). Europeans do not take on heroic roles as actors in history, who are passionate about their decision to become Europeans or who fervently resist the pull toward Europeanization. For most people, Europeanization is neither choice nor destiny but just a blurred backdrop to everyday practices and taken-for-granted realities, one that requires no specific engagement or forms of collective identification.

Cross-border mobility and education have been analyzed as key dimensions of European social integration, which involve 'ordinary citizens' as movers within the common market.[18] The everyday reality of Europe is best represented by the EU regime of citizenship and free movement, which, in the words of Adrian Favell (2014: 283), has become a "mass middle-class

phenomenon." He observes how free movement has become part of Europeans' banal consumption through holidays, short-haul travel, knowledge of
other places, and expanded networks of friendships. In similar terms, mobile
EU citizens distinguish themselves from migrants from other places by taking for granted their range of rights and practices within the European free
movement area (Duru et al. forthcoming). A traveler in the Europe of free
movement is no longer the adventurer of former times (who, according to
Bauman [2004], still dominates the imaginary Europe[19]) but is instead a
routine passenger, who sometimes knows foreign cities better than her own
neighborhood. Studies have further emphasized how major cities have become hubs for intra-EU mobility (Favell 2008). Northern cities in particular,
such as London, Paris, Amsterdam, Berlin, and Copenhagen, have been
transformed into transnational social spaces for testing out new cosmopolitan
lifestyles and expanding cross-border cultural and economic activities.

The most complete empirical picture of the impressive range of everyday
transnational practices and the degree to which Europeans are involved in
them is given in the work by Steffen Mau and Roland Verwiebe (Mau 2011;
Mau and Verwiebe 2010). Mau and Verwiebe analyze "horizontal Europeanization" in terms of "contacts, interactions and social relationships between
different European countries, as well as various forms of pan-European mobility" (Mau and Verwiebe 2010: 303). The infrastructure of horizontal Europeanization becomes tangible, for instance, in the numerous transport projects that connect Europeans (such as the Øresund Bridge and the Channel
Tunnel), in the tight road and air traffic networks, in the preferred target of
European tourism, and in the transnational friendship and family networks
(now more easily maintained through social media and other means of communication). Mau (2011) provides a sociostructural analysis of the emerging
transnational social lifeworlds on the basis of Eurobarometer data, which
posed the following questions: "In the last 12 months, have you visited
another EU country?" and "In the last 12 months, have you socialized with
people from another EU country?" He then identifies a mix of explanatory
variables that either strongly or slightly affect Europeanization: social factors
like education, social class, age, gender, and citizenship are all positively
correlated to the likelihood of having foreign social relationships. Structural
factors such as size of the country of origin (people from Luxembourg are
more likely to travel abroad than people from France), degree of modernization, and length of EU membership further help explain differences in social
transnationalism among European populations.

Building on Mau's survey, Favell et al. (2014) measure social transnationalism within the following dimensions: transnational travel and mobility,
transnational social relations (friends and family abroad), transnational communication and consumerism, and transnational human capital (knowledge
of languages and watching foreign-language television). Their findings con-

firm that the everyday reality of horizontal Europeanization is not restricted to particular privileged countries or strata of the population but can also be found at a high scale and intensity, providing evidence of a broader diffusion of opportunities for mobility, among Europe's middle and lower classes (Favell et al. 2014: 166).

The sociogeographic map of Europeanization provides us with a complex picture of an emerging European social space that is no longer adequately described within the familiar confines of the national. The existing quantitative survey data is often based on a categorization of Europeans as nationals divided into subcategories of class, education, or gender. One possible effect of Europeanization is, however, the transformation of such subcategories into primary categories of emerging transnational groups, which consciously or subconsciously share important characteristics or are involved in similar practices because they are carriers of the same rights, make use of similar opportunities, or are exposed to similar consequences that are interpreted as negative. One example of how such categorizations work is the notion of vulnerability, which is applied to particular groups of citizens like minorities, young people, and certain gender categories. Such categorizations of individuals become often meaningful in relation to the formulation of EU policies, for example, the fight against youth unemployment. In implementing these policies, the contours of these groups are further specified, and the application of policy programs related to these groups generates similar practices across European social space.

Another example of how categorizations substantiate transnational social groups is EU citizenship, which defines bearers of rights as well as opportunities to exercise these rights. The free movement area, for instance, introduces a general distinction between EU movers and stayers, who find themselves in similar life situations. In fact, a framework of citizenship enactment can be addressed in terms of the possible multiplicities of Europeans' allegiance to political institutions and entities, stretching from the domestic sphere through the national and European levels to the global (Saward 2013). European citizenship practice not only is manifested in relation to political mobilization and advocacy for rights and justice (Wiener 1998) but also comprises a wide range of 'acts' arising from people's social lives, which address their vulnerability (Isin and Saward 2013; Saward 2013). As such, citizenship can be 'enacted' not only through explicitly political claims by groups (such as minorities) but also through individual choices for education, mobility, or work. The EU citizenship framework places emphasis on the social rights of EU movers and workers, which adds an important social dimension to European integration in terms of equal treatment, nondiscrimination, and solidarity. Through this focus, the various practices that develop in relation to EU citizenship and the development of particular groups of vulnerable or empowered people linked to it can be addressed as a trans-boundary phenomenon that is linked more to socioeconomic precariousness or possibilities than to predefined national political membership.

Differences and variations on the sociogeographic map of Europeanization are thus drawn not only along national lines but also frequently correlate with cross-cutting factors such as education, class, age, or gender. Europeanized social lifeworlds are more than just an enclave for privileged elites; they are a playground for quite different social groups and their daily encounters (e.g., Poles working in Scandinavian countries, Germany, or the UK in sectors as diverse as agriculture, health care, elderly care, or services, some as temporary guests and others determined to settle). Instead of an elite bias for Europeanization, Favell et al. (2014: 13) find in countries like Denmark and the UK evidence for a 'massification' of the effects of European integration, which is not in line with the simple polarization of winners and losers suggested by Fligstein (2008). Far from being the preserve of a small elite of entrepreneurs, middle classes are the most enthusiastic users of free movement rights. Exchanges for studies, internships, or (temporary) work in other member states have become a normal part of many young people's life planning, and pensioners from the North find it increasingly attractive to reside for more or less extended periods in second homes in the South of Europe. With growing levels of unemployment in crisis-ridden Europe, this massification effect is reinforced, and again, the descendants of the middle classes, young, and educated people from the South are those who make the most of free movement opportunities, (temporarily) seeking work in the North. Favell et al. (2004: 18) point out that, in contrast to the expectation of a class bias for Europeanized elites, persisting differences in transnationalism are related to education rather than class. Those from lower-class backgrounds generally perform well in utilizing their Europeanized opportunities to achieve education, and when exposed to transnational experiences, they change values even more rapidly than middle-class descendants, who have already acquired higher social capital. At the same time, the North-South population exchange that is currently shaping European social space also undoubtedly reflects a North-South divide in terms of the unequal distribution of life chances and wealth in the European Union. The Europe of equal living conditions, which was promised with the establishment of the Common Market, has perhaps lost credibility, but it still looms behind the expectations of many Europeans, who grew up in a banal European reality. The new North-South divide thus does more than simply divide European populations. Economic divisions do not automatically translate into social and political divisions between the populations of Europe. Mobile citizens of the South are not socially or culturally segregated in the Northern European cities that receive them, and the mobile cosmopolitan elites do not develop a class consciousness against the immobile nationalist underclasses. What these divisions instead signify is that a European society has developed beyond the fragmentation of national populations or classes. Mobility within this developing social space regularly bridges not only territory but also class and national belonging. Beyond the conscious identification of groupness or class lies a whole range of unconscious practices, which are part of Europeans' life trajectories.

THE LIMITS OF EUROPEANIZATION AS NORMALIZATION

This chapter has shed a different kind of light on the rise of European society, not as a progressive force based on the shared values of Europeans in search of self-realization but as a by-product of European market building and the social and structural effects of Europeanization on citizens' changing life-worlds. Europeanization proceeds as a quiet revolution of everyday life, through which an increasing number of Europeans are entrenched in a dense network of horizontal exchanges, developing similar lifestyles and expectations. New generations of Europeans acquire similar knowledge of Europe and go through the same experiences of socializing in a European context of travel, education, social and cultural exchanges, and labor. A European frame of reference is applied to many contexts of social and private life and developed, for instance, through cultural dialogues and communications (Eder 2011).

However, I have also argued that everyday Europeanization is not always a harmonious process. There is no development path toward a European society, and Europeanization could face several turning points or ruptures. First of all, the contours of Europeanization remain somewhat blurred in the wider context of denationalization, transnationalization, or cosmopolitanization. In many of the practices described in this chapter, the distinction between 'banal Europeanism' and 'banal transnationalism' is difficult to uphold. The question of whether there is any meaningful way to demarcate European social space against the outside world is therefore not simply one of empirical measurement through social scientific indicators (Delhey et al. 2014). Europeanization as space-building and space delimitation must also be rendered politically meaningful. Delineation of the European against the non-European or the global is, last but not least, a normative and political undertaking of the self-imagination of a European society that is rendered visible as a self-organized meaningful entity. The idea that transnational practices need to be geographically and socially confined is part of this self-imagination, even if such distinctions between the European and the non-European are regularly disputed and demystified.

Secondly, tales of Europeanization as normalization involve the risk of institutional stalemates. Banal Europeanism clearly lacks the mobilizing potential of nationalism, socialism, and other '-isms,' which have in the past constituted successful political forces. Such a postheroic tale of contemporary European history might result in a weak form of collective alignment, for example, a constitutional patriotism, which supports some constitutional essentials but for which people are no longer asked to make greater sacrifices or to build the kind of solidarity that is necessary for shared welfare and redistribution (Müller 2009). Similar postheroic accounts of identification have been also proposed as substitute identities for the national community. However, 'banal nationalism' is different as it is often contrasted to the template of dominant national narratives, which for substantial portions of the population are no longer convincing (Billig 1995). 'Banal Europeanism' cannot easily draw upon such negative templates and lacks a common positive reference point that could guarantee a degree of political commitment (such as positive identification with the constitution). Europeanization through market exchanges privatizes individuals' transnational experiences. It relies upon individual initiative but creates only shaky balances of social relationships and only low degrees of collective responsibility. In the long run, a postheroic Europe might also increase people's disengagement from or dissatisfaction with politics. The deadlocks and routines of banal Europeanism risk forming a bulwark against innovation and initiative. European bureaucracy is experienced by many as an 'iron cage.' In this sense, banal Europeanism also reflects the deadlock in which European integration is caught. There is no easy way out of the banal once you are trapped within it.

A third related danger of banal Europeanism is that the European construction remains fragile, especially when compared to the still convincing force of national constructions and their appeal to people's emotions and identities. There is no strict correspondence between postheroic accounts of Europeanism and nationalism but instead numerous nationalist backlashes against the perceived threats of identity loss through transnationalization. Important in this context are the oft-perceived negative effects of market liberalization implicit in many of the practices of everyday Europeanization described in this chapter. The liberal market Europe points to another trend of Europeanization, which increasingly shapes inequalities across the market of free movement and thus divides European populations into specific groups of winners and losers.

In post-constitutional Europe, EU institutions and member-state governments have committed to a low-profile and conflict avoidance strategy, renouncing the promotion of symbols of Europe and trying to keep EU politics out of the media and public debates. There is thus a deliberate attempt by EU elites to routinize and depoliticize EU politics and regulation, in contrast to previous strategies to make them relevant and to seek public attention. The question is whether and under what condition this self-imposed routinization and depoliticization strategy, which reverses previous trends of politicization, also risks creating a popular backlash (de Wilde and Zürn 2012). There is perhaps no need for an explicit consensus concerning European integration, but this can hardly prevent expressions of dissensus. Market and free movement opportunities for exit and entry are also linked to the opportunity to voice opinions, which is indeed intrinsic to EU citizenship in the form of political rights and democracy. If EU citizens are socializing through European integration, they are also learning about opportunities to make their voices heard, to protest against Europe, or to become rebellious. There are times of prosperity when the European Union 'delivers,' but there are also times of crisis when the performance of the European Union 'suffers.' Europeanization as adaptation, as a *deus ex machina*, or even worse as an 'iron cage of bureaucracy' creates resistance. Many thus experience Europe not only as dull and boring but also as annoying and pretentious. The European Union's promise that it is profitable for everyone and preferable to alternative arrangements might be proven wrong and can easily be contested. Instead of creating equal living conditions across the territory of the European Union, the effects of EU policies might contribute to the worsening of living conditions in some parts of Europe or be directly related to people's suffering. This is what I will describe below as the desacralized or skeptical tale of Europeanization.

NOTES

1. An institutionalist account of EU multi-level network government has been promoted in the post-Maastricht years by Jachtenfuchs and Kohler-Koch (1996), Kohler-Koch and Eising (1999), and Marks et al. (1996).

2. Europeanization as domestic adaptation is the empirical framework used by Börzel and Risse (2003). The routines of a supranational administration are analyzed by Egeberg (2006).

3. On the agenda of Europeanization as diffusion see Börzel and Risse 2011.

4. For the strategies of Europeanization through social mobilization from below see Liebert and Trenz (2010), Marks and McAdam (1996), and Trenz (2007b).

5. There is a broad literature on how long-term Europeanization shapes political attitudes and contributes to the development of a civic component of European identity. For the range of attitudinal research see Bruter (2005), Duchesne et al. (2013), McLaren (2005), Petithomme (2008), Rumford (2003), and Sanders et al. (2012).

6. The concept of banal Europeanism is developed in Cram (2001; 2012).

7. The call was published under the FP7 programme in 2010: http://cordis.europa.eu/programme/rcn/864_en.html.

8. The narratives of EU cultural policies are analyzed by Sassatelli (2009; 2015).

9. See Michailidou and Trenz (2015), who show that politicization of the EU citizenry is still constrained by huge knowledge deficits. There is, so to speak, a lack of competence, which explains that citizens across member states are increasingly prepared to challenge the fundamentals of European integration while the EU's day-to-day activities remain largely non-politicized.

10. See Dutceac Segesten's documentation of Eurosymbols at: https://www.facebook.com/pages/Eurosymbols/250762764970197?fref=ts (last accessed on August 15, 2015).

11. See the online documentation provided by the FREE project (Football Research in an Enlarged Europe) http://www.free-project.eu/Pages/Welcome.aspx (last accessed January 3, 2015).

12. The cultural framing of EU and foreign news coverage is analyzed by De Vreese (2001), De Vreese and Kandyla (2009), Hannerz (2004), and Trenz (2007a).

13. All references are adapted and rephrased by the author. For other examples, see Trenz (2005a; 2006a).

14. For the full documentation of my earlier work on banal references to Europe in media news coverage see Trenz (2005a; 2006a).

15. The correlation between involvement in social transnationalism and adherence to cosmopolitan values has been tested in the comparative surveys by Favell et al. (2014), Mau et al. (2008), and Recchi and Favell (2009).

16. Within the Framework Programme for collective research, see, for instance the INTUNE and PIONEUR projects (Rother and Nebe [2009] and Sanders et al. [2012]).

17. See the results of our series of interviews with so-called 'crisis refugees' from Southern Europe in Denmark and Norway (Duru et al. 2015).

18. See the encompassing comparative surveys on intra-EU mobility by Favell (2006), Favell and Recchi (2011), Mau (2011), and Recchi and Favell (2009).

19. See my discussion of the imaginary of the European traveler in the introductory chapter.

Chapter Four

From Triumph to Trauma

Resistance to Europeanization

Europeanization as triumph inevitably involves an element of drama because the story of the rise of the new can only be told in relation to the fall of the old. There are different versions of drama, which relate to the intrinsic conflicts and divisions within European social space. One popular mode of dramatizing history is to emphasize the power struggles that have accompanied European integration. Contemporary Europe is a result of the fall of old powers, which has facilitated the flourishing of new powers. Similarly, we can distinguish between the winners and the losers of European integration, the net contributors and the net receivers, the big and the small member states, or the hegemonic center and the periphery. This contradicts the official credo of triumph that European integration would create equal living conditions for all and promote an 'ever closer Union.' Many scholars insist that there is a case for bringing power back in and that Europeanization is not just to be perceived as a "smooth transition" and mutual learning for the benefit of all (Mahoney 2004; Moravcsik 1998). Such an account of power that is exercised by the EU is implicit in many studies of Europeanization that analyze how the EU impacts subordinated entities such as regions and member states. Intergovernmentalist or political economy approaches to European integration, for instance, are often schematized in accordance with a quantified relationship between winners and losers, for example, the beneficiaries of EU policies; those who get support from the European Union to impose their interests and identities; or those who gain power, salience, and legitimacy in contrast to those who must pay the price of adaptation, face structural hurdles to compete in the EU game, or adjust their interests and identities.[1]

In contrast to these power games, Europeanization also unfolds as the drama of history. The story of the rise of Europe is related to the parallel story of the fall of the nation-state. In the original heroic tale, the demise of nationalism was embraced as a story of emancipation that would help to transcend the insufficiencies of the nation-state and complete the project of modernity (Beck and Grande 2007). The hope that Europeanization will end the national era and establish a more just and democratic post-Westphalian order (Habermas 2001) also evokes fear among the still-numerous defenders of the nation-state, who instead regard EU bureaucracy as threatening their sovereignty and way of life.

The drama that grants new salience to Europe's internal conflicts cannot be analyzed separately from what I have previously discussed as triumphant or banal affirmations of European integration. If Europeanization of life experiences results in a new taken-for-grantedness of the boundary constructions of European integration and a new mode of constructing social belonging, then drama again broadens the perspectives, introduces new significance, and contests taken-for-granted meanings and interpretations. Drama thus inevitably relates to boundary contestations and identity conflicts.

From a storytelling perspective, it makes sense to base tales of Europeanization on conflict. If there is an attempt to glorify the success story of European integration and to ground a common Europe in values, then these values can also be contested. The saga of Europeanization is not only open to interpretation; it is also open to contestation. Such contestation brings Europe to the attention of the European publics, which are more readily mobilized by enthralling plots of conflict, involving stories of both elites and ordinary citizens. Resistance to Europeanization frequently builds upon schematized polarizations that are inherent to the European project: the European versus the national or the elite versus the people. This creates the possibility that Europe is shaped by the internal conflict between European forces of change and openness versus national forces of persistence and closure (Münch 2008: 113).

Europe's political and cultural history provides several templates for telling the story of Europeanization as related to social struggles and conflict. These consist not just of the wars that underlie the making and unmaking of the modern European order (Tilly 1990) but more broadly include the struggle over European modernity and the strong linkages to tradition, anti-modernity, and counter-Enlightenment, which continued as powerful social and political forces during long periods of the nineteenth and twentieth centuries. It is part of the success story of Europeanization that radical critiques of modernity gradually lost their persuasive power or became marginalized as irrational or residual expressions of opposition in the postwar period. Looking back at the postwar reconciliatory period, the triumph of Europeanization over residual forces of nationalism and anti-modernism was perhaps merely a stalemate and not a lasting form of conflict resolution. The European Union's territorial expansion and its failed constitutional settlement once again opened the Pandora Box of identity conflicts, through which European modernity and the secular tradition of the West once again became contested.

Most forcefully, the emancipatory account of Europeanization is challenged by the Eurosceptic account, which dismantles the false promise of Europeanization and seeks to protect the nation-state's achievements in terms of welfare, democracy, and popular sovereignty. Eurosceptics translate the success story of Europeanization as a triumph into a story of drama that is driven by deep and fundamental conflict. The contested nature of Europeanization for which Euroscepticism stands is only insufficiently captured within the notion of class or interest conflicts. Euroscepticism is not simply a continuation of the eternal conflicts between the governments concerning the net payer contributions to the European budget. For many observers, Euroscepticism stands instead for a new quality of identity politics, one that revives the old national animosities between Europe's countries and peoples (Fligstein 2008; Hooghe and Marks 2009).

The observation that Europeanization (in terms of deepened integration and enlargement) results in fundamental identity conflicts is emphasized in the recent literature. In fact, as I shall argue below, it is overemphasized. It is, of course, easy to give examples of the new salience of identity politics, be it in the form of new nationalist and regionalist movements, new populism, or anti-immigrant and anti-Islam mobilizations. All of these movements are also often explicitly anti-European. They occupy what can be called the Eurosceptic agenda. It has furthermore been emphasized that the so-called new identity politics have a negative impact on European integration or at least on the functional mechanisms that have long driven European integration. In the literature, this is referred to as the breakup of the permissive consensus.[2] The new identity politics are thus seen as the driving force behind the EU's politicization, which is more than simply an elite affair (Hurrelmann et al. 2015). To understand the new constraining dissensus that has replaced the permissive consensus in EU governance, we need a sociohistorical perspective that situates EU governance in the wider context of societal support and resistance. The 'drama' of EU identity politics is closely related to the 'trauma' of a perceived loss of identity and the forms of collective resistances and mobilizations related to it:

> The concept of trauma, borrowed from medicine, suggests that change per se, irrespective of its content, but provided that it is sudden, comprehensive, fundamental and unexpected, may produce painful shock for the social and particularly cultural tissue of a society. Paradoxically, this applies also to changes which are otherwise progressive, welcome, and intended by the people. Cultural trauma begins with disorganization of cultural rules and accompanying personal disorientation, culminating even in the loss of identity. This condition

is made more grave by the traumatizing events or situations which occur as the effect of major change in areas other than culture, and affect the whole "life-world" of the people. (Sztompka 2000: 4)

Events that have traumatized Europeans' collective memory are usually related to experiences of the Holocaust and fascism. As such, the traumatic drama of history plays a key role in the constitution of a European community of memory, which commemorates past excesses of nationalism. Commemoration of the traumatic past does not, however, provide sufficient grounds for collective departure into a post-national future (Giesen 2003; Closa 2010). Sociologists have emphasized that events are not 'quintessentially' traumatic but are always linked to processes of cultural interpretation. This implies a temporal aspect to trauma, which must be related to collective experiences of humiliation and loss of autonomy over time. If Europeanization is experienced as collective trauma, this can hardly be located in concrete events or in statistics about the worsening of material living conditions. It instead exists in the experiences and interpretations of many Europeans, who feel that they 'suffer' from Europe (e.g., as an effect of economic crisis, see chapter 5) or feel humiliated and limited in their autonomy. Europeanization might in this sense trigger a process that has been termed "cultural trauma" (Alexander et al. 2004), characterized by a number of collective emotions, orientations, and attitudes, which are used to defend national life projects against perceived outside threats or perpetrators. Most important here is the cultural interpretation given to trauma, helping confine the perceived threats to collective identifications that underlie Eurosceptic responses.

Euroscepticism provides a collective interpretation of the Europeans' traumatic experiences with European integration, but it is also linked to new forms and practices of political mobilization. In dealing with these new contentious dynamics of European integration, my argument is the following: If popular contestation and discontent is part of the saga of Europeanization, this is not the end of the story but instead an enthralling new plot within it. New heroes enter the scene: no longer the political leaders who represent us but the people of Europe themselves. Through contestation, we imagine the European project in a different way, provide new reasons and justifications for or against it and link it to different emotions. Europe becomes much more our own story, not only at the subconscious level in terms of affirmations of everyday life but also in confronting us with a choice, forcing us to reflect upon whether we wish to support or oppose the European project and upon what might be good reasons for our support or opposition.

FROM 'PERMISSIVE CONSENSUS' TO
NEW 'CONSTRAINING DISSENSUS'?

The spread of Euroscepticism has been an invitation for debate among scholars concerning how to theorize European integration. The success of political parties that fundamentally oppose European integration has, in fact, inspired many scholars to rethink European integration in terms of power and conflict and no longer in terms of an incremental process driven by functional necessity. In relation to this, a postfunctionalist theory of European integration has been formulated, postulating the new salience of mass politics, which mobilizes around core areas of state sovereignty and national identity (Hooghe and Marks 2009). Euroscepticism would thus be *prima facie* the expression of a new identity politics challenging the functional, efficiency-based rationale of European integration, which is no longer seen as 'inevitable' but is instead linked back to power and political choice. Euroscepticism stands for the politicization of European integration. It is about debating the choices related to European integration and not taking them for granted or embracing them with a 'permissive consensus.' Euroscepticism is about contesting the intrinsic value of these choices, not in the form of policy debates among political actors and experts but in the form of public debates involving a wider mass audience and the media (de Wilde 2011). Euroscepticism as a form of resistance to European integration is in this sense a simple reminder of alternative pathways to integration at the national and global levels. Eurosceptics prompt us to rethink Europeanization in terms of progress, "which is very much an empirical matter rather than simply an a priori assumption" (Downs 2011: 279).

One might thus be tempted to define Euroscepticism in relation to everything that slows down the locomotive of European integration, undermines institutional capacities, or disrupts the automatism of deepening and widening. Two assumptions are made: first, that politicization has constrained European integration, and second, that it is primarily expressed as a new form of 'mass identity politics.' As we have argued elsewhere (Statham and Trenz 2014), both assumptions are problematic.

The expectation that politicization has constrained European integration and affected its institutional autonomy is not supported by the expansive dynamics of EU crisis governance, which instead enhances the autonomy of executive actors and bureaucracies. In handling the current financial and monetary crisis, EU institutions and governments have been even less responsive and have indeed shown a surprising capacity for shielding integration from public demands and containing the "constraining dissensus" (Schimmelfennig 2014). Several commentators have highlighted this mismatch between politicization as measured in public unrest, discontent, and negative public opinion on the one hand and the day-to-day policymaking process in Brussels, which continues its "business as usual" on the other hand (Haverland 2013). In confronting its deepest crisis, the EU administrative apparatus opts for more technocracy and seems to rely even more on stakeholders and experts, thereby disrespecting public opinion. One could ironically conclude that the 'constraining dissensus' thesis was too optimistic with regard to the democratic quality of the EU, assuming that EU officials and bureaucracy could be constrained and become more responsive to public demands. The 'politicization' scholars underestimated the perseverance of the EU's democratic deficit, the symptoms of which imply that EU institutions can be (and some would claim 'need to be') shielded from public opinion. In times of crisis, the EU institutional apparatus can even more readily disregard lack of public support in formulating and implementing its policies (and is even encouraged to do so by the banks and governments) by drawing upon justifications of emergency and so-called TINA ('there is no alternative') decisions. Symptoms of the EU's democratic deficit thus perpetuate. In a political system where accountability deficits underlie a detachment of the formal legality of procedures from the legitimacy of public visibility and control, there is, strictly speaking, no necessity to respond to public demands.

Instead of focusing (perhaps too optimistically) on Euroscepticism as an engine for institutional change, we must thus take into consideration the structural mismatch between the 'functioning' of the EU institutions, which remain 'shielded' from politicization, and the public responses to European integration, which barely impact EU governance. The legality and the public legitimacy of EU governance are disconnected; there is, so to speak, a representative gap, which is only insufficiently bridged by procedures of public accountability and control. While there is but little evidence that the functioning of EU institutions in governing the financial and monetary crisis is constrained by the necessity of taking into account mass-level domestic politics in member states, the negative impact of EU crisis governance and the austerity measures taken on public support and legitimacy seems undeniable, and it is here that Euroscepticism must be conceptually anchored.

A second assumption made by the postfunctionalist school of integration has been that the new politicized dynamics of integration are mainly expressed as a form of identity politics. Again, the recent events of contesting crisis-related austerity policies seem to indicate rather the return of redistributive conflicts shaping both the national and the European political landscapes. This is also supported by opinion polls, which show that economic determinants and very palpable material concerns and not a diffuse feeling of threat of identity account for the loss of public support with the EU (Braun and Tausendpfund 2014; Statham and Trenz 2014). The people of Europe do not fear losing identity, they simply fear the loss of material life chances. More important than these attitudinal measurements, the people in Europe also mobilize a collective 'we' against the state and the market. This collective 'we' marks however not a delimited ethnic or identitarian space, but rather a societal space where rights are claimed and citizenship is enacted often quite indiscriminately of origin. Euroscepticism can from this perspective be conceptualized as a case of "creative destruction"—a process of fission and fusion, that makes visible ruptures of social relations but also possible departures and through which society is transformed and not simply contained in the national (Eder 2015).

Hence, the type of conflict for which Euroscepticism stands is more deep seated as simply a momentary slowing down of the locomotive of European integration. If EU scholars, who conceptualize European integration from a perspective of administrative science, feel no need to rewrite a theory of functional integration, this is ultimately also explained by the successful implementation of protective measures, which shield off EU decision-making practices from society constraints. The EU administration can continue to operate in relative autonomy and does not need to respond to demands raised by the Eurosceptic opposition. Euroscepticism should therefore not be conceptualized in relation to its putative impact on EU governance but in relation to its wider societal resonance and the type of contentious politics it generates. From this latter perspective, it is precisely this autonomy of the EU apparatus of decision-making that is targeted by the Eurosceptic account. The triumph of Europeanization, which is still reflected in the progressive-functionalist account, cannot be detached from the drama of those who are left behind. Euroscepticism, from this perspective, is formulated in defiance to the powerful narration of the postwar triumph of Europe and of Europeanization as linked to progress, emancipation, and empowerment.

EUROSCEPTICISM AND THE UNFINISHED DEMOCRATIZATION OF THE EU

When theorizing Euroscepticism below, emphasis will therefore be less on the ways in which it affects EU governance and decision-making and more on the explanation for the contested legitimacy, ruptures, and bifurcations that European societies are undergoing as a consequence of this contestation. By shifting emphasis from a theory of governance to a theory of legitimacy and society, Euroscepticism can be variably related to a type of constitutional conflict that shakes both the EU and its member states. While functional integration continues, and the building of executive power for a new type of supranational administration remains largely unconstrained (Egeberg 2012; Schimmelfennig 2014), the foundations of the structure are becoming increasingly shaky (Menéndez 2013). Euroscepticism thus stands as a form of systemic stress for the evolving unit. It is manifested as a legitimation crisis, which *prima facie* affects neither the regularity and routine of *governance* nor the struggle over composition of the *government* but instead, in the sense of David Easton (1975), influences recognition of political authority.[3] In systemic terms, such a crisis of regime is measured in lack of support (input) and not in lack of decision-making (output). Diffuse support "refers to evaluations of what an object is or represents (. . .) not of what it does" (Easton 1975: 444). As such, manifestations of Euroscepticism are typically detached from short-term 'output' or 'performance.' 'Eurosceptics' are, for instance, not easily impressed by a proclaimed increase in the 'output legitimacy' of EU governance. They do not care whether a particular regulation is beneficial since they would oppose the principle that EU institutions have regulatory competences in the first place. Euroscepticism, as a 'crisis of regime,' is a reminder that the EU's legitimacy is not simply coupled with the 'functioning' of its institutions but also linked with a third instance that provides such legitimacy. This third instance is what emerges from popular contestation involving a diffuse category of 'the people,' who engage in communication over the legitimacy of the underlying unit (Eder 2015). It is in this sense that I will conceptualize Euroscepticism as a form of 'polity contestation' that is no longer restricted to constitutional debates among intellectuals but involves, in the final instance, the 'people,' who grant legitimacy to the economic and political order. Euroscepticism, in short, reminds us that the logics of institutions and decision-making practices that contribute to the 'functioning' of European integration are related back to ideational constructions and discursive interactions of identity and community, which attribute general legitimacy (Schmidt 2013: 3).

MAKING SENSE OF EUROSCEPTIC OPPOSITION: ANOMIE, PARTISAN CONTESTATION, OR POPULAR RESISTANCE

In order to proceed with the conceptualization of Euroscepticism as a form of polity contestation, it is crucial to determine where the processes that are necessary for the generation of political legitimacy are allocated. The overview of the academic literature on Euroscepticism provides us with three responses: the first approach discusses political legitimacy in relation to trust and shared identities of citizens, measured through the methods of attitudinal research. The second approach views political legitimacy as an outcome of the strategic mobilization of collective actors, in particular of political parties. The third approach discusses political legitimacy in relation to welfare and material well-being, which accounts for the emancipation of individuals. Placing these three lines of research in a wider social-scientific context, we can distinguish a Durkheimian account of Euroscepticism based on attitudinal research, a Rokkanian account based on the reconstruction of ideological divisions and partisan mobilization, and a Marxian account based on a critical reconstruction of the EU's political economy.

The Durkheimian Account: Euroscepticism as Anomie

Socio-psychological or attitudinal research on Euroscepticism is based on the assumption that enhanced political conflicts over European integration correspond to citizens' changing attitudes. Existing surveys often approach public opinion in terms of support for and identification with European integration, EU actors and institutions, or specific EU competences and policies (Eichenberg and Dalton 2007; Hooghe and Marks 2007). Especially in Eurobarometer and European election surveys, European citizens' attitudes are treated as predispositions embodied by particular groups, using the common standards of classifying people along national lines or using relatively invariable indicators like education and social class (McLaren 2005; Petithomme 2008). Attitudinal research on European integration has thus aimed to trace general patterns of group polarization and especially to identify those groups within the larger population that present Eurosceptic attitudes.

Sociopsychological explanations of Euroscepticism are furthermore often intended to 'rationalize' the 'irrational responses' of some groups of people. As such, they ultimately end up in explaining Euroscepticism in relation to the 'collective consciousness' of Europeans as primarily national and not yet ready to embrace the benefits of European integration. They draw upon the old Durkheimian understanding of anomie, which affects modern society like a disease of the collective. Anomie is, in fact, seen as a side effect of modernization, which is not only progress (the triumphal account of Europeanization) but also undermines social cohesion, thus leading to collective irrational responses. The Durkheimian account of Euroscepticism as a state of anomie or a 'collective mental disorder' operates through the attribution of psychological characteristics to particular groups within society. Anomie as a societal account of normlessness is linked to alienation as a condition of powerlessness, both leading to a collective response by the individuals or social groups that are placed in such an 'objective' condition. This opens Euroscepticism to a kind of research that relies upon attitudinal surveys for a sociopsychological diagnosis of the aberrations of European electorates. The normlessness of anomie is related to diffuse fears of a loss of national identification, powerlessness when confronted by the transfer of sovereignty to European institutions (Bruter 2008; McLaren 2007). The lack of diffuse support for the quality of the political system correlates with expressions of cynicism, as David Easton (1975: 447) observed. Similar explanations of cultural anomie are also used to explain the rise of right-wing extremism and xenophobia or the passage from the welfare state to disembedded markets and neoliberal governance, which have deprived affected individuals of agency and voice (Burgi 2014).

The clear advantage to such a sociopsychological explanation is that it tends to be broadly applicable as it can be more easily detached from the material living conditions of many Europeans who still live in relatively wealthy societies. Anomie as an experience of normlessness and disempowerment does not necessarily need to be linked to 'objective conditions' of economic hardship. It can be used to explain the 'welfare chauvinism' of Scandinavia as much as the sudden and dramatic change of public attitudes in a situation in which literally the entire population turns Eurosceptic overnight, as discussed in relation to crisis-ridden Italy (Castelli and Froio 2014). The claim that Euroscepticism is an expression of resistance by people who 'suffer' from disorientation or even loss of identity also has a vindicatory component for the so-called defenders of European integration, who wish to disclose the 'irrational character' of the Eurosceptic response. The perception of Euroscepticism as an anomic reaction of collectives thus primarily serves to ensure the defenders of European integration of their own 'rationality' while at the same time simulating understanding of the humiliated.

The literature has sought to test several variables on the basis of Eurobarometer opinion surveys, seeking to explain why some groups tend to be more Eurosceptic than others (Fuchs et al. 2009; Hooghe and Marks 2007). The observation that Euroscepticism is not directly related to material suffering can be backed by various opinion polls such as the European Social Survey and Eurobarometer. Analysts seem to agree that the pro-European and anti-European division is not an issue of social class. In the UK, for instance, even though business tends to be pro-European, supporters of the Conservative Party—including the most fervent Eurosceptics—are to be found among wealthy and influential families (Anderson 2004). In Scandinavian societies as well, voters from all strata of society back Eurosceptic parties (Sitter 2001). In the Netherlands, electorates are found to show high levels of welfare chauvinism (de Koster et al. 2013). Werts et al. (2013) find only a weak correlation between social class, education, and the propensity to vote for right-wing extremist parties and that cultural and identitarian concerns in general tend to lose significance in times of economic hardship. The upper strata of society continue to be on average more pro-European than the lower strata, but as demonstrated by the distribution of votes, Euroscepticism nevertheless seems attractive to some of them.

If there is no stable positive linkage between pro-European and anti-European attitudes and social class, other sociostructural variables might play a role in explaining Euroscepticism. Hakhverdian et al. (2013), for instance, have tested the impact of educational attainment on Euroscepticism, showing that higher-educated strata of the population are less likely to base their opinions on questions of national identity and less likely to be influenced by cues from Eurosceptic parties. Euroscepticism can also simply be explained as an information deficit among some parts of the population, and fighting existing educational asymmetries would be the best means of keeping the locomotive of European integration going (Downs 2011).

The anomic account of Euroscepticism is ultimately popular among those policy actors and institutions that seek viable therapies to cure Euroscepticism as a form of irrational group behavior. The programs of 'enlightenment' that are launched by the European Commission to make European voters more rational are either designed as general campaigns, meant to balance information asymmetries (Brüggemann 2010), or they target specific groups (especially young people) through education, civic engagement, and cross-border exchanges, which are seen as conducive to long-term changes of Europeans' attitudes.[4]

The Rokkanian Account: Euroscepticism as Partisan Contestation

Turning away from sociopsychological explanations, which associate Eurosceptic attitudes with particular categories of people, another important tradition among scholars discusses Euroscepticism in relation to political mobilization. In the tradition of Stein Rokkan (1999), Stefano Bartolini (2005) has described the political structuring of European political space in relation to collective actors' strategies and capacities for mobilizing large segments of the population. As only few people experience Europe directly, the issues related to European integration need to be made salient by someone, the knowledge that people have about Europe needs to be formed, and the controversies need to be made explicit. In short, Euroscepticism is seen as a consequence of political mobilization, not as a state of mind. Its new salience marks the turn from elite politics backed by a permissive consensus to mass politics, which expresses dissent and constrains the functioning of the EU. The conceptualization of Euroscepticism relative to the ongoing politicization of European integration draws attention to the restructuring of political spaces within which political parties and their electorates align. In contrast to the old 'mass politics,' which were organized around ideological (left-right) alignments, the new mass politics are primarily expressed as a form of 'identity politics' over Europe. The new identity mass politics are related to the counter-forces to globalization and Europeanization, which have been mobilized by popular parties on the left and the right. This, in turn, explains the salience of a new division structure, which divides the European electorates into fervent defenders of national identity and promoters of European integration. The idea that European integration polarizes the European population along a pro-European and anti-European dividing line also underlies Neil Fligstein's (2008) 'Euroclash' thesis. This thesis considers how globalization and open liberal markets (for which European integration stands) have produced new groups of 'winners' and 'losers' within society, which increasingly politically self-identify themselves as such and mobilize on this basis within domestic national politics. Likewise, for Hanspeter Kriesi et al. (2008), opposition to European integration is shaped by competition between the winners and losers of 'de-nationalization' processes.

These publications all call for the study of Euroscepticism in relation to citizens' reactions (rather than attitudes) and an analysis of political stances expressed in public discourse (rather than privately held opinions) (Duchesne et al. 2013: 24–26). Discarding all sociopsychological explanations of 'identity loss,' 'irrational group behavior,' and 'anomie,' Euroscepticism is explained by either strategic action mobilization or collective action logics. From the first (rational choice) perspective, political parties, interest groups, and voters behave rationally by marking their positions in the political struggle along a set of preferences for the EU's constitutional and institutional design.[5] Euroscepticism can thus be derived from voters' utilitarian considerations in relation to cues received from Eurosceptic political parties (de Vries and Edwards 2009). From the second (Bourdieuan) perspective, party-based Euroscepticism is investigated as a field of practices through which resistance finds expression and is publically justified.[6] Building upon cultural-institutional approaches, such explanations also take into account how such resistance is discursively framed, how political cues resonate with and are taken up and amplified by the media. The cultural-institutional understanding of Euroscepticism considers, for instance, the possibility of an inverse relationship between political cues and Euroscepticism. It is not just political parties' negative cues that inform voters; even positive cues can provoke cultural resistance. Euroscepticism, in some instances, could then be explained as a public reaction to pro-European elite discourse (Trenz 2007a).

The Marxian Account: Euroscepticism as Popular Resistance

Political economy approaches to European integration relate Euroscepticism, populism, and right-wing extremism to macroeconomic changes that European societies are undergoing in times of crisis. Critical scholars typically start by classifying the beneficiaries of European integration into the elite classes of highly mobile and educated people who profit from free movement and the exchange of goods and knowledge on the one hand and those many who remain excluded and suffer from material hardships as the 'underdogs' of the liberalized and deregulated market on the other hand. Euroscepticism is thus shared by those who suffer from economic hardship and have difficulty seeing European integration as a process of emancipation and well-being. The salience of a pro-European and anti-European division is primarily a vertical division between the beneficiaries of European integration and the victims of open neoliberal economies.

Political economy approaches are a useful corrective to essentialist interpretations, which seek to explain 'inherent qualities' of Euroscepticism or its defenders. Euroscepticism is not a self-sufficient phenomenon; the explanatory focus is on the externalities that generate it. There is no sense in researching Euroscepticism as an attribute of particular actors or parties. Instead of a descriptive account of Euroscepticism and its various manifestations, we need to engage in a critical inquiry of the structural and material conditions that empower or disempower particular population strata and generate reactionary collective responses.

This interpretation of Eurosceptics as the 'victims' of neoliberal market deregulation can be read as a revival of a Marxian account, which explains why particular strata of society are cut off from the possibilities of emancipation and disempowered as both market participants and as citizens (Daianu et al. 2014). Eurosceptic voting preferences are understood as a form of 'silent protest' by the disempowered citizens. The progressive narrative of Europeanization as emancipation is rejected, raising concern about structural impediments to emancipation and empowerment (Somek 2013). Under current socioeconomic conditions, resistance to European integration cannot be formulated as a progressive force but instead takes the form of populist and right-wing backlashes. The European Union, as just another variant of capitalist government, has engaged in "empowerment light" (e.g., stakeholder participation in policy formulation or anti-discrimination) that is removed from the ideals of human emancipation (Somek 2013: 51). The activation of the individual through various training and support programs has replaced the Marxian vision linked to full-bodied empowerment of the citizenry (62). Under these circumstances, political mobilization remains necessarily fragmented. Euroscepticism is seen as a distorted form of class consciousness among people who take refuge from international capitalism in safe national harbors. Inspired by Marxist explanations of fascism, these interpreters of the EU's political economy would concede that the followers of right-wing Eurosceptic parties have chosen the right target (the European Union as the main promoter of neoliberalism) but would hold that they are not in the position to formulate an emancipatory project, partly because their media environments do not support such radical expressions of resistance (Fuchs 2014).

The 'anti-modern' and 'reactionary' character of oppositional politics to global capitalism is thus explained as an effect of the patronizing attitude of liberal elites and the media as well as their domination of official channels of communication. Under conditions of hegemony, class conflict is turned into 'agonistic politics,' through which the opponent to the hegemonic project is marginalized and demonized. Europeanization, as linked to the progressive rationalization and technocratization of all aspects of our lives, is thus seen as an ideological force of capitalism, operating in such a way as to exclude the opponent or the repressed person from the realm of 'legitimate discourse.'

The Marxist interpretation is used to account for the absence of an emancipatory project of the left, which could effectively challenge the hegemony of European integration as an expansion of liberal-capitalist markets. Instead of proposing a new left-wing project, critical scholars analyze the failures of various political movements to formulate a radical political alternative. Such an analysis is useful for identifying the discursive constellations and structural conditions of hegemony, which block emancipatory politics and drive repressed people into the arms of nationalist and populist parties (Arditi 2007). The rise of Euroscepticism and the extreme right is also related to a new strategy of depoliticization on the part of European governments and the so-called TINA ('there is no alternative') emergency decisions taken in relation to governing the financial and monetary crisis (see chapter 5). Eurossceptics and populists take part in repoliticization in response to technocratic governance and offer themselves to electorates as the truly 'democratic' alternative (Pérez 2013: 28).

Euroscepticism as an element of 'agonistic politics' is thus interpreted as an important deviation from representative democratic politics; in fact, it is seen as a potential force for undermining liberal democracy and capitalist markets. Unlike the representative system of democracy, the opening of the EU to 'agonistic politics' would not require the pre-existence of a European demos. The latter is seen as an ideological construct, which further inhibits expression of the popular voice. Populists are in this sense not to be blamed for undermining the system of representative democracy or disrespecting individual citizens' rights but should instead be praised as the only possible form of opposition under conditions of capitalist hegemony that attempt to articulate the "authentic voice of the people" (Laclau 2005).

EUROSCEPTICISM AS EU POLITY CONTESTATION: FROM NORMATIVE ASSESSMENT TO COGNITIVE FRAMING

These various sociological accounts reflect the ambiguous and elusive character of Euroscepticism as a form of polity contestation that can neither be reduced to stable attitudes or identities of the people who subscribe to it nor be ideologically confined as a discourse informing the strategic mobilization of a specific group of political actors (de Wilde et al. 2015). Several attempts have been made in the literature to conceptually grasp the phenomenon, to categorize the 'soft' and the 'hard' Eurosceptics, to confine its analytical dimensions or approach its ideological core.[7] All of these approaches have their own value for inquiring into the range of concepts, contexts, environments, and actors through which Euroscepticism can find expression and endure over time. But none of these approaches can claim to capture the 'essence' of Euroscepticism or understand the 'core' of its ideological expression. Euroscepticism is not an ideology but instead stems from political actors' difficulties formulating ideology and mobilizing their adherents on the basis of firm political beliefs. Euroscepticism is also not confined to particular arenas, actors, or discourses but is instead ubiquitous. Nor is it a fixed attitudinal pattern or the identity of a confined group of people but is instead often accrued from quick attitudinal change and a general disorientation of particular segments of the population. For the same reasons, Euroscepticism can only with difficulty produce stable party alignment and in most cases stands for a diffuse division in the party landscape, along which actors temporarily align.

Several observers have furthermore noted the difficulties involved in formulating EU resistance as an emancipatory political project but have sought its origins in people's disempowerment in European politics. In this sense, Euroscepticism does not provide an alternative account of the official project of progressive Europeanism but is instead linked to diffuse practices of the delegitimation of this project. It would therefore also be illusive to expect discursive coherence in the formulation of a Eurosceptic political counter-project. The strength of Euroscepticism is not an argumentative power that convinces people but is instead its vagueness and ideological indeterminacy, which draw upon people's unarticulated feelings and emotions. Through such an inbuilt elusiveness, proponents of Euroscepticism can reach out more easily to a diffuse public than would be possible for a political party, which relies on written manifestos to target specific groups but, on the basis of these programmatic statements, can be also tested for coherence and held publically accountable.

In most of its variants, both left and right, Euroscepticism is paired with a strong notion of anti-elitism. This is used to explain the affinity between Euroscepticism and populism (Ruzza 2009). Populist rhetoric is primarily meant as a challenge of representative democracy and technocracy. As such, Eurosceptic parties also often change their targets and mobilize, for instance, against national elites. Populist rhetoric is furthermore used to articulate the unitary voice of the people in disregard of all its multiplicity and factitiousness. Euroscepticism provides a framework for turning the various critical accounts of Europeanization into one political voice that can be properly identified and attributed. If Euroscepticism can hardly be considered a marker of collective identity and its historical narration, it nonetheless works as a marker of popular voice and resistance. Euroscepticism is a defensive and protective movement that opposes the dismantling of the national project of identity and democracy. It builds upon an account of Europeanization as inherently conflictual. There is a fundamental conflict line that structures politics between power holders and the people. Representation is not meant as reconciliation but indicates the alienation and exclusion of the people from democratic politics. Representation therefore provokes legitimate popular resistance, disrupting not only the myths of peaceful coexistence and equal living conditions among Europeans but also the routines of conflict settlement implemented by EU institutions and member-state governments. The anti-elitism of Euroscepticism as a unifying denominator comes closest to the political economy explanation of diffuse popular resistance to market logics. The Eurosceptic account of the people as the eternal losers of European integration could thus be given meaning as a form of 'class consciousness' that reflects the objective condition of disempowered electorates.

As an alternative to attitudes, it has been proposed that Euroscepticism should be considered a legitimation discourse. Several attempts have been made to classify such discourses along different lines of content and to confine them to particular actors. Glyn Morgan, for instance, distinguishes between conservative Euroscepticism and social democratic Euroscepticism, both of which seek to transform the project of European integration but remain unable to provide a democratic justification of the alternative form of polity that they promote (Morgan 2005; 2007). Others have sought to root Euroscepticism in discourses of nationalism, populism, or right-wing extremism but have had to conclude that the many sides of Euroscepticism can scarcely be brought under one common denominator.[8] Our own research on discursive expressions of Euroscepticism in the media underlies a classificatory scheme for discourses of legitimation of the EU polity within which Euroscepticism appears as a diffuse and residual category. As we concluded: "EU polity contestation dominantly spreads an under-specified negativism about the EU and European integration. We are witnessing many unfocused expressions of discontent, rather than precisely formulated and substantiated evaluations of EU legitimacy and we get only little information on the kind of European polity that would be supported or that is opposed by the participants in the examined online media debates" (de Wilde et al. 2013: 53). Euroscepticism reflects in this sense a debate in which the EU polity is strongly contested but in which this contestation is indiscriminate with regard to the dimension of the EU polity being targeted and the criteria of justification underlying the evaluation.[9]

As I argue below, this fuzziness is indeed symptomatic of the way in which Eurosceptic resistance to European integration is promoted and made salient in public and media discourse. The reason why neither attitudinal nor discursive approaches can fully grasp the 'meaning' of Euroscepticism is that there is often no such 'meaning' in the form of a story line that can be fixed beyond the *ad hoc* expression. There is, so to speak, no '-ism' of Euroscepticism. While ideologies seek to formulate a coherent belief system combined with a positive mandate to act, Euroscepticism is "totemic" (Usherwood 2014: 7). As such, it needs no meaningful plot and no constructive vision but merely builds upon a negative vision of that which is collectively disliked. There is thus no coherent narrative thread for adherents to follow, take up, and continue. As part of the saga of Europeanization, Euroscepticism often appears like a troll, which in Internet slang denotes an individual who makes provocative or inflammatory statements, which are mainly used to derail the official plot and discontinue its narration.

This is not to suggest that meaning and interpretations cannot be variously attributed to Euroscepticism's contribution to ongoing public debates that contest the contours and legitimacy of the European project. The purpose of applying a discursive understanding to Euroscepticism is, then, to account for these practices of contestation and the various techniques (normative argumentation, cognitive selection, and framing biases) that are applied to draw the attention of European publics.

Euroscepticism as Polity Contestation: Defensive and Reactive

In line with the overall argument of this book, I wish to relate Euroscepticism to societal practices of legitimation and justification of the project of European integration, its institutional-constitutional setting, and its future trajectory (the 'EU polity' dimension). Euroscepticism can thus be approached as part of a discursive practice that contests the legitimacy of European integration as a project and of the EU polity as an institutional and constitutional entity, which exerts political authority over member states and the people.[10]

Such legitimacy contestations concern deeply grounded conflicts about the rightness of a political order. They are the religious conflicts of our modern times. As the nation-state framework, which for so long provided the settlement for such modern religious conflicts, is challenged by processes of transnationalization, we observe a new salience of 'polity contestation,' which reallocates popular sovereignty in relation to state order and constitutionally guaranteed rights. 'Polity contestation' is thus about a restructured relationship between the national and the international. It can be defensive in the sense that existing constitutional arrangements are protected against the perceived negative effects of transnationalization or Europeanization, but it can also be transformative in the sense of undermining the functioning of established systems and promoting alternative arrangements. Euroscepticism as a form of polity contestation is thus not self-sufficient but frequently correlates with systemic opposition at the nation-state level. The way that nation-state legitimacy is challenged in many member states (the UK, Belgium, Spain, and Italy, to mention just a few) and the way that EU legitimacy is challenged bear many similarities. This does not mean that many regionalists are also Eurosceptics, only that they position themselves in the same arena in which state and popular sovereignty are redefined in relation to the national and the international.

By locating Euroscepticism as part of the ongoing legitimacy contestation of the EU, two defining elements can be discerned: its negative (defensive) and its reactive character. Euroscepticism is meant to shield off the protected area of national democratic politics and to reassert popular sovereignty within such national democratic protectorates. Attention should furthermore be directed from the contestants to the arenas in which such forms of system opposition are promoted. The negativity of 'polity contestation' that undermines EU legitimacy cannot be simply attributed to particular actors (the 'Eurosceptics') but must instead be considered a structuring element of public and political discourse. It is, as I shall argue below, a cognitive foundation of public legitimation discourses, not an explicit justificatory element that can be tested or refuted by strength of argumentation. The emphasis is then on the discursive arenas for this type of contestation. These are primarily the mass media. Euroscepticism unfolds under conditions of mediatized democracy, as a by-product of media negativity. Actors, institutions, and publics involved in the 'making of' Euroscepticism are constrained by the media logics that apply to their conflicts and are not intentionally seeking to achieve anything through the media (Michailidou and Trenz 2013).

While recognizing that the European project is in need of justificatory arguments, the particular linkage between Eurosceptic discourse and pro-European discourse comes to the attention. Euroscepticism is in this sense not simply negative; it is also reactive. One could from this perspective interpret Euroscepticism as an 'act of defiance' of excluded, humiliated, and vilified publics. National publics feel naturally attracted by dissensus when confronted with the "culture of total optimism" that prevails in the EU (Schulz-Forberg and Stråth 2010; Majone 2014). They engage in a "discursive exploration of dissensus" under the restricted conditions of public discourse imposed by the EU. As a consensus-building machine, the EU has enormous difficulties accommodating dissent, and those who fall outside of the consensus tend to be ignored or disdained (Usherwood 2014: 5). Euroscepticism is an act of defiance by such stigmatized publics. It is a reaction to 'triumphant Europeanism' and is staged as the profanation of the sacred. As such, it is part of the ongoing legitimation struggle that debates what European integration is good for and whether and why we should support it. Stating that Euroscepticism is reactive emphasizes that it reacts to and often explicitly responds to the public legitimation discourse that is launched in support of the EU. It is made possible because there are European leaders and institutions that try to promote the legitimacy of the EU (for instance, through public communications or PR strategies). In other words, the more the EU tries to be legitimate by promoting its own success story, the more it also provokes a Eurosceptic reaction. Furthermore, Euroscepticism is staged as a form of constitutional conflict. What is contested is the legitimacy of the EU polity, its underlying principle that justifies integration, its current institutional and constitutional setup, and its future trajectory (5). As such, Euroscepticism is placed outside the institutional arena of the EU and unfolds within the public and media sphere that is open to this kind of contestation.

EUROSCEPTICISM AS A DELEGITIMIZING PRACTICE: THE NORMS THAT UNDERLIE AND THE KNOWLEDGE THAT INFORMS EU POLITY CONTESTATION

This notion of EU polity contestation represents a significant advance over other approaches that measure Euroscepticism as attitudes or behavioral patterns belonging to individuals or groups and not as attributes of discourse. It also extends the agenda of a normative political theory of the EU by taking into account the legitimation practices through which the validity of norms that apply to a particular political order are negotiated within a particular sociohistorical context. Instead of presenting a static assessment of the 'object' legitimacy of the EU, it turns to the sociohistorical practice of legitimation, its institutional underpinning, and its cognitive-cultural determinants.

The underlying assumption is that legitimacy is an *essentially* contested concept (Gaus 2011: 3). Legitimation is a process designed not only to justify the existing political order but also to explain it (Gaus 2011: 10). Social cognitive structures, which are linked to the generation of knowledge, tell people why they should appraise a particular order and not another but also why things are as they are within that order. Legitimation has, then, a normative and cognitive element: It provides good arguments for the justification of political order, but it also provides knowledge and constitutive rules to apply that knowledge and translate it into a normative evaluation that is understood and shared by others. Normative discourses are in this sense shaped by cognitive structures that specify the "constitutive rules for how society or specific groups think and interact" (O'Mahony 213: 302–311). It then makes a decisive difference whether societies can apply ready-made and culturally rooted normative templates for claiming the generalized validity of their political order or whether they must engage in processes of fundamental learning about the content and applicability of norms. The latter entails the need for collective cognitive reorientation, which, however, is often blocked by the perseverance of the established cultural-cognitive apparatus (as sustained, for instance, by the education system or—even more effectively—by the mass media). As a complex transnational and multicultural arrangement, the European Union has arguably entered such a process of collective cognitive reorientation. This requires more than just a new normative settlement of its quality of democracy. It also entails the need to respecify its cognitive orientation as a polity that could take over the normative template of liberal democracy but could also experiment with all sorts of other templates and even use cognitive and normative models to turn such experimentalism into a permanent quality (O'Mahony 2013: 307; Dorf and Sabel 1998).

The observation that knowledge precedes values in the legitimation of political order (Gaus 2011: 10) adds to the character of essential contestation of 'polity legitimacy,' which we encounter in the specific case of Euroscepticism. As I have argued above, EU polity contestation is not simply about the applicability of norms but is more fundamentally about their essential content. Discussing Euroscepticism in relation to the sociocognitive underpinning of political order helps explain why change of value preference is so difficult: society's cognitive structures are protected by the nation-state's existing institutional arrangements, which frequently block learning potential and slow down cognitive reorientation.

One important implication of this 'cognitive turn' is that Euroscepticism is not simply the manifestation of a normative dispute but is instead evidence of a contestation of core concepts that underlie the coherence of social and political order. According to Collier et al. (2006), such disputes about "essentially contested concepts" concern meaning and correct usage rather than simply the application of norms. As such, they are locked in a principally unfinished dispute and often preclude a rational settlement:

> The strong normative valence associated with some concepts, often combined with other considerations, motivates users to strongly prefer a particular meaning. They may energetically defend their own usage, whereas others will contend that an alternative usage is correct—hence the idea of a contested concept. Examples of such concepts are democracy, justice, rule of law, citizenship, war, genocide, abortion, rape, and hate crime. (Collier et al. 2006: 212)

Inquiries into such disputes about essentially contested concepts must address the cognitive frames, prototypes, and complex and often mutually exclusive sources of knowledge by which they are informed. Polity contestations in David Easton's sense, outlined above, concern such essentially contested concepts, more specifically the meaning of democracy, popular sovereignty, and (universal) rights for the national and the European (global). The essentially contested character of EU polity is entrenched not only by the EU's 'unfinished' democratization but also by the zero-sum character of the available alternatives for resolving such polity disputes. Struggles between the nation-state and Europe over the allocation of popular sovereignty and the validity of norms are more than just unsettled. The particular polity alternatives at the disposition of an institutional and constitutional EU settlement rely on mutually exclusive projects. If the EU is to democratize, it cannot at the same time be a Europe of sovereign nation-states, a federal Union, or a cosmopolitan project. While the question of the project's *finalité* requires a definite answer, democratization itself is ambiguous, and its underlying processes and contents are contradictory and conflict-laden. In daily legitimation practice, the exclusivity of a particular polity design furthermore frequently implies the delegitimation of its rivals (Morgan 2007). Democratization processes translated into public legitimation practices involving political parties and the media are therefore rarely reconciliatory and consensual but usually highly conflictual and exclusive.

Euroscepticism reflects the rupture of the existing institutional-constitutional order's routine sense-making practices and the difficulties in coming to terms with polity alternatives. Legitimacy contestations within the nation-state framework usually relate to the same type of political entity (the state or the government). As long as the polity dimension of legitimacy disputes is considered stable, only the value attributed to that polity is contested. In the case of the European Union, however, essential legitimacy contestation is far reaching as a result of changes in the polity objects of legitimation practices. Contestation is, then, not simply about different beliefs in legitimacy but also about different entities within which these beliefs are validated.

The notion of 'EU polity contestation' needs to account for the fact that the people of Europe evaluate the EU not just in terms of the quality of its outputs and inputs but also often rely on various cultural and cognitive models for constituting legitimate political order between the national, the European, and the global (Morgan 2007). These cognitions vary along national lines, yet they also evolve around mutually exclusive notions of legitimacy applied to the EU. The problem is, as Morgan continues, that different "types of polity—'the EU' (however it is described), 'the sovereign nation state,' and 'a Federal Europe'—cannot coexist in Europe; they are mutually incompatible" (Morgan 2007: 22). In other words, "the EU cannot vindicate its own claims to 'polity legitimacy'—its status as 'a self-standing political community'—without delegitimating its conceptual rivals, including a Europe of nation-states" (22).

By conceiving of democracy in EU integration as an idealized consensus within normative political theory, such essential conflicts about polity legitimacy have been banned or reframed in terms of integration's reconciliatory logic. Debates in political theory have been processed in such a way as to inquire into the relative merits of each of these "polity models."[11] On the basis of such a validity test of the strength of arguments, the Eurosceptic option is rejected through the "register of normative justification." The Eurosceptics, in Glyn Morgan's terms, defend a transformative project, that is, they advocate a "different" European Union or plainly reject it (Morgan 2005: 58). These transformative implications also constrain their ability to meet the democratic requirements of justification, that is, to provide people with sufficient reason to lend support to or reject the project of European integration. Claiming that a particular political entity is legitimate or illegitimate activates a 'register of justification' derived from normative reasoning. There is, however, also a second 'register of cognition,' which is disregarded by this type of exercise in normative theorizing and which matters in the contestation of political legitimacy.

Conflicts over the 'right application' of norms have furthermore been appropriated by legal scholars, normative theorists, and civil society representatives and removed from the competence of the public, which is seen as unprepared to enter into a normative debate about Europe. The tendency of such intellectual debates has been to abandon mass democracy and to protect from public and media logics the discursive spaces in which normative choices about the future of European integration are taken (Chambers 2009; Olsen and Trenz 2014). The EU's democratic deficit is from this perspective based on a voluntary restriction of the contentious space of democratic politics. It is an attempt of pro-European elites to uphold their idealized consensus against the logic of dissent and essential conflicts that apply in public and media debates.

A normative theory of European integration, which focuses on justifying the European Union as a political arrangement, must be supplemented at this point by a sociocognitive theory of European integration. Such a theory of European integration must analyze both how symbolic communication influences the legitimacy beliefs of European elites or citizens and how the beliefs and values that inform perceptions of political legitimacy are themselves culturally framed and symbolically communicated. *Cognition* is understood here as the selective application of knowledge and beliefs in contesting political legitimacy. As such, cognition relies on a selective mechanism and a framing device for applying knowledge. In the contestation of political legitimacy, mass media represent the central communicative infrastructure for the selective application and framing of political knowledge.

It follows from this that the study of Euroscepticism as legitimacy contestation should embrace not only a normative assessment but also an analysis of the sociocognitive structures that define Europeans' knowledge repertoire and the type of meaning and interpretations that are attributed to Europe. Euroscepticism as normative evaluation cannot be detached from the analysis of Euroscepticism as a cognitive foundation. While this agenda is also taken up in other chapters of this book, and has in fact informed the program for a sociology of European integration outlined in the first chapter, I will pay particular attention in the remainder of this chapter to EU news coverage through mass media and news media as a principal infrastructure of the cognitive-cultural structuration of Europeans' mind-sets.

EUROSCEPTICISM IN THE MASS MEDIA: THE SOCIO-COGNITIVE FOUNDATIONS OF EU POLITY CONTESTATION

Account must be taken of the knowledge-mediating mechanisms involved in contesting contemporary Europe's political order if we are to embrace the cognitive element of EU legitimacy contestation. Such research into the cognitive-cultural structures underlying the negotiation of political legitimacy could take different directions. It could be developed in the form of a "sociology of critical capacity," which explores the cultural repertoire of justification of normative order that is at the disposal of European actors and institutions (Boltanski and Thévenot 1999; Boltanski and Thévenot 2006). It could also proceed in the form of a cognitive-cultural analysis of knowledge formation within political parties, movements of various kinds or civil society (Marks and Steenbergen 2004; Topaloff 2012). Finally, it could explore the generation and distribution of knowledge through the media (old and new) and how learning potentials are either blocked or freed by media infrastructures and their transformations. It is this latter tradition that I wish to follow when setting forth some thoughts on the relationship between Euroscepticism and the formation of knowledge and opinions about Europe through the mass media.

In order to further contextualize Euroscepticism in relation to the contested notion of EU polity legitimacy, we can draw upon studies of political communication and journalism. Mass media are considered the central arena for propagating Eurosceptic content and interpretations. News coverage on the EU provides most citizens with their basic repertoire of knowledge, through which perceptions of legitimacy are given expression and meaning. Public opinion formation with regard to central questions of European integration is thus heavily dependent on the systematic biases of EU news coverage, upon which media scholars have elaborated in their reconstructions of EU media debates. Existing research has, firstly, emphasized a selection bias in the operational modes of journalism, which produces and distributes news primarily within the confines of the nation-state, and secondly, a cognitive bias in the framings and interpretations of EU news, which lean toward negativity.

News-making practices are biased in the way in which journalists apply particular selection rules to cover EU affairs. Journalists are professional nationalists: The drawing of national geographic and economic borders between societies remains fundamental for the organization of political journalism, which needs to provide specific news formats for national and local audiences who are willing to pay for their products. Qualitative content analyses point to a strong nationalistic and ethnocentric bias in foreign and European news coverage, and journalists tend to defend national interests over normative ideals of a just world order.[12] Journalism's selection bias furthermore accounts for the high saliency of domestic political actors as the main informants about the EU. Journalists are usually not trained to deal with EU sources and prefer to rely on familiar names as the protagonists of their stories, which theoretically also make the stories more accessible to their audiences. This is paired with a focus on official-governmental sources in regular EU coverage and a general disregard for civil society.[13] Eurosceptic actors at the fringes of the domestic political spectrum can, however, easily overcome these agenda-setting hurdles by providing sensationalist cues for the journalists. Örnebring speaks in this regard of three mutually reinforcing categories of failures that explain why journalists respond primarily to the demands of national media systems and cannot meet the requirements for adequate EU news coverage: a) failures of news production that is organized in such a way that EU topics are often ignored, and EU journalists are not backed by the institutional rewards system to cover the EU in a complete and fair manner; b) failures of news representation, meaning that national actors and governments are disproportionally represented in EU news, and the role of supranational actors and institutions is downplayed; and c) failures of participation, with citizens being unprepared to focus attention on European news and, if inadequately informed, unprepared to engage with Europe (Örnebring 2013: 5).

European journalism's nationalist selection bias furthermore explains the focus of EU news stories on the intergovernmental arena of power politics and the systematic disregard for the many secondary stages of institutional politics. The highly selective salience that is given to EU politics focuses on the drama of constitutional politics (for instance, questions of enlargement or Treaty change) and tends to disregard the everyday reality of EU decision-making. There is thus a generally low salience granted to so-called 'policy issues' and an overemphasis on constitutional politics that involve member-state governments. EU politics thus often appear to have a high impact and to disproportionately affect the 'powerless people.'

While this selection bias is often contingent upon political events and could in principle be overcome by a more European socialization of journalism, a more fundamental problem seems to be the general cognitive bias manifested in the framing routines of journalism with regard to the negativity of political news. The observation that media content and public opinion tend to be focused on negative information is reported from various contexts and encompasses both quality and tabloid news formats.[14] Political journalism is frequently found to be far from devoted to fair judgment and substantive critique, preferring instead polemicism, excessiveness, and general negativity. By and large, media coverage delivers a distorted image of politics as a world of scandals, intrigue, dishonesty, and lies. By inflaming public mistrust, anger, and frustration, journalism contributes to an erosion of political legitimacy. The problem with this negativity bias in the public representation of politics is not only that it creates systematic inaccuracies (Soroka 2014: xv). There is also a "tendency for news to be both sensationalist and negative; a consequence not just of the preferences of individual journalists and editors, but of the entire structure of the practice of journalism, as well as of the mediums themselves—newspapers, but especially television" (Soroka 2014: 20). This news-making negativity bias seems universally applicable and is aggravated by recent trends in the media industries toward a more competitive market and a general dumbing down of news quality (Anderson et al. 2013). Critical media scholars accuse news media industries of being "out of order" and systematically undermining trust in democracy (Patterson 2011).

The question is why the European Union and political debates linked to it are likely victims of this negativity bias in news coverage. While there seems to be almost universal agreement that media in different cultural contexts lean toward negative news, a double bias applies to the EU in the distribution of negative over positive news. There is, firstly, the overall negativity bias that applies to political news-making and, secondly, a selection bias in focusing on more critical or Eurosceptical domestic actors as informants for EU news-making. There is thus a tendency to apply more critical standards to EU institutions and to be less critical with regard to the performance of domestic actors as protagonists in EU news stories. The magnitude of the negative bias is thus amplified with regard to EU news coverage by the tendency of journalists to reward national politicians with more positive news framing and to punish EU institutions with negative framing.

In the EU, the dominant media negativism leads to systematic misrepresentations of the EU governance system's performance. EU politicians are portrayed as Machiavellian figures, unconcerned with the public good. When the heads of government come out of a Council meeting late at night, there are national reporters waiting for them who do not want to know whether anything was resolved for the betterment of the EU but who instead want to know who tricked whom, who was beaten, and who gained the most. In similar terms, strategy coverage produces systematically unfavorable news about the European Commission, which is punished by journalists for its rationalistic, consensual style of policymaking. Content analyses of routine European news coverage reveal the dominance of strategic news framings, which stress the power game aspects of politics—winning and losing, self-interest, maneuvers and tactics, performance and artifice (Kevin 2003). Experimental designs in audience research indicate that such repeated exposure to strategic news coverage about the EU produces political cynicism and declined readiness to support the EU (De Vreese 2004). In the end, the public expects to get only negative news from Brussels and automatically associates the EU with dysfunction and corruption.

Just as public cynicism and civic disengagement are seen as likely by-products of news coverage negativity, Euroscepticism can be interpreted as systematically related to the negativity bias of EU news-making. Negative news coverage about the EU, Eurosceptic campaigning by political parties, and public cynicism about EU politics are causally related. Our own findings on media campaigning in the context of European Parliamentary elections show, for instance, that news coverage in the member states awards high salience to Eurosceptic actors and political parties, while the performance of EU actors and institutions is misrepresented. The Eurosceptic voice might be overrepresented with regard to some news formats (especially tabloids) because they respond more easily to news values than could EU actors and institutions, with their focus on the functionality of governance.[15] The coverage of European Parliamentary election campaigning furthermore focuses on the EU's alleged elite biases, democratic deficits, and crises whereas there is a near silencing of the candidates themselves and their programs (de Wilde et al. 2013).

The negativity bias of political news coverage has important repercussions for the design of political and legal institutions and their routine ways of seeking publicity and interacting with journalists. Especially among regard to EU actors and institutions, we observe a protective attitude to shield themselves from the negative effects of mediatization (Michailidou and Trenz 2014; Trenz 2013). Withdrawal from the media stage is, however, risky and might create even more negative news in the long run. It also contradicts attempts to hold EU governance publically accountable. The application of accountability mechanisms in turn tends to create even more negative news coverage. This has to do with an emphasis on error monitoring in the design of political institutions. The whole democratic system of checks and balances is organized in such a way that political representatives and institutions are easily penalized for negative trends but not similarly rewarded for positive ones (Soroka 2014: 31). The negativity bias furthermore contributes to the rise of Euroscepticism in the context of crisis, when negative news is paired with citizens' first-hand negative experiences of economic hardship. The victims of crisis are not, of course, simply victims of media negativity, but they are exposed to news coverage that journalists and political actors systematically use to enhance negative stereotypes of the EU and of those European neighbors which are to blame for the negative effects of the crisis. European institutions are in turn highly vulnerable to negative events in such moments of heightened public attention and have little or no possibility of counteracting them as no amount of positive information seems capable of undoing the damage.

Studies on political behavior also emphasize that negative attitudes matter more in shaping voters' choices.[16] Changes in public opinion and voter behavior with regard to negative news tend to be very quick, whereas positive news induce no immediate change in public opinion. Negative policy change is found to have a strong impact on citizens' evaluation of the political system, whereas positive policy change is difficult to communicate and has problems influencing public opinion. Negative political attitudes are also more persistent and difficult to change through more positive information. Citizens' trust can decline very quickly but is difficult to build up.

These insights into the negativity bias of EU news coverage are also understood by political campaigners. The anti-European campaign will often defeat the pro-European campaign in terms of newsworthiness and the public's willingness to pay attention. Drawing upon these experiences, candidates and political parties often opt for negative campaigning strategies when standing for election for the European Parliament. The Eurosceptic campaign is thus not only made more salient by the news media; it is also rewarded with the selective attention of the voters over the more neutral or positive contents diffused by pro-European mainstream parties. This latter finding is also relevant for explaining the success of the anti-European movement in countries like Norway and Switzerland, where membership is blocked by a systematic negativity bias that applies to the EU both in terms of selective news-making and public opinion.

It is thus important to note that the media and their publics are mutually reinforcing in the application of negativity bias and its effects. In the "spiral of cynicism," the preference of journalism for negative news is seen as corresponding to the preference of the public and its demand for the sensational (Cappella and Jamieson 1997). In a situation of media market competition, this can trigger a journalistic race for political intrigue and scandal. For journalists who work under increasing pressure and time constraints, negative news is 'cheap' news, whereas facts, fairness, and evaluation require more expensive journalistic investigations. As a result, political news coverage in fields of imbalanced attention and uncertain public preferences becomes less reliable and tends to create easily applicable strategic frames, incoherent stories, and political mayflies. Cynical publics in turn require ever-more negative news. They develop expectations for mainly getting bad news from Brussels, and these expectations guide their selective news consumption.

The "spiral of cynicism" is turned under these conditions into a "spiral of Euroscepticism" (De Vreese 2007), which is driven by the high salience of EU issues in the media. Under a 'constraining dissensus' of public opinion (Hooghe and Marks 2009), even neutral or fact-based news coverage that brings the EU to the attention makes people alert of the potential negative impacts and undesired effects of European integration, which they tend to oppose rather than support (Lubbers and Scheepers 2010). Paradoxically, expression of Euroscepticism would thus be linked to the very process of EU democratization and the various ways in which EU actors and institutions claim public legitimacy. The "constraining dissensus" takes effect whenever the EU becomes salient in public and media discourse. An EU democracy that seeks publicity for its operations would thus be self-defeating.

The proposed analytical focus on media dynamics of polity contestation explains inherent biases in the legitimation of the national and international (European) order. Media frames are important for attributing responsibility and ascribing political legitimacy. Media can, in this sense, be made responsible for negative cues about the EU and an inherent 'nationalist bias' in the representation of politics. This type of coverage in turn excites particular cognitive and emotional reactions from audiences, which lean toward hostility regarding the European project. Euroscepticism can thus be partly explained as an effect of negative learning through media inputs. The negativity bias of media news coverage of EU politics is not, however, entirely independent from audience cognitions and judgments, for audiences often receive information from different sources and process media content selectively on the basis of collective interpretations and emotional reactions (Kepplinger et al. 2012). These public judgments and emotions can equally be made responsible for the news coverage's negative bias, in turn informing the media frames and content. Negative learning through media discourses is thus a complex process in which providers of media content (journalists and political informants) and audiences interact and equally contribute to the structuring of public debates and expectations.

One last question to be addressed in this context is whether new and online media provide alternative cognitive frames for evaluating EU news and content, thereby reconstituting European audiences and allowing different learning paths. This question is relevant, not least from the perspective of EU institutions, which develop online media strategies to counteract the negativity of traditional mass media and to launch image and PR campaigns, which are designed to stimulate collective learning or to actively involve segments of the European public (e.g., positive image campaigns targeting young people). Without wishing to exclude the possibilities for positive cueing through the use of online media,[17] our own findings indicate that the negativity bias is replicated in online news making (Michailidou et al. 2014). The diffusion of EU news on the most popular and salient online news sites is even more constrained by the rules of the attention market, which explains the selective bias of media companies' journalists to focus primarily on negative news coverage in their online editions. Negative and EU critical news is not only the news that is most liked and shared by social media users. In addition, the Internet offers a platform for voicing people's discontent through social media and through the highly popular commenting forums that mainstream newspapers offer their readers. Online discussions regularly play out a dynamic of EU bashing through highly negative and often insulting language. They frequently tend toward populism, portraying a fundamental conflict between citizens and elites and positioning the former against the established system of representative democracy. In addition, online readers and commentators primarily present national arguments and interpretations of national interests. In contrast, we find that the negativity bias potentially unites Eurosceptical publics in their aversion to political elites, at both the national and at European levels. Under certain circumstances, negative publics may feel united and can even express solidarity across borders. They not only share cognitions and a particular repertoire of cultural frames, which is used to bash political elites and the EU, but they also fight the familiar struggle of ordinary citizens against the elite. As such, they might develop a shared awareness of being part of a 'deceived European citizenry' where the Germans, British, Dutch, and Greeks alike 'suffer' from demands of the EU, the International Monetary Fund (IMF), the European Central Bank (ECB), or their own national governments. The possibility of translating cynicism into criticism is at least not excluded and could be triggered off external events such as the financial and monetary crisis. The unprecedented crisis in which the European Union and its member states have been mired since 2008 has without a doubt further enhanced the type of fundamental legitimacy contestation that distinguishes Euroscepticism from 'politics as usual' in the EU and in its member states. This raises the question as to whether Euroscepticism can be translated into a tale of solidarity of the 'common people,' who suffer from the negative consequences of European integration and see themselves as sitting in the same boat: as the victims of banks, elites, and the EU. Reformulation of the tales of Europeanization as radical rupture and failure in relation to crisis as well as the possibilities for popular mobilization and resistance linked to these new visions, shall be explored in the final chapter of this book.

CONCLUSION: TOWARD A SHARED
EUROPEAN NARRATIVE OF SKEPTICISM?

This chapter has argued that Euroscepticism is best understood as a delegitimating practice that unfolds through normative assessment and cognitive framing of the legitimacy of the EU polity. In contrast to the Durkheimian account and its focus on irrational group behavior, emphasis has been placed on the responsive and often consequential character of Euroscepticism, on its reaction—rather than passive submission—to perceived normative breaches of democracy. In contrast to the Rokkanian account and its focus on the role of strategic actors, who align along ideological or identitarian dividing lines, emphasis has been placed on the cognitive and cultural framing of Euroscepticism, which influences strategic action frames. In contrast to the Marxian-inspired political economy approach and its focus on externalities that condition popular responses, emphasis has been placed on the internal dynamics of liberal-representative democracies, which enter into a new phase of normative self-understanding when facing the current challenges of globalization. The recent rise of Euroscepticism and the extreme right in many EU countries thus cannot simply be explained by the negative and external impact of the financial and monetary crisis on people's life chances and material living conditions. Euroscepticism is also informed by the cognitive filters, by the frames and discursive dynamics that apply to public contestation of democratic legitimacy and that are inherent to Western democracies and part of their repertoire of norms and values. Euroscepticism research should thus explore the generation and distribution of knowledge through the media (old and new), which underlies evaluations of the EU's political legitimacy.

If Euroscepticism in David Easton's terms indicates a lack of diffuse support for the EU political system, then the 'unfinished democratization' of the EU must be deemed the major obstacle for resolving this kind of fundamental conflict, which undermines EU legitimacy. Any conflict resolution would rely upon the successful constitutional appeasement of a complex entanglement between national, European, and international orders in such a way that people again feel empowered. The problem is that such a constitutional settlement of the deficits of democratic politics and the implicit problems of transnational political representation cannot be achieved through short-term political reform. As a rule of thumb, a lack of diffuse support cannot easily be compensated by creating specific support through policies or political representatives. Easton himself emphasizes that diffuse support cannot be generated but usually arises from an existing condition. In particular, he mentions two sources from which diffuse support can arise: first, through socialization in a political community, and secondly, from experience, more specifically "from the evaluations of a series of outputs and of performance over a long period of time" (Easton 1975: 446). Long-term gains in diffuse support for the EU and the arduous building of a European identity through socialization (Risse 2010; see also my elaboration in chapter 2) can be quickly reversed under less favorable conditions. Taking into account the EU's severe output crisis, which affects hundreds of thousands of Europeans, a new salience is granted to contestation of the EU's legitimacy, which may not constrain the functionality of EU governance in the short term (Schimmelfennig 2014). However, in the long term, this could undermine the sustainability of the political project of integration. As a complement to attitudinal research on Euroscepticism, the interpretative approach elaborated in this chapter emphasizes how European citizens' negative experiences are expressed through particular norms, ideologies, cultural patterns, and cognitive frames. In other words, negative experiences of Europe are narrated in such a way as to link them to the collective life histories of Europeans. It is here that our tales of Europeanization materialize as part of ongoing practices of EU legitimacy contestation.

The argument that has been presented in this chapter is furthermore that popular contestation should not be seen as a new sequence—a new historical phase—of European integration, distinct from earlier 'functional integration.' We must instead understand how support (diffuse or specific) and opposition are interrelated. Euroscepticism does not introduce a new phase of renationalization that is disconnected from previous phases of Europeanization. The enhanced proneness to conflict of EU polity contestation instead evidences an ongoing Europeanization that has become more multifaceted and more conflictual and that affects more strata of the population. From a perspective of Eurosceptic opposition, we must thus dramatize the saga of Europeanization, must account for how European integration and the European Union can be contested.

In this light, the new resistance movements to European integration are not necessarily anti-modern or occupied by the enemies of Enlightenment. They also encompass resistance that is mobilized because the European project no longer convinces or because it lacks progressive force and normative drive. As an expression of people's generalized mistrust of and resistance to processes of Europeanization, Eurosceptic counter-narratives explicitly reject the heroic account and challenge the prevalent "culture of total optimism" (Majone 2014). They are part of a critical-normative discourse, which dismantles self-interest behind the 'incorrect promise' of European leaders, their immorality, or their normative misconduct. However, they also build upon alternative cognitive frames, blaming the 'other' for relying upon values that are not 'ours' and posing a threat to 'our' identity. The cognitive frames and concepts underlying EU polity contestation are relatively uniform (e.g., conceptual metaphors for popular sovereignty as 'we, the people') and easily translatable across the European discursive arena. They are themselves part of the conceptual universe of Europeanization and, as such, account for Euroscepticism's public resonance, shaping the thoughts of a public that is European and not merely nationally fragmented.

Finally, it would be a misunderstanding to regard Euroscepticism merely as an explicit rejection of the 'heroic account' of Europeanization and the imposition of a powerful counter-narrative. As has been emphasized throughout this chapter, the dynamics of EU polity contestation rarely follow the rules of rational discourse. Euroscepticism is not a unitary counter-discourse but instead a piecemeal narrative. It is also often less dramatic than an open confrontation of oppositional identity projects. Sometimes, Euroscepticism is simply based on an intuitive rejection of European lifestyles by segments of the European public. Other times, it is an 'escape' from banal Europeanization, which imposes itself on Europeans' everyday lives, and the attempt to evoke 'heroic' national accounts of popular sovereignty.

In recent times, we have experienced several situations in which not only the heroic account but also the regular and linear processes of Europeanization have been deeply disrupted. The EU went through a series of crises that brought into question the underlying credo of Europeanization in terms of a correlation between 'deepening' and 'widening' and the creation of equal living conditions across European social space. The automatism through which the European society was imagined to come into being came under challenge. As I will argue in the next chapter, the new salience of Euroscepticism in crisis-ridden Europe is explained by these experiences of disruption of everyday Europeanization. This implies a translation from Euroscepticism as 'resistance' to an account of Europeanization as crisis and 'failure.'

NOTES

1. Such strategic accounts of 'winners' and 'losers' of Europeanization can be found in Jones and Verdun (2005), Koopmans (2007), and Thatcher (2004).

2. The breakup of the permissive consensus and its impact on EU politicization is dicussed by Hooghe and Marks (2009), de Wilde (2011), and Risse (2014a, 2014b).

3. This is also the original meaning associated with Habermas's legitimation crisis (Habermas 1975). I will explore this shift of narration from EU opposition to crisis in chapter 5. There obviously is a continuity from "system opposition" as promoted by Eurosceptic actors and "system breakdown" or "failure" related to the account of crisis. The notion of a legitimation crisis of the EU thus combines a voluntaristic account of EU opposition with a structural account that measures EU output and performance. The Euroscepticism narrative and the crisis narrative are in this sense not neatly distinguished but often interchangeable. It is, however, important to stress that Eurosceptic narration can unfold in a way that is decoupled from the material conditions of integration and the performance of EU governance, as much as the crisis narration does not rely on the support of the Eurosceptic opposition.

4. See the Youth in Action Programme, which "aimed to inspire a sense of active citizens, solidarity, and tolerance among young Europeans, as well as involve them in shaping the future of the European Union" (http://ec.europa.eu/youth/tools/youth-in-action_en.htm).

5. For this rational choice perspective on partisan contestation see Hix (2007) and Hooghe (2007).

6. For this Bourdieuan school of party contestation see Crespy and Verschueren (2009), de Wilde and Trenz (2012), Leconte (2010), and Vasilopoulou (2013).

7. See Crespy and Verschueren (2009), de Wilde and Trenz (2012), Hooghe (2007), Hooghe and Marks (2007), Kopecky and Mudde (2002), Szczerbiak and Taggart (2008), and Usherwood and Startin (2013) for the state-of-the-art literature of conceptually grasping the phenomenon of Euroscepticism.

8. Varieties of Euroscepticism in relation to nationalism, populism, or right-wing extremism are discussed by Krouwel and Abts (2007) and Szczerbiak and Taggart 2008).

9. We have developed this classificatory scheme further in de Wilde et al. 2015.

10. For the further elaboration of this idea of Euroscepticism as EU polity contestation see de Wilde et al. (2013); de Wilde and Trenz (2012).

11. See the so-called RECON models of a democratic design of EU governance proposed in different versions by Eriksen and Fossum (2008) and Eriksen and Fossum (2012).

12. This nationalist bias of journalism has been repeatedly shown in comparative analysis of foreign and EU news coverage. See Page and Shapiro (1992), Kevin (2003), Trenz (2005a), and Koopmans and Statham (2010).

13. See the Europub findings on EU contestation in news media documented in Koopmans (2007; 2010), Statham (2010), and Koopmans and Statham (2010).

14. For an overview of the literature on the effects of the negative bias of news coverage see Cappella and Jamieson (1997: 32).

15. See in particular our case studies on the UK, Germany, and Austria in de Wilde et al. (2013).

16. For a literature overview on media negativism, see Soroka (2014, chapter 2).

17. For some positive experiences with EU online campaigning through social media, reaching out to substantial segments of the European population, see the relatively successful Facebook profile of the European Parliament (Tarta 2014).

Chapter Five

The Crisis of Europeanization

The dramatization of the triumph of Europeanization, which I have reconstructed under the heading of "Euroscepticism," is negatively constructed through dissent, which expresses deep aversion to the idea of European integration. Eurosceptic accounts use various opportunities to express principled opposition. When Eurosceptic opposition first found expression in the post-Maastricht years, its proponents offered little more than a disruption of the official story line of Europe's triumph. For most people whom this counter-story addressed and who perhaps felt drawn to it, the European Union and its policies remained abstract and unexperienced. Euroscepticism has been successful because it is vague and there is no need to put it to the test. It is intuitive and emotional and only loosely related to people's life histories and experiences. What has been discussed as the 'mainstreaming of Euroscepticism' since 2008 points instead to a qualitative turn in EU opposition, which draws upon a deep legitimation crisis of the project of European integration, a crisis that has shattered its input and output dimensions.[1] The drama continues in a form that goes beyond an intuitive rejection of the success story of European integration by embracing the possibility of its deep crisis, disruption, and failure.

Many politicians as well as political analysts have concluded that this deep crisis challenges the very foundations of European integration. Accounts of crisis vary with regard to where the crisis ought to be located (internationally, on a European plane, or domestically) and how to understand its causes and consequences. There has been a recurrent difficulty in sketching the contours of the crisis since the nearly banal insight is that EU-related crises are multiple and multifaceted. With reference to the specific historic time frame since 2008, we can identify overlapping and mutually reinforcing processes of systemic disturbance and uncertainty, which have

113

been unfolding at three levels: the global economic and financial crisis, the EU political and constitutional crisis, and the public debt crisis of the Euro-zone countries.

Another controversy revolves around the causes of crisis. There is the natural history of crisis as destiny: the international order underwent the major shock of the 2008 financial crisis, which consequently turned into a crisis of the Eurozone in 2009–2010. Yet there is also the homemade story of crisis and attributed responsibility. The crisis is related to deficiencies in the construction plan for European integration and, in particular, for the Euro-pean Monetary Union's institutional inadequacy, economic unsustainability, and democratic deficit. There is a double-edged sword of criticism in the sense that Europeanization either went too far or not far enough.

With regard to the consequences of crisis, the legitimacy of the European political and economic order is challenged not only in the input dimension but also in the output dimension. Europeanization is no longer automatically linked to better and more efficient governance. We have experienced that Europeanization is not only the path to progress, the motor of peaceful Euro-pean coexistence, the rational solution to our collective problems, the guaran-tee of our welfare and security. Europeanization can also disrupt ordinary life, affect us privately, and increase our fears and general sense of uncertain-ty.

MAKING SENSE OF CRISIS: BETWEEN EXCESSIVE DOOMSAYING AND ACADEMIC APPEASEMENT

At first glance, the EU crisis governance regime, established in 2008, re-verses previous trends of Europeanization. Just as the crisis has brought the era of growth to a halt, it has also blocked the incremental transfer of political authority, legitimacy, and identities from the national to the European level. When markets collapse, countries contract as well. Many analysts have hailed a new era of renationalization, which is seen as the inevitable result of the 'failed Europeanization' of previous decades and the diagnosis that the EU has simply gone too far in establishing a multilevel governance regime that is neither efficient nor democratic (Majone 2014). Renationalization might be destiny, but it can be also seen as normatively required to resolve the legitimacy conundrum, into which we have been delivered by two decades of enhanced Europeanization (Chalmers 2013). That said, technocra-cy, as the EU governance regime that has been set up to deal with crisis and its consequences, is transnational in its design, including international organ-izations, for instance, in the case of the *Troika* of the International Monetary Fund, European Central Bank, and European Commission. Europeanization in the form of expert governance harks back to earlier forms of functional integration and is thus continued at the price of depoliticization (Schimmel-fennig 2014). Europeanization through expert governance is manifested in the displacement of politics with regard to a great number of regulatory fields (such as monetary policy, the entire field of EU market integration, and security). One effect of technocratic Europeanization is that politics are re-duced to rigid regulatory action, legal obligations, and compliance mecha-nisms, excluding popular votes or reducing them to forced consent. We can call this the "outsourcing" of Europeanization, which as a "no-choice situa-tion," becomes increasingly detached from democratic process within our established systems of political representation and contestation of political choices. The displacement of politics in these areas increases the sense of impotence among citizens, who remain formally empowered to exercise con-trol but are *de facto* forced to either consent through symbolic side politics or turn to populist protest votes (which again increase the uncertainty of the situation).

In the EU scholarly literature, references to Europeanization are mainly used to sketch out several rescue scenarios, which explain why European integration continues despite crisis. The vocabulary of institutional theory, for instance, provides a reading of crisis as catharsis. Instead of putting an end to European integration, the economic and monetary crisis is frequently discussed as a filter of institutional reform and learning. Such shocks may have a revelatory function for the institutions and collective actors involved: waves of crisis clearly travel between economically interwoven countries and raise a collective awareness of innovative solutions (Grant and Wilson 2012). In similar terms, neoliberal thinking praises the curative effects of shock therapy, which is needed to regain control over the financial markets, to return to a strategy of 'fiscal realism,' and to build a more sustainable and stable monetary union (Pickford et al. 2015). Such a catalytic function is also emphasized by cultural analysts, who see the crisis as a facilitator of the Europeanization of the public sphere. Crisis-related events and experiences not only account for the heightened salience of European affairs in the media (Meijers 2013), but the financial and monetary crisis furthermore triggers normative debates, which contest the legitimacy of the economic and politi-cal order, nationally and transnationally. Such Europeanized public spheres thus offer a promising means by which politicization can be recoupled to the EU's democratization.[2] Lastly, the integration paradigm is upheld through the historicization of crisis experiences. It is recalled that the European inte-gration process already underwent several crises in the past but that integra-tion still continues. Through such retrospective post-crisis accounts, it can be maintained that the European integration process is fed by crises or even purified by them. There is thus no return in history once one has set out upon the path of integration. As John Erik Fossum (2014a: 1) critically para-phrased this position: "The upshot is that integration is not only a fairweather phenomenon; it is equally a bad-weather phenomenon. Through sunshine and storm, the EU continues to integrate."

It is striking that, in most of these scholarly accounts, the saga of Europeanization falls short of imagining the unthinkable: the Eurocrash and the collapse of the European Union are not foreseen and can hardly be envisaged without a major rupture of the narrative. Despite these disruptions to the architecture of EU governance and the evident shortcomings of problem-solving techniques, mentioning the possibility of system failure remains heretical. The terminology of Europeanization is used to confirm the *telos* of integration and belief in the steering capacities of a supranational governance arrangement. Europeanization research is still used directly or indirectly, consciously or unconsciously to legitimize the European Union as a "governance system," which through management, intervention, and regulation develops superior problem-solving capacities and higher legitimacy in terms of output and efficiency. The task for the EU studies community is then to define the conditions under which the temporary weakening of the EU can be turned into a new moment of strength: the crisis as a case of collective learning and catharsis from which the EU will emerge even stronger (Champeau et al. 2014; Eriksen 2014).

At the same time, Europeanization indeed remains literally with no alternative, as the vision of a new paradigm or of a paradigm shift is blocked. Even if the monetary system is out of control and the framework for policies and regulation provided by the EU appears to create more problems than it is able to resolve, the EU studies community seems to agree on the principle that the way out of crisis can only lie in deeper integration and intensified cooperation. Europeanization has led us into crisis, and only more Europeanization can lead us out of crisis, so the story goes, even though in practice, and beyond the shared rhetoric, interests differ widely.

These academic appeasement strategies can themselves be seen as symptomatic of a reluctance within the EU studies community to apprehend crisis as a turning point, a failure and a loss of paradigm that simultaneously affects the cohesiveness and routines of the discipline. The reservedness of EU scholars is also explained as a demarcation from the Eurosceptic opposition, which refers to Europeanization as a negative template for illustrating the risks of national integration. The symptoms of crisis are, of course, fuel for the "mainstreaming of Euroscepticism" in many European countries, but their interpretation as a turning point in the drama of Europeanization at the same time reaches beyond the Eurosceptic account of negativity. While opponents of the European Union seize the opportunity to call for a reversal of Europeanization, the possible end of European integration becomes an increasingly attractive scenario for many. Under this new constellation, the EU studies community is ill prepared to enter the discussion concerning the current crisis, not just in relation to questions of "crisis governance" and "management" but also in terms of putting the macroframework of democratic politics to the test.

The linearity of the account of Europeanization, according to which EU member states are trapped in an "iron cage" of EU governance, can only be questioned at the price of deep rupture and heresy. The European studies community has only just begun to recognize that this last scenario of a failure of Europeanization and its possible reversal is a thinkable option (Krastev 2012). The debate concerning the failings of the system has started undermining the strength of the saga of Europeanization. By reinterpreting the financial and monetary crisis as a symptom of system failure, the agenda of disintegration research has been set, and the likelihood is discussed that a period of more-or-less intensive Europeanization might be followed by a new phase of renationalization (Majone 2014). Crisis stands in this regard for two types of failure: the EU's system failure and its democratic failure, both fundamentally undermining the credo of the triumphal saga of Europeanization, which was reconstructed in chapter 1. From the first perspective, the crisis fundamentally challenges the output dimensions of European integration, that is, the promise of growth and efficiency related to European market building. From the second perspective, the crisis fundamentally challenges the input dimensions of European integration, that is, the promise of an automatism between market integration; political integration; and social integration, inclusion, and equality. The tense drama of crisis thus relates Europeanization to the tragic failures of its protagonists, be they the elites, who misrepresented the people of Europe by precipitating integration and pushing Europeanization forward, or the people who withdrew their support and are no longer willing to follow their political leaders. Crisis accounts are thus used to place the triumph of Europeanization in a historical context and to highlight its structural limitations. The Europeanization of the masses has purportedly failed (Majone 2013), and the people not only regularly reject the choices of their political leaders (e.g., when they are asked in a referendum) but also are increasingly structurally excluded and marginalized. Europeanization is thus no longer expansive and inclusive but experiences serious backlashes. The idea of a reversal of integration is, then, not simply discussed as a political choice (the Eurosceptic option); it becomes destiny. The heroic play of an expansive Europe is removed from the program, and the tragedy of Europe's decay enters the stage.

According to Majone, the heresy of 'thinking the unthinkable' would be an unforgivable breach of the dogma of EU studies, which only few scholars have so far dared to propose. Ignoring the impact of what he calls 'failed Europeanization,' EU scholars have become dogmatic in postulating a correlation between the ever-closer union of member states and an ever-closer union of the people of Europe. His explanation for this disregard of all empirical evidence to the contrary is the elitist bias of the EU studies community, which replicates the elite bias of the European integration project. Most scholars are accustomed to seeing elites as agents of Europeanization but pay insufficient attention to the negative attitudes and resistance of 'ordinary people' (Majone 2013). As EU scholars, we closely interact with these elites, often meeting them at conferences, receiving research funding from them, and educating them or implicitly or explicitly defending their choices or explaining their rationale in our academic writing.

Another reason for the EU studies community's reluctance to question the integration paradigm and diagnose failures in democracy or identity might be sought in the absence of viable counter-projects, which could replace the expansive account of Europeanization with a new progressive collective endeavor. This results in desperate rescue attempts for nearly lost causes, such as Jürgen Habermas's (2012) and Ulrich Beck's (2013) pleas for a return to the old ideals of fraternity among the people of Europe ('more justice through more Europe'). Or it results in statements of disillusion or almost fury regarding the political elite's failure to comply with the project of European Enlightenment, such as Hauke Brunkhorst's denunciation of a 'new bonapartism,' blaming European elites and capitalism for having turned the original project of emancipation into a new master plan for domination (Brunkhorst 2014).

THE TRAUMA OF CRISIS

The symptoms of crisis are in this sense slowly turning the drama of expansive Europeanization into a trauma of collective failure and breakdown. The new trauma of crisis is directly related to the life histories and experiences of the Europeans. As such, it does not remain in the abstract (Europe as something remote and diffuse, which affects our collective identifications as in the Eurosceptic account) but instead becomes concrete in the way it visibly affects the Europeans' material life chances. The trauma of crisis not simply distracts from everyday life and brings the negativity of European integration to the attention of European publics (as emphasized by the Eurosceptics). It actually disrupts life experiences and leads to deep frustration and disenchantment with politics. The drama played out by distant political elites in Brussels becomes, so to speak, a drama that affects us all. The drama becomes the trauma of those who feel affected by "heteronomy" or suffer from unexpected ruptures and consequences. Europe's triumph and Europe's fall are closely related. The crisis adds in this sense a situational component to the Eurosceptic account, through which "the trauma" is made real and is directly experienced by the Europeans. In contrast to the other three narratives of Europeanization, "crisis" is primarily defined in situational terms, namely with reference to a specific historical event (the Eurozone crisis), but it draws upon historical narrations of "what makes a crisis" and how it can be collectively handled. At the same time, the crisis has a unique capacity to overcome distance in the way the Europeans' suffering comes to our immediate attention and calls for our reactions. Crisis accounts are in this sense constantly shifting between despair and hope, between denial and the call for collective renewal. On the one hand, they can be read as an application of trauma narratives and remain closely tied to the negative (Eurosceptic) interpretations of history. On the other hand, crisis accounts can draw upon a cultural repertoire of interpretation that goes beyond the collective trauma and nourishes references to utopia by envisaging sometimes radical alternatives of the resurrection of Europe after the crash and the great recession. The revived promise of Europe's triumph is then often sought in anti-politics to global capitalism or in popular resistances. As discussed in chapter 4, these movements differ from Euroscepticism since they often seek to go beyond the categorical rejection of Europe. As I will elaborate in this chapter, they nevertheless often promote a strong anti-Brussels rhetoric and express the outrage of the people of Europe who suffer from austerity. But we also often find them united in cross-national alliances under the common European umbrella and mobilized by the belief that "another Europe is possible" (Della Porta 2009).

In emphasizing crisis's cultural interpretations as part of the drama of Europeanization, I do not wish to doubt that harsh austerity and humiliating bailouts are at the same time traumatic experiences that can lead to dramatic falls in support for the EU. People who undergo unexpected hardship in their personal lives have good reason for withdrawing support for the level of government to which political responsibility is attributed. The collective practices that are commonly categorized as "crisis responses" are, however, defined in relation to these ascriptions of responsibility and collective interpretations of crisis. There is a strong correlation between capitalist market dysfunction and the ways in which responsibility is attributed to political institutions that are in charge of market regulation. In the context of financial and monetary crisis, citizens' vulnerability is defined in relation to who suffers how much from the negative consequences of market failure. Market failure as system failure lies at the core of crisis perception and interpretation. The meaning of the notion of a 'crisis of Europe' remains, however, vague (Eder 2015). To speak of "crisis" is apparently more than to just negatively identify with the project of European integration. Crisis is not simply another enthralling plot of the drama of European integration (the "Eurosceptic" contribution) but instead turns the drama into a trauma that affects material life chances beyond merely altering Europeans' attitudinal predispositions. The notion of "crisis of Europe" points in this sense to a lack of capacity for collective action as Europeans, and as such, it returns society to the market dynamics of European integration (Eder 2015). This reminds us that there is a Europe beyond the market, which is the Europe of social relations and which has evolved in a routine and "banal" manner (see chapter 3) but is now being disrupted by the externalities of crisis governance. The way in which "crisis" takes society back thus relates to the disruptions to Europeans' everyday lives and the types of social practices that result from them. Europe is not only talked about; it is also acted upon, and these actions are not nationally confined but have a European dimension. The collective experiences of the negative consequences of crisis break the routine of Europeanization and create the potential for the extraordinary, which is in need of interpretation, comprehension, and possibly action.

In the next section, I review the academic and public intellectual debate over the current crisis in relation to a postulated paradigm shift in integration studies. Crisis accounts are produced by scholars for illustrative purposes. For those who teach European integration in schools and at universities, Europe's crises are a boon as they are inherently instructive.[3] Retrospective interpretations of crisis are often designed as invitations to collective learning. Current interpretations of crisis instead evoke moments of catharsis through which repressed emotions can come to the surface to overcome the trauma and permit collective renewal.

Paradigm Lost? European Crisis as a Case of Destruction

Reflection upon the causes and consequences of crisis is at once a reflection upon the dynamics of European integration and an invitation to formulate alternative accounts of the European project. The intellectual debate surrounding the project of European integration echoes a deep disenchantment with the liberal market Europe combined with a passionate and almost desperate defense of the European Enlightenment vision (Brunkhorst 2014; Habermas 2012). However, European studies scholars also acknowledge the huge gulf that has opened up between the market Europe and the Europe of *égaliberté* and admit that there are indeed good reasons to doubt the EU's wider cosmopolitan ambition. This uncertainty reflects a general normative disorientation with the project of European integration. Do crisis accounts then point at a paradigm shift in terms of how we make sense of European integration?

Crisis is a category of diagnosis and critique from which decisive normative, conceptual, and institutional implications follow. The crisis calls for a paradigmatic change of Europeanization as envisaged through the categories of progress and expansion. Yet how can we formulate such a paradigm shift if our critical and diagnostic capacities are at the same time limited by loss of the old paradigm? We speak of crisis precisely because the old paradigm can be neither regained nor straightforwardly replaced by a new paradigm. Crisis thus relates to the diagnosis of a paradigm shift in a situation of paradigm loss (Kompridis 2006). As such, crisis accounts of Europe are not simply a negative template of pro-European accounts (which is, as I have argued in chapter 4, at the heart of Euroscepticism). They instead question Europeanization in a paradigmatic manner, within several of its core dimensions. The paradigm loss for which European crisis stands encompasses the following:

1. *The return of power politics*: Crisis has dismantled the credo that Europe would overcome the long-established enmities among its nations. The austerity measures imposed as part of the crisis rescue measures by international institutions founded partly outside the Treaty framework, such as the European Financial Stability Facility (EFSF) and the European Stability Mechanism (ESM), are experienced by many as a new form of authoritarianism. Authoritarian capitalism is also discussed in relation to the mandate of the European Central Bank (ECB) and the role played by the German government, representing the major creditor country in the Eurozone. Germany's rise as a new hegemonic power might be seen on the one hand as an involuntary and unplanned product of the financial crisis (Beck 2013: 54). On the other hand, Europe's 'reluctant hegemon' is far from being perceived as a 'benign ruler,' and the Merkel government in particular is accused of a harsh and populist austerity policy, which follows no economic rationale but is mainly used to achieve greater power in Europe and 'aimed at the German electorate with its ingrained fear of inflation' (Beck 2013: 55). From Germany's perspective, however, the country's political leadership sees itself as an 'involuntary hegemon,' seeking to avoid any impression of authoritarianism and emphasizing the country's responsibility in Europe as an "enlightened ruler" (a position shared by those who call for leadership in the crisis situation, not least the many voices in the debtor countries, from those who do not trust their own elites and governments).[4]

2. *The failure of social cohesion*: Crisis has dismantled the credo of Europeanization as cooperation among equals, based on a win-win situation for all and the creation of equal living conditions across the continent. Austerity policies are not only seen as demands by creditor countries; they are furthermore interpreted as a form of legislating inequality, an emergency legislation that is meant to rescue the banks yet widens the gap between populations, drawing a new dividing line between the debtors at the periphery and the creditors at the core of Europe. In this sense, the Eurocrisis represents a failure of EU cohesion policy, not just a failure of the EU's financial and monetary system (Zielonka 2012: 21–41).[5] Instead of the Europe of equal living conditions, there is an unintended Mathew effect of a downward spiral of increasing inequalities: he that has plenty of goods shall have more

(Bach 2014: 6). The only visible effects of the Euro rescue measures are short-term economic gains in the creditor countries, with cheap loans, low unemployment, and general increases in welfare while the long-term rescue that has been promised to the debtor countries remains vague and concealed beneath ongoing recession. Questions of justice and fairness re-enter public debates and divide public opinion. What is worse, the EU is turning into a humiliation regime, with the bailouts degrading not only states but also ordinary citizens. The austerity policies are thus deeply at odds with the self-image of the EU as a regime that respects its citizens, takes care of its poorer and less developed areas, and facilitates a peaceful and happy coexistence (D. Smith 2015). Last but not least, social cohesion is damaged by the depreciation of EU citizenship, the questioning of the European free movement area and rights, and the free riders within the common market, for whom internal economic competitiveness has greater value than European solidarity (most notably, the case of the UK).

3. *The failure of modernization*: Crisis has furthermore dismantled the credo of Europeanization as modernization, enhancing the global competitiveness of the European market through innovation and the promotion of knowledge. The renewal of the European common market was scheduled with the Lisbon strategy of 2000, which devised an action and development plan for turning the European Union into 'the most competitive and dynamic knowledge-based economy in the world capable of sustainable economic growth with more and better jobs and greater social cohesion by 2010.'[6] The Lisbon strategy has been proclaimed as the common point of departure for the European Union into the new millennium, but its modernization agenda in fact merely adds rhetorical adrenaline to the economic rationale that has driven integration since its very beginnings. In instrumental terms, the long-term strategy goals of innovation could not be implemented as EU institutions were constrained by budgetary cuts and structural blockades of necessary constitutional reform. Concrete initiatives like the Framework Programs for Research and Technological Developments primarily created new playgrounds for societal elites but rarely addressed citizens. Since 2008, political analysts and the media increasingly speak of the failure of the Lisbon strategy. As exemplified by crisis, Europe has not managed to secure employment, income, and knowledge, while single-country opt-outs are becoming a viable alternative. Free riders such as the UK have begun dismantling the credo of Europeanization as modernization and of the higher competitiveness of the Common Market. Progress is sought in differentiated integration, renationalization, or disintegration. Modernization has also allegedly failed with regard to protecting the welfare state, a key marker of

European modernity (in contrast, for instance, to the United States) (Crouch 1999) but now being dismantled by free market dynamics, privatization, and the undermining of state social security infrastructures.

4. *The new insecurity:* The fact that the Eurocrisis has consequences far beyond the EU's economic architecture is best illustrated by the general weakening of the EU's foreign and security policies. This is partly related to direct effects of budgetary cuts, which weaken the ability of the EU to act as a crisis manager in other parts of the world. The retreat of the EU as a foreign policy actor is a gentle reminder that the "normative power" of Europe is closely related to the economic strength of the union. Some of the EU's humanitarian missions, especially in the Mediterranean area, were heavily affected by budgetary cuts.[7] In particular, the EU has lost face for ignoring the refugee drama at its southern borders and leaving the burden of accommodating refugees to its weakest members. The flagging of the EU's foreign and security policy agenda can only be properly understood as a symptom of the general crisis of credibility of the European integration project. In this last regard, the longest-lasting and most engrained credo of European integration as a promoter of peace and security has been challenged in the aftermath of the 2008 crisis. This not only concerns the erosion of the image of EU foreign and security policy as a "normative power" engaging in peace-making missions and 'doing good in the world' (Sjursen 2007). In confronting Russia, the EU is set to enter a new Cold War as its strategy of seeking dialogue over Ukraine has proven insufficient for preventing military conflict in the region. A new geopolitical confrontation between the EU and Russia is also fought along cultural and identitarian lines between (Western) Europe and Eurasia as opposing poles of a fundamental civilizational clash. This clash has been cemented by the drafting of sanctions against Russia, as the pragmatic appeasement strategy and dialogue of the past no longer prove convincing as guarantors of peace and security in Europe. The change in Europe's security structure in connection with the new confrontational style with Russia also makes the EU more vulnerable to critique, for not only has the historical achievement of European integration at securing peace in the postwar world order been shattered, but the EU can also be made directly responsible for instilling insecurity and risking new military confrontations in Europe.

5. *The failure of democracy:* Last but not least, and related to all of the previous discussions, crisis fundamentally dismantles the credo of Europeanization as democratization. The democratic deficit of the European Union has always been discussed in light of the possibility of the

European Union as this deficit's potential solution and rather than as its irremediable cause. Such solutions were sought in a balance of national and supranational forces and the strengthening of constitutional rights and procedures of participation and representation. The economic and financial crisis points instead to a more fundamental dilemma between the functional necessity of integrating in response to crisis on the one hand and the democratic will of the voters on the other hand. Practical necessities are increasingly difficult to square with morality. European integration is trapped: in order to guarantee continuity of functional integration that delivers outputs in terms of stability and problem-solving efficiency, we need democratic legitimation. In order to achieve democratic legitimation, we must convince and enlighten citizens about the EU's greater problem-solving capacities. The balance between national and EU democracies no longer provides solutions. The European Union's democratization is no longer linear but instead interrupted by antagonistic forces. At the same time, measures taken by the Eurozone countries to stabilize the common currency are seen as illegitimate from the perspective of national democracy. The European Union is both held responsible for its interventions intended to violate democratic standards and for its unintended democratic failures. This makes the EU increasingly immune to democratic interventions and reform. The democratic deficit is thus no longer interpreted as a challenge that can be remedied by constitutional reform but is instead a matter of destiny. It becomes a fundamental dilemma of supranational governance that is detached from democracy. The automatism between Europeanization and democratization is interrupted. There is new evidence for the old fear of a negative causal relationship: the observation that Europeanization inevitably means the continual dismantling of democracy.

Paradigms do not change because they are internally contested but because their capacity to explain basic facts and beliefs is eroded. If we are currently witnessing the dismantling of the integration paradigm, this need not be the result of the successful mobilization of the Eurosceptic opposition. The paradigm is instead challenged by the unintended consequences of external shocks or developments. These might not at first glance affect the EU's routine internal functioning. Administrations continue to function, even if the premises upon which they claim public legitimacy are no longer deemed valid. The quasi-automatism through which the EU responds to crisis still follows the old construction plan, which prescribes financial and monetary stability as the means of holding the monetary union together. The architecture of European integration has, however, been shattered in such a manner that legitimacy requirements have changed, not simply in the sense that the

EU fails to meet the normative expectations (the EU's output legitimacy is *de facto* found to be much lower than expected). It is instead in the sense that there is a default logic in relation to the *principle* of integration, which is displayed in the growing imbalance between the needs of the common market and the needs of the citizens who populate this market. In light of this fundamental incongruence between market Europe and social Europe as well as the lack of political steering capacities for mediating between the two, any attempt to recover the old integration paradigm may well produce the opposite effect, contributing to the crumbling of the EU's fragile constitutional architecture. A return to the old construction plan might rescue the union from the dangers of immediate collapse, but it will not halt the erosion of the groundwork and will instead merely prop up the facade.

Perceptions of crisis thus fundamentally disturb the imagination of Europeanization as a confined and controlled process. Out of such disturbances, social scientists are tempted to translate the old paradigm of integration into a new paradigm of disintegration.[8] The natural history of integration is turned into a natural history of disintegration, explaining the unmaking of the union as a consequential and incremental process dictated by the social laws of crisis. From a traditional Marxian perspective, the irreversibility of crisis results from an endemic conflict between capitalist markets and democratic politics (Streeck 2014). From a more Weberian-inspired institutional perspective, the crisis of state and capitalism is not cyclical but patterned, possessing a self-perpetuating dynamic that is reproduced over time. The destructive dynamics can be explicated by multicausal mechanisms such as unintended effects, recouplings, vicious circles, escalation processes, circular stimulations, contagion, and paradox (Bach 2014: 4).

The automatism of disintegration is often described as a vicious circle, which comes into play in the sense that crisis rescue measures rely on prerequisites, which the EU in itself can no longer guarantee. In particular, the implementation of austerity policies would rely upon the stability of political systems—a prerequisite that is, however, undermined by the social consequences of crisis and the kinds of political responses crisis generates. Depoliticized crisis governance provokes repoliticization in political side arenas, which cannot easily be controlled and often escape the logics of established representative politics. The vicious circle of European inequalities is thus interlocked with a vicious circle of social and political conflict (Bach 2014: 7). EU crisis governance has important democratic side effects: it undermines democratic legitimacy and inevitably intensifies what I have discussed in chapter 4 as "polity contestation," affecting the legitimacy of the democratic system at both national and European levels.

Such a process of creeping disintegration as the unintended side effect of the rescue measures undertaken by the governments and the *Troika* is also described by Zielonka (2013), who argues that the EU is doomed. His compelling argument is that the EU governance apparatus might well be able to continue for some time and even pretend to function as usual, but this reduced technocratic vision will be but a shadow of what the integration project originally stood for. The EU's major problems are therefore lack of cohesion, trust, and imagination, not just the financial supervision needed to run a common currency (Zielonka 2013: 7–12). Read from this perspective of paradigm loss, the EU's proposed solutions out of the crisis remind us of the "government of the blind" or of Napoleon's attempt to reassemble his lost troops on the map. The common journey for which this map was drawn has changed in fundamental ways, and the fellow travelers have lost sight of their destination.

The interpretation of history as a case of destruction is, however, asocial in the sense that it overlooks the forces of catharsis, re-equilibration, and reorganization of social relations (Eder 2015: 272). From a sociological perspective, a crisis is an accelerated moment of social evolution, which implies destruction and reconstruction. Crisis then appears as a moment of somewhat open-ended institutional transformation: instead of disintegration, the European Union seems to follow a pattern of permanent differentiation (Fossum 2014b: 65), involving state and society at different levels of aggregation. Crisis as state transformation and crisis as societal transformation are obviously interlinked, which is why sociologists have also spoken of the crisis as a case of 'creative destruction' (Eder 2015). The sociological imagination thus invites us to relate crisis as a case of destruction to moments of societal creativity. This creativity of crisis as a case of society-building through social evolution and learning shall be traced back to its roots in the next section.

THE EUROCRISIS: AN EXPERIMENTAL DESIGN
OF EUROPEAN SOCIETY BUILDING?

In the development of modern sociology, the notion of crisis has always been intrinsically linked to accelerated social change and mobilization. Crises are open and complex constellations of conflicts, which break from the iterative structures of social change.[9] Crisis as paradigm loss brings interpretations back into play. Such interpretative moments are at the same time moments of social imagination and creativity. The driving forces for accelerated social change are then the varying interpretations that are offered to make sense of crisis and the negative experiences (the collective suffering) associated with it. Crisis diagnosis and interpretation are ambivalent because crisis is an open conflictual constellation, in which the existing paradigm for "objective" scientific interpretation and normative evaluation no longer applies. The sociological analysis of crisis can in this sense only be a second-order observation of the various social forces that develop and apply crisis interpretations and diagnoses in an open and non-institutionalized transnational conflict constellation (Vobruba 2014: 4–5).

Adding to these dimensions of openness and ambivalence in the Eurocrisis is that the societal spaces for interpretation are transnationalized by the negative consequences and experiences of crisis. This goes beyond the original idea of a 'legitimation crisis of late capitalism,' which discussed crisis dynamics in relation to global capitalism while discussions of societal impact remained confined to national welfare states (Offe 2000). In the case of Europe, not only the origins of crisis and the measures taken to combat it but also its social dynamics and consequences stretch beyond the nation-state. This new scale of social forces requires an approach to crisis and crisis resolution in terms of problems of social integration and institutionalization in the European framework. Crisis does not, however, simply indicate the transformation of social and political order but also implies a notion of risk for established institutions (EU and national), the control capacities of which are under stress. Social change is expected to become discontinuous as an effect of crisis. In the EU context, for instance, functionalist notions of gradual accumulation of the *acquis communautaire* and progress toward deeper integration no longer apply. At the individual level, crisis is typically experienced as a threat to material well-being and social and cultural identities. Crisis-ridden social relationships are at risk of breakdown or disintegration. As such, the current crisis represents a gradual disintegration of the European social and political space and reinforces a trend of renationalization, which drives political identities and preferences. Instead of economic and social harmonization, the European crisis has exposed the asymmetries of European political space and the seemingly insurmountable divisions between the peoples of Europe (Risse 2014a, 2014b). The potentially explosive social conditions generated by the European crisis threaten to derail the future of the European integration project over the next decade on the basis of economic development and social welfare and cohesion. From a political sociology perspective, we must ask which social groups are at risk of social exclusion and how they are exposed to the long-term implications of crisis.

Interpretations of crisis are contested within the EU studies community but are at the same time taken up as reflections concerning assumptions that have been taken for granted. The paradigm loss implied by the interpretation of crisis is not to be equated with a loss of social imagination or even a silencing of its interpreters. It is instead grasped as an opportunity for new social forces, which profit from the open constellation of crisis to promote their interpretations and mobilize collective action around them. Such an open interpretative context is characteristic of what is discussed in critical social theory as a legitimation crisis. The sociological question resulting from such an open interpretative constellation involves the manner in which crisis is transformed into an opportunity for collective learning. How is the interpretative openness taken up by social actors as an invitation to join their efforts to interpret crisis, to cope with crisis, to resist crisis, and to define ways of overcoming crisis? Such a perspective on crisis-induced societal learning differs from the dominant paradigm of progressive European integration. It simply assumes that the perceived destructive effects of crisis affect societal self-organization and thereby facilitate new methods of social evolution and learning (Eder 2015). Whether these processes should be described in terms of integration or disintegration remains undetermined. In sociopsychology, such moments are described as catharsis, through which repressed emotions can come to the surface to overcome trauma and permit collective renewal. From a sociological research perspective, the focus will be on what Klaus Eder (2015) has called a sociological inquiry into the European crisis as a 'case of creative destruction.'

One straightforward means of developing the sociological agenda of crisis as a case of social evolution and 'creative destruction' (Eder 2015; Vobruba 2013) would be to search for society in relation to institutional transformation and reform. Crisis as an open interpretative constellation thaws institutional configurations (Rokkan 1999); it marks the point where institution-building takes a detour through societal mobilization. Crisis makes issues of European integration more salient in the public sphere and keeps institutions in a state of alert. Enhanced attention replaces European publics' mutual indifference with a new conflict orientation and a readiness to contest the legitimacy of the EU's institutional and constitutional setting. Enhanced attention is further paired—as we have argued in relation to Euroscepticism—with a polemical orientation on the part of sensitized publics, but polemics are mobilized with a view beyond society's national confines and intensify publics' mutual observation along the lines of transnational solidarity and divisions. Following the sociological conflict paradigm, the conditions for turning this enhanced attentiveness and polemics into a case of society-building are in place whenever intensified collective action is conducive to the building of supplementary institutions for collective problem solving (Vobruba 2013: 13). A case for social evolution is thus made from a process of institutional thaw, which is at the same time a driving force for the building of new and supplementary institutions. These dynamics of societal institution-building are contributed to less new institutions being created than by existing institutions being rendered meaningful, that is, used as reference points for collective practices and mobilization.

Next, we will follow this path from deconstruction to social evolution. In order to approach the crisis as part of the experimental design of Europe's social evolution, I will reconstruct the nexus between the EU's system crisis and legitimation crisis, which sets the general cultural and interpretative framework for the repoliticization of crisis experiences and grants insight into the state of solidarity in Europe and new coalitions and frictions within

European social and political space. Based on this reconstructive reading of the normative and cognitive structures that help collective actors pursue legitimacy, I will then collect selected empirical evidence on how legitimation crisis engenders new social practices and builds new social relationships. Social experiments take place in three related fields: the resilience practices of EU citizens, the articulation of voice and resistance by selected groups affected by crisis, and the media contestations of public legitimacy.

The Challenge of Democratic Legitimacy

Academic focus on this crisis has very much been on its handling by EU institutions and member-state governments as well as on the consequences for welfare state provisions and the socioeconomic status of ordinary citizens. These are relevant issues to address as we need to understand both the institutional and human effects of crisis politics and its impact on democratic reform of the EU.[10] There are lacunae, however, in terms of understanding the effects of the crisis on changing state-society relationships, the rights and empowerment of citizens, and the transnational contestations that link individuals and collectives across national borders. Such an investigation into the transnational dynamics of crisis-related legitimacy contestations can grant insight into the state of solidarity in Europe and new coalitions and frictions within European social and political space.

The idea that social developments in capitalist markets and societies involve contradictions or crises is a basis of Marxist political economy. With the development of advanced capitalism and the consolidation of the democratic welfare state, this debate has, however, shifted from the fundamental contradictions of capitalism to the crisis tendencies of late capitalism and the possible renewal of democracy through economic, social, and democratic reform (Habermas 1975; Offe 1972). In late capitalism, we experience the 'naturalization' of the 'system of purposive rational action,' which comprises the iron cage of bureaucracy and capitalist market forces (Habermas 1975: 30). The EU common market and, more specifically, the EU monetary system have acquired this status of objectivity of a "system of purposive rational action." Through naturalization, the ideological core can no longer be challenged by reflection. The economic and administrative apparatus not only becomes autonomous; it also becomes immune to societal intervention and the demands for participation and co-decision. Under these conditions, a system crisis breaks forth as a natural catastrophe, as 'inexplicable, contingent, natural events' (30). The question, then, is whether and under what conditions social forces can be reactivated in crisis, which is a matter of the possibilities for reinterpretation and repoliticization that break from the naturalized and—as a consequence—depoliticized logics of the market.

One of the basic insights of Habermas's influential book *Strukturprobleme des Spätkapitalismus* (originally published in 1973 and translated in
1975) was that an economic crisis is not simply an *objective* force or a
process that can be impartially viewed from the outside. A crisis can only be
described in relation to the individuals who are *subjectively* undergoing it
and who, as subjects, are condemned to passivity and temporarily deprived
of the possibility of being in full possession of their powers (Habermas 1975:
1). From this perspective of the crisis as a 'deprivation of sovereignty,' there
is an intrinsic normative element in the conception of crisis and its possible
solutions. We cannot speak of crisis in general system terms but only if the
experiencing of system disturbances is critical for members of society, who
feel their continued existence and identities threatened (3). A crisis puts
social integration at stake: it impairs society's 'consensual foundations of
normative structures' (3).

By building upon this idea of a legitimation crisis as an open interpretative context, the question is not simply how crisis is experienced by members
of society but more specifically how these experiences are interpreted and
assessed, which normative and cognitive structures underlie these assess-
ments, and how these norms and cognitions are themselves contested. The
crisis is interpreted in light of the people's suffering and the unequal representation of Europeanization as a triumph of the elite few and a trauma of the
many. These normative translations take place in the public sphere, where
crisis experiences are narrated, interpreted, and contested. It is through these
processes of narration and interpretation that an economic or system crisis is
translated into a legitimation crisis through which society's normativity is
fundamentally contested.

Raising this question of how the Eurocrisis is experienced, interpreted,
and contested by members of society broadens the perspective of a crisis of
"output legitimacy," which political scientists sometimes apply to explain the
failures of the EU political system and the structural deficits of its performance (Scharpf 2012). Popular perceptions matter in the assessment of EU
output legitimacy (Jones 2009). Steering problems of the political-adminis-
trative apparatus of the EU thus cannot be assessed independently of the
norms used to evaluate "output legitimacy." At stake is the validity of the
underlying ideologies and identities through which the EU project has been
carried forward. In line with this research program, Habermas called already
in the mid-1970s for a new crisis theorem, which departed from the legitimation problems of late-capitalist societies, the democratic means available to
them in pursuit of legitimacy, and their potential/limits to integrate complex
societies (Habermas 1975: 45–60). The program for a sociological inquiry of
crisis-related social experiments in contemporary Europe is included in this
statement.

Of increasing importance here is not only the experience of material loss and risk of life chances but also the subjective experiences of crisis governance as a heteronomous intervention that affects the autonomy of social spaces. EU legitimacy contestations are increasingly framed as confrontations between epistocracy (governance through experts) and democracy (government of the people). Epistocracy as the regime of EU governance that is set up to deal with crisis and its consequences is transnational in its design, including international organizations, for instance, in the case of the *Troika*, the International Monetary Fund, the European Central Bank, and the European Commission. Governance through experts is manifested by the displacement of politics from a great number of regulatory fields (such as monetary policy, the whole field of EU market integration, and security). One effect of EU crisis governance is that politics are reduced to rigid regulatory action, legal obligations, and compliance mechanisms, which exclude the popular vote or reduce it to forced consent. "Governance through experts" thus systematically restricts the possibilities of "government by the people." The "no-choice" decisions of EU governance, which are taken to rescue the common currency, become increasingly detached from the democratic process within our established systems of political representation and contestation of political choices. The displacement of politics from these areas increases citizens' feeling of impotence: Although they are still formally empowered to exercise control, they are *de facto* either forced to consent through symbolic side politics or to turn to populist protest votes (which, again, increase the uncertainty of the situation). There is thus sensitivity not only to perceived external threats and the deterioration of material life chances but also to perceived breaches of cultural codes or normative rules as part of the functioning of democracy.

A further reflection that merits attention here is the interrelationship between the European crisis and the crisis of legitimacy of national political systems, which is affecting most Southern European countries as well as, to some extent, the old member states at the core of Europe, like France, Belgium, and the UK. The crisis of legitimacy of the EU is simultaneously a crisis of legitimacy of the nation-state. There is, in short, a structural democratic crisis of both the EU and the nation-state, manifested in the growing mismatch of their normative aspirations to act in a way responsive to democratic will formation (Menéndez 2013: 463). The signals sent out by several national elections since 2009 (most prominently the Greek legislative elections in June 2012 and the Italian elections in February 2013) are that disintegrating dynamics at the EU and national levels are deeply interwoven. The demise of the EU political project is closely related to the demise of (some of) its member states and their incapacity to represent the collective will. In the Italian and Greek cases, the past legislative elections must be seen as a plebiscite against Brussels and Berlin as much as a plebiscite against Rome and Athens. From a European perspective, such a situation is paired with an unprecedented level of mutual misunderstanding between the peoples of Europe. In Europe's prosperous north, particularly in Germany, many politicians have praised their noble act of rescuing of the south in the spirit of European solidarity. In the crisis-ridden south, such "rescue measures" are experienced quite differently. Election results in Greece and Italy mobilize political parties and electorates, which reject the "false" solidarity of the north, which they understand as relief for the creditors by safeguarding the liquidity of the debtors at the expense of the wider population (Streeck 2014). As emphasized by Dennis Smith (2015), the so-called acts of solidarity are furthermore linked to dynamics of degradation and humiliation, which can unleash a highly destructive and disintegrative force.

What is the way forward? In order to further develop this research perspective on the Eurocrisis as an open interpretative context for societal contestation, the key issue is not normative, in the sense of seeking to identify the kind of polity that should be designed to overcome crisis and its negative consequences. The issue is instead analytical, in the sense of seeking to identify how crisis accounts are developed and promoted by particular actors, giving rise to new social relationships, shaping conflicts, and distributing resources and power. In the following, we will look at three types of practices that result from crisis and can be meaningfully related to processes of social evolution and society-building: practices of social resilience, social resistance, and media contestation.

Crisis and Social Resilience

The concept of social resilience has risen to prominence in the social sciences in the wake of the financial and global crisis, not least with regard to a recent call for research under the European Commission's FP7 program and collaborative European research projects linked to it.[11] What went unnoticed in these Commission efforts to occupy a new research agenda was a redefinition and a slight shift of emphasis from "individual" or "social" resilience to what the Commission calls *citizens'* resilience. The Commission, which is often criticized for promoting a kind of 'disciplinary neoliberalism,' replacing the public good with individual responsibility (Gill 2003), actually does just the opposite when it encourages networking and community through the *collective* use of rights and legal entitlements. What the Commission explicitly or implicitly suggests here is that there exists a link between the development of resilience capacities and the enactment of EU citizenship. The new emphasis on citizens' resilience is thus designed as part of a 'new politics of civil society,' which turns citizens into carriers for Europeanization from below (Liebert and Trenz 2010).

Resilience is not a new concept in the social sciences but has thus far mainly been analyzed within the fields of sociopsychology to measure the ability of individuals or small groups (like local communities) to mitigate the effects of hazards (like an environmental disaster). While it is widely recognized that social and political context are vital for understanding the development of individual coping strategies (e.g., Mitchell 1995), the resultant models and indexes typically measure individual capabilities linked to degrees of vulnerability of particular categories of actors. Usually, these individuals are statistically aggregated (like "young unemployed") but not analyzed in their quality as groups that build social relationships and networks. "Resilience" relates, then, mainly to the capabilities of individuals or collectives to tolerate failure, disruptions, or dysfunctions in local settings.[12] Yet the global scale and deep political and social ramifications of financial crises such as the one that broke out in 2008 demand that we rethink the context within which resilience is examined. Resilience is then maintained not only through cognitive strength or group support (the sociopsychological approach) but also through institutional provisions or sociocultural repertoires (the institutional approach) (Hall and Lamont 2013). The question is therefore whether the EU provides particular tools or action frames for developing capabilities collectively, to create and activate new networks of social relationships, and to empower them politically.

Rendering resilience sociologically meaningful in the current context of crisis requires us to understand not just individual but also collective responses generated in a transnational (European) context of interaction and communication. Díez Medrano (2015) categorizes sociological answers to this question as either Durkheimian or Weberian. The Durkheimian account conceives of resilience as resulting from particular structural conditions, which are culturally defined and interpreted. As explicated in a groundbreaking book by Mary Douglas and Aaron Wildavsky, resilience is less strategic and directional than it is explained by cultural perceptions of risk and crisis (Douglas and Wildavsky 1982). In the neoliberal era, for instance, social resilience can be analyzed as a collective reinterpretation of free market ideologies and their emphasis on individualized responses (Hall and Lamont 2013). It emphasizes the cultural value of collaboration instead of competition. Although the Weberian approach would not object to this cultural interpretation, it regards resilience more as a result of contingent social action. Individuals or collectives within a particular institutional setting are then analyzed as both mobilizing against the negative aspects of neoliberal market policies and seizing upon its opportunities. The latter becomes important in the Europe of free movement, which is indeed not just a constraint upon life chances but also an opportunity for many citizens (whether in vulnerable positions or otherwise) to build new capacities, make use of rights and legal entitlements, or simply expand their networks of activities. There are thus specific advantages of the market of free movement, which can be seized by citizens to engage in cosmopolitan lifestyles or claim for transnational justice with both a redistributive and an identitarian dimension (Favell 2014). It is this "fourth freedom" that truly makes a difference when it comes to explaining how citizens can develop resilience capacities in a free market Europe that is open not only to the movement of capital and goods but also to the movement of people. The development of the European labor market becomes a reality for the definition of citizens' life chances and expectations and in this sense is the most important driving force for rebalancing growth, political control, and social cohesion at a new postnational scale (Favell 2014: 284).

Arriving at a sociologically informed answer to the question of how resilience can contribute to European society-building requires that we further relate to the political and institutional context within which collective capabilities are developed and employed. Resilience practices rest upon specific skills and know-how, which apply within a particular institutional environment and make use of legal entitlements and rights protected at the community or polity level (Te Brake et al. 2008). Citizens' resilience defines a capability to cope with crisis by *collectively* utilizing different types of legal entitlements and social, political, and economic resources. The term "citizens' resilience" refers in this sense to social practices, linking individualism with collectivism and asking not simply how individuals can be statistically aggregated to particular categories (like "young" people) but also how they can be empowered as social groups within a given institutional framework.

From this vantage point of resilience as a collective practice, the European Commission is not just seeking to ideologically occupy research agendas but also displays sociological intuition when introducing the new framework of citizens' resilience and asking the EU research community to identify the role of European citizenship as mitigator of crisis-related negative effects. The 'resilience agenda,' which was originally developed in the framework of humanitarian aid policies (Keohane 2011), has been applied since 2010 to encompass the responses of a broad range of actors: trade unions, civil society, cities, neighborhoods, and households. All of these collective actors can be also reached and addressed by specifically designed policies at the EU community level. By putting its resilience program into practice, the EU's program for building state-society relationships is thus normatively reinterpreted and developed.

Understanding how collective resilience practices develop in relation to EU citizenship means reappraising the agenda of bottom-up banal Europeanization that is driven by ordinary citizens. The EU legitimation crisis is confronted by ordinary citizens who do not necessarily mobilize politically or openly resist the elites (as in the form of Euroscepticism discussed in chapter 4) but instead seek to seize remaining opportunities (like mobility) or accommodate through a range of 'coping' practices (such as developing language skills and new forms of entrepreneurship) (Díez Medrano 2015). Resilience can then be discussed as a capacity that develops out of the qualities of banal Europeanism. It can develop because citizens are Europeanized in terms of their life expectations and identities and can adapt to the European free movement area.

Resilience is thus interpreted as a form of uncoordinated and nonpurposeful collective action under conditions of high uncertainty. European societies and welfare systems are unsettled by a multitude of destabilizing factors to which affected citizens often can only respond in a spontaneous and experimental manner rather than with strategies guided by clearly defined purposes (Schimank 2011). Often, the long-term impact of individual decisions is difficult to assess. Under these conditions of uncertainty, many individuals simply wait, others improvise with no major fixed expectations, and still others experiment by taking more collective choices (like engaging in alternative economic practices at the community level, see Conill et al. [2011]). Even if these individuals have no clear master plan, they nevertheless react. They must be ready to adapt and learn at any moment and see how the crisis unfolds (Schimank 2011: 22). Resilience thus involves very different reactions to welfare instabilities, ranging from passive acceptance, muddling through, experimentation, or development of more proactive strategies.

Resilience practices related to EU citizenship range between exit, entry, voice, loyalty, and their possible recombinations (E. Olsen 2015). Exit as a resource is created through transnational rights of free movement. EU citizenship is, however, unique in also providing equal rights of entry (admittance, study, work, and settlement) (Bauböck 2007). EU citizenship is furthermore unique in creating rights of voice as a resource for civil and political rights of participation, which give citizens tools for *mobilization* (Shaw 2007). This innovation runs counter to the clear-cut boundaries of inclusion and exclusion in the traditional understanding of national citizenship. Noncitizens—that is, citizens of any EU member state—have an inherent right to have rights in other EU member states (E. Olsen 2012). Exclusion based on a uniform formula of citizens/noncitizens is no longer possible in the EU setting. This not only constrains the member states and EU institutions but also creates an added source of rights for EU citizens. In sociological terms, such individual backing by a distinct set of rights creates ideal conditions for the development of new forms of citizens' engagement (Vobruba 2013). EU citizenship thus accounts for a particular combination of coping practices, allowing citizens to enter new transnational alignments and recombine exit, entry, and voice opportunities and resources. This has the potential to mitigate traditional conflict lines—for example, status quo-oriented groups and change-oriented groups or mobile and immobile groups within the nation-state framework. Far from being grounded in a clear-cut opportunity structure for individual choices or collective action, EU citizenship constitutes a transnational social and cultural infrastructure for seeking opportunities, which are discovered along the way and are in constant need of readjustment to new circumstances.

Citizens' resilience in the current crisis can, then, be identified in various coping practices employed by particularly vulnerable groups within the Europe of free movement and citizenship. As mentioned above, EU citizenship is particularly interesting in this context of defining vulnerable citizens' coping practices because it bestows the right of free movement and thus lays the groundwork for the unique European *social* space of free movement, which increasingly comprises its citizens' transnational life experiences and expectations.[13] On the one hand, the EU is thus far the only "international" polity that bestows transnational rights upon its citizens and embeds them in a system of participation and representation. Political and social rights, as defined through EU citizenship, supplement national citizenship rights and aim to solidify political and socioeconomic integration at the supranational level. Nevertheless, EU citizenship also impinges upon the everyday ways in which individuals experience their being part of this transnational polity. EU citizenship facilitates various ways of "doing Europe." New patterns of interaction and communication emerge, for instance, within so-called expat communities, composed of EU citizens (and others) in the wealthy cities of the north like London, Berlin, Copenhagen, and Amsterdam, which offer various job opportunities and educational programs to young, often multilingual, and highly dynamic people (Duru et al. 2015). EU citizenship in this sense comprises the practices, values, and expectations that are attributed to it by individuals and groups. To be (or to aspire to be) a citizen of the EU is to understand one's self, whether positively or negatively, as a member of a transnational community.

The current crisis in Europe thus also stands for continued Europeanization of social relations. It might be seen as activating social networks of those groups which are affected by social exclusion, thereby testing new forms of solidarity and social cohesion beyond the national. The "enactment" of EU citizenship—that is, the wide and disparate range of means by which citizens' rights can be exerted (Saward 2013)—in this sense always relates back to opportunities for political participation and systems and structures of representation. The Europe of rights and citizenship confronts the Europe of increasing inequalities. Practices of coping and institutional adaptation are thus only one side of the coin of crisis, which also gives rise to acts of defiance, political voice, and resistance.

From Resilience to Resistance

In categorizing the range of possible collective reactions to crisis, resilience is often distinguished from *resistance*. While social resilience is generally described as a "silent" and incremental process of adaptation and coping by individuals, groups, or even social systems undergoing unwanted change (Chandler 2014), resistance is usually conceived of as an expression of political will. As such, it is manifested by the active mobilization, noncompliance, or civil disobedience of particular groups, which strive for social change instead of restoration. Social movement scholars therefore typically link resistance to disadvantaged groups (Bieler 2011), while resilience is primarily used by those groups that wish to maintain the status quo or re-establish previous order. Resilience is an adaptive response to the unexpected effects of crisis after they have become manifest, while resistance is reactive and proactive. Social resilience remains beneath the surface of incremental societal change while resistance takes on political form.

This does not mean, however, that social resilience as it develops in response to crisis should necessarily be considered a nonpolitical manifestation of citizens' passive submission to market forces.[14] To the extent that resilience does not individualize European citizens but is turned into a social experience, it also makes likely forms of collective action that are politically meaningful. There is thus a pragmatist reading of resilience as an experimental form of democratic self-governance, which not only enables collective learning but also contains within itself the possibility for democratic renewal by empowering a transnational group of affected citizens (J. Schmidt 2014). The crisis then creates a common platform of experiences, needs, and aspirations, which unites citizens in their political demands for equal life chances and social solidarity. The EU framework of rights might thus become a platform for citizens' mobilization and empowerment to shape a collective will that resists inequalities born out of crisis.

Following this logic of democratic self-renewal, the return of "civil society" can be expected in a context of depoliticization driven by crisis governance. The upshot is that the technocratization and depoliticization of EU crisis governance will inevitably result in repoliticization. In the following, I will critically test this assumption of the collective mobilization potential of the European crisis and follow up by considering how EU politicization has developed on national and transnational levels.

The politicization of the EU in response to crisis is often predicted (and sometimes even emphatically announced), but it is unclear when and under what conditions it occurs.[15] In discussing the democratic implications of EU crisis governance and its societal repercussions, citizens give collective expression to their individual experiences of injustice and express dissatisfaction with representative structures of national and EU democracy. As I have elaborated elsewhere, such dissatisfaction with existing representative arrangements of democracy is a breeding ground for civil society (Trenz 2005b). We have seen how, in the framework of EU crisis governance and its efforts to regain financial stability and control over the efficiency of outcomes, new lines of input-oriented legitimation are often ruled out by the governments, driving an "avoidance strategy" that shuns public salience and confrontation. Under such conditions, we might expect established civil society organizations to return from governance to protest while new protest actors emerge transnationally. [16]

Of particular interest in this context is the way in which social responses to crisis and mobilizations are translated into political conflict and division. In the new sociopolitical constellation of crisis-ridden Europe, we observe that the (re)politicization of technocratic governance accounts for the simultaneous appearance of new conflicts over income and distribution, which are combined in specific ways with new identitarian conflicts over different life projects. [17] This would indicate the dismissal of a "new politics of European civil society," which in many ways seems closer to the old functionalist logic of integration, relating European institution-building to the development of problem-solving capacities in response to "new" grievances about gender equality, civil liberties, and discrimination or technological and environmental uncertainty (Liebert and Trenz 2010). Functionalism allowed for the development of policymaking competencies in these areas, with contestation being restricted to an institutional arena populated by EU professionals, experts, and stakeholders. However, as Lahusen has argued, recent advances in European integration and enlargement have been "putting 'old' grievances on the public agenda again, such as economic disparities, social inequalities, poverty and social marginalization, interethnic conflicts and xenophobic anxieties" (Lahusen 2013: 156). In the current context of crisis, this functionalist logic of stakeholder contestation transforms into a postfunctionalist logic of public contestation (Hooghe and Marks 2009). The new contentious logics once again follow the pattern of "class politics" and "identity politics," tending to disregard postmaterial civil society concerns. The increased cross-border mobility brought about by the Eurocrisis (Recchi and Salamońska 2015) may mobilize, for instance, protectionist movements on the receiving end of this intra-EU migration. These movements often express opposition in populist terms as the "resistance of the people" against *transnational* integration and in favor of an exclusive application of national welfare provisions and the reservation of social and political rights to members of the national community.

EU politicization occurs in this triangular energetic field between civil society politics, class politics, and identity politics. Social responses and mobilizations in times of crisis depart from 'organized civil society' by articulating citizens' concerns in terms of struggles over redistribution combined with struggles over belonging (Ancelovici 2015). The new identitarian and redistributive conflicts are, as noted by Georg Vobruba (2014: 11), only weakly institutionalized. They find a common denominator in the diffuse term of "the people," and they rely on an equally diffuse identification of the "other" as the "elites" and the "establishment." The "other" that is opposed by such populist struggles is rarely narrowed down to specific names or groups. It is instead variably identified as the established political representatives at the national level; the EU or Brussels; the banks and the big capitalist enterprises; the "rich" or the "corrupt"; the *Troika* or the International Monetary Fund (IMF), the European Central Bank (ECB), or Germany. The new populists also frequently shy away from institutional representation. In 2014, representatives of new populist and anti-European parties on the left and the right fringes of the political spectrum have triumphed in European Parliament elections, but they have been notoriously unsuccessful in occupying the parliamentarian arena for coalition building or making use of its procedures of control (Kietz and von Ondarza 2014).

How EU politicization develops in the current spiral of political and financial crises depends on the ways in which these redistributive and identitarian conflicts unfold at national and transnational levels. In its most salient forms, and taking on elements of both class politics and identity politics, EU politicization has led to a rise in populism at the nation-state level. As I argued in chapter 4, EU crisis governance has intensified the confrontation between the Europeanization of the experts and the defenders of popular democracy. EU technocracy meets popular democracy. The repoliticization in response to EU crisis governance defies the progressive account of Europeanization by questioning both the viability (efficiency) and validity (democratic legitimacy) of common market integration. The question is whether this fundamental challenge can be interpreted as a paradigmatic change (e.g., in an attempt to launch alternative stories of renationalization) or whether it instead provides another sequence to the story of Europeanization through its inherent conflicts.

Despite the divisions between the populist and Eurosceptic parties and the struggles between their prominent representatives, the popular resistance of the south indeed provides strong evidence of a Europeanization of the populist anti-austerity agenda. The culturalist reframings of redistributive conflicts take place in public and media debates that clearly transcend the national arena. Questions of austerity, debt, and hegemonic power are given a broader cultural meaning, which is interpreted from a European perspective. Such culturalist reinterpretations are seemingly more pronounced in the South of Europe, where people are in search of scapegoats for their suffering from austerity. For the many people suffering from economic hardship, such a Europeanized culturalist reframing is provided by the idea of a new German hegemon, which for many Europeans is more convincing than the idea of the sinful and lazy South that is sometimes evoked by tabloids in Germany (Michailidou et al. 2014). The prominence of cultural reframing in public discourse in the South might also be explained by the political impasse these countries face and their difficulties resisting the political and economic demands of the creditor countries. Culturalist struggles partly follow an escapist logic to reinterpret political and economic dominance as an imposition of different (Protestant) values of a merciless economy. The Italian philosopher Giorgio Agamben went so far to publish a pamphlet in several European newspapers in which he calls for a Latin empire to resist German hegemony. This Latin Europe should strike back and act as a counterweight to the dominant role played by Germany in the European Union. Resistance by the South is thus evoked as adherence to a different way of life, interpreting the EU common market as fundamentally contradicting the value system of 'Mediterranean societies,' which are based on other forms of solidarity—not only rational calculation but also forms of leisure and different speeds that are unknown in the Protestant North:

> Not only is there no sense in asking a Greek or an Italian to live like a German but even if this were possible, it would lead to the destruction of a cultural heritage that exists as a way of life. A political unit that prefers to ignore lifestyles is not only condemned not to last, but, as Europe has eloquently shown, it cannot even establish itself as such. [18]

These culturalist reframings of popular resistance matter, however, within a framework of redistribution in which recognition often becomes secondary. For many citizens, there is a deficit of justice, fairness, and distribution, in the sense that the EU has not fulfilled its promise to guarantee equal living conditions. The rise of populism is therefore intrinsically related to the transformation of power relationships among the countries in the periphery and at the center of Europe and the questions of redistribution related to it. The various manifestations of populism in Europe, ranging from left-wing welfare protective to nationalist-ordoliberal parties, develop a common denominator in mobilizing the 'politics of the people' against the 'other' (Canovan 2002). This "other" is a potential unifier of populists across Europe, who in the depoliticized context of crisis governance wish to reconquer politics against the TINA ("there-is-no-alternative") decisions imposed by experts and technocrats. Claims for recognition of the "people" as a political force are not intrinsically "nationalist" or anti-European. In most countries, they target the heart of the state, blame the corruption of the established political parties and the malfunctioning of national democracy. The new populist parties across Europe remain, however, isolated and diverse. They are less united in their struggle against the "political system" and "the EU" than this shared cultural framing would suggest. It remains to be seen whether this propensity for reinterpreting the populist struggle in terms of class politics and drawing an antagonistic border between Europe's core and peripheries can be also translated into a new "Euroclash," structuring patterns of political mobilization and guiding voters' preferences.

In addition to these new populist mobilizations and their characteristic move between redistribution and recognition, mobilizations in response to crisis have begun to formulate an agenda of global counter-politics. This is the kind of participation seen in the global justice movement, in counter-summits, social forums, and most recently the democracy of the square as represented by the Occupy and *Indignados* movements (Ancelovici 2015). These phenomena have been widely interpreted as anti-politics to global capitalism: anti-neoliberal, anti-globalization, anti-austerity, and anti-Euro. Civil society is taking up the concerns of a new generation of young Euro-peans, who are deeply disillusioned with the EU but even more so with the established political parties in their home countries. In Spain, the name of the protest movement is the program itself, *Indignados*, that is, the people who are outraged and filled with indignation. Yet the *Indignados* and *Wutbürger* are ubiquitous, no longer supporting the representative system of democracy but fundamentally undermining its legitimacy. A brief look at some of their slogans is revealing: "They don't represent us!" (*¡Que no! ¡Que no! ¡Que no nos representan!*); "Don't vote for them!" (*¡No les votes!*); "We are not antisystem, the system is against us!" (*¡Nosotros no somos antisistema, el sistema es anti-nosotros!*).[19] Once this *Wut*, this anger and indignation, is politically organized, it can become very powerful, the most successful ex-ample of which is Italy's Five Star Movement (Conti and Memoli 2015).

Resistance and political mobilization in the context of crisis as manifested in a new politics of civil society, a new identitarian politics, and a new politics of redistribution contribute to and amplify the perception of a deep legitimation crisis, which fundamentally affects citizens' patterns of loyalty to and diffuse support for the EU representative system and democratic insti-tutions in general. The crisis of legitimacy is not, however, a consequential outcome of protest and political mobilization. The way in which public opin-ion and perceptions of democratic legitimacy are formed is much more com-plex. Central to the crisis, both in terms of offering core mediating capacities and providing the public stage for crisis conflicts, are Europe's available media spheres and infrastructures—new and old media, offline and online, news and social.

The Unfolding Media Drama of Crisis[20]

Delving into a media perspective of the crisis is paramount to understanding how Europeans understand the challenges facing the EU and express public opinion that is more than just an aggregate of individual attitudes.[21] Firstly, we can expect that media coverage of the EU and its institutions becomes more salient during times of crisis. Crises, as threatening situations that belie expectations of normality and have widespread negative repercussions, focus the media's attention and increase the public's demand for information (Seeger et al. 2003). Secondly, we can assume that enhanced media coverage profoundly affects citizens' views of EU legitimacy. The media play a fundamental role not only in shaping the perceptions and development of the crisis itself but also in driving political and social (re)actions to the crisis and any measures taken to counter it at the elite level.[22] The media function as agenda-setters (for example, highlighting particular aspects of crisis and actors who are dealing with crisis); as crisis actors themselves (for example, by exacerbating a critical situation or creating financial "panics"); and perhaps above all, as the general "interpreter of public voice" (amplifying popular perceptions of blame for crisis). Thirdly, we can assume that perceptions of crisis responses and solutions vary between countries and constituencies and that differences in crisis coverage between countries and different media outlets (e.g., online-offline) matter. The mass media and increasingly also social media are in this sense the main drivers of public contestation between the countries of the EU, supporting a confrontational style between national media audiences and, quite often, reinforcing national identity stereotypes. German and Greek media users in particular are familiar with the populist style of some of their main media outlets regularly labeling Southern Europeans as 'lazy' and 'unreliable' and Northern Europeans as 'calculating' and 'vindictive' in the context of the Eurocrisis.

Drawing on a country comparison of most salient online news coverage and commenting in France, Germany, Greece, the Netherlands, and Norway, the author and collaborators have found strong evidence on how the public legitimation process of the EU polity is shaped by the way media spheres are reacting to the Eurocrisis (Michailidou et al. 2014).[23] Our comparative findings indicate a strong technocratic hegemony of journalistic news framing on the Eurocrisis. EU spokespersons, governments, and professional journalists often communicate about EU public policy choices as the 'only available alternative.' The question of public consent becomes secondary, as expert choices cannot be negotiated or compromised. Public communication about EU politics is in this sense used by professional communicators (e.g., PR specialists or EU correspondents) to translate the EU jargon of elites and experts into a common language to be understood by those who are in a less privileged position and lack the knowledge and insights of the experts. EU political mediation requires some exercise of translation, which includes the use of political rhetoric, trust-generating symbols, and mass-mediated messages but which often disregards the possibility of entering into an argumentative exchange with the lay public. In the current situation of crisis, such a technocratic regime of governance by default has been set up by the enhanced cooperation between the International Monetary Fund (IMF), the European Commission, and the European Central Bank (ECB) (the aforementioned *Troika*). Politicians, and in particular the governments of the member states, act as the principal mediators of the *Troika*. Their use of the mass media is mainly restricted to transmitting the 'no-choice' rescue packages but not to contesting it or pointing out possible alternatives. This declamatory style of communication of the governments reverses previous trends of politicization and the hesitant steps taken to open EU governance to electoral authorization and control. Mylonas, in his critical analysis of the German tabloid *Bildzeitung*, speaks of a "hegemonic discursive construction of the EU's current [2012] economic crisis, as it is articulated by political and economic elites and by mass media" (Mylonas 2012: 646). From a political economy perspective, journalists are seen as entrapped in a 'free market economistic ideology,' which determines the hegemony of news production and interpretation.

Crisis publicity is interpreted here by critical media scholars as an instrument of social control. Through the 'culturalization' of crisis and the creation of country scapegoats (such as Greece), the hegemonic center of Europe is accused of fighting political struggles of capitalist restructuring of the EU, diverting from the roots of global crisis and reiterating neoliberal worldviews as the only available alternatives (Brunkhorst 2012). In our own study of Eurocrisis reporting in online news media, we could confirm that technocratic and political elite actors (that is, political actors in decision-making positions) dominate media coverage of the Eurocrisis in professional news platforms, and their public statements virtually never contain any critique or hint of doubt of their own actions. This combined with the seemingly 'neutral' crisis framing that news reporters adopt—namely, most frequently simply presenting the actions of various decision-makers as facts rather than provide commentary or analysis of those—leaves the technocratic hegemony discourse virtually unchallenged (Michailidou et al. 2014).

The technocratic governance of crisis combined with the depoliticizing strategies of governments has thus resulted in a communication vacuum. The transparency of EU crisis governance is low, while at the same time the demands for publicity by increasingly concerned citizens are rising. How can EU and national governing institutions be held accountable under these conditions and how are responsibilities attributed in public-media discourse?

The new secrecy of government can be seen as the hour of critical journalism. Journalists from several countries can help forge a common European public discourse on the causes and solutions of the crisis, which is different from the official discourse promoted by the *Troika* that is in charge of crisis governance. This is where the role of online news media is key, as they provide an alternative but not marginal sphere for crisis discourse that does not necessarily follow the narrative and frames found in mainstream offline media reporting. The online media sphere gives voice to investigative and critical journalists who may no longer be welcomed in established media organizations because they do not follow the preferred crisis narrative. In a vicious circle, quality journalism in many parts of Europe enters itself in its deepest crisis because many newspapers or television, due to crisis-related recession, can no longer afford it,[24] and even in the richer countries of the North only few news organizations are willing to pay for expensive cross-border investigations (Örnebring 2013). In response to these deficits, the online media sphere offers the alternative to open a more participatory arena of news-making and distribution, where readers' views appear alongside those of professional journalists but do not necessarily coincide in their perspective of the crisis. Under these conditions, the *Troika* faces constraints of publically justifying their choices and policies in response to investigative journalism and the critical attention of the public. It is then unlikely that the concerted action by the *Troika* to create publicity by forced consent can impose a hegemonic discourse on the media. The public controversy around the highly unpopular measures taken to rescue the Euro rather opens the possibility that ideas of 'alternative Europe' or of 'European resistance' also become salient in public discourses across the European press. In addition, the press in different European countries can present perspectives from other member states to foster a cross-national understanding on the crisis.

This picture of a 'repoliticization' trend uniting critical journalists and protest actors would be incomplete, however, without also paying attention to the polarizations and structural divides of European elites and audiences. As regards the emerging divisions, a structuring element of politicization in the Eurozone debt crisis is related to the new transnational elite divisions between executives from creditor and indebted countries. The inter-Eurozone conflict field is structured around a powerful European core of "strong" countries (especially Germany and France) on the one hand and a European periphery of "weak," relatively indebted countries (Greece, Portugal, Spain, Ireland, and Italy), which have harsh austerity measures imposed upon them, on the other hand. Overall, there is very high potential for deep and long-term divisions between these blocs over the terms of EU membership. Populist backlashes are likely in the media frenzy to attribute blame to other countries and to return to "identity politics" pitting pro-integrationist elites against nationalist and/or xenophobic publics. In all Eurozone countries, the bailout measures are contested by populist parties, which evoke publicly held stereotypes and possess positions that are often given prime exposure in mainstream media discourse. Nationalist populism is in this sense represented not only by a general rise in populist nationalist parties but also, sometimes even more prominently, by the spread of media populism as manifested in tabloids and new social media formats (Mazzoleni 2003).

The specific collective identities that tabloid media mobilize (for example, "sovereign national people versus EU financial technocrats" or "Greeks versus Germans") are constructions that tell us about the groups and relationships forming within the conflict. They publicly communicate emergent conflicts between groups over the new structural inequalities generated by neoliberal financial capitalism (manifested in monetary union) in the region. Mediatized public contestation is in this sense a crucial element in the attribution of responsibilities; the salience of new divisions (North-South, Nordics vs. the rest of the EU, etc.); and the demarcation of new national or transnational spaces of democracy, belonging, and solidarity. Cultural, social, and political norms are brought under public scrutiny through media debates. Their meanings are contested, dismissed, reconfigured, or strengthened (for example, the principle of solidarity among EU countries and questions of justice and popular sovereignty with regard to the repercussions of the Stability Pact for the weaker Eurozone countries). Crisis contestation in the media sphere can furthermore facilitate transcultural encounters and exchange of meanings (for example, organization of protests across countries and the mingling of diverse cultures across linguistic divides).

Relating media dynamics back to the contentious dynamics of EU crisis communication, our findings indicate that new and old media play a crucial role in meeting the needs for recognition, political expression, and economic well-being of European citizens affected by crisis. The role of media here goes beyond their effect on individual users, defining personal preferences and identities; it encompasses the collective, which is embraced by these evolving media practices and cultures, giving expression to the economic, social-identitarian, and political needs of vulnerable citizens (Couldry 2012). By mediating between a politics of civil society, a new politics of redistribution, and a new identitarian politics as well as by amplifying these conflicts in an often sensationalist way, the mass media form Europeans' collective consciousness and knowledge concerning their mutual dependencies and responsibilities in times of crisis. A trend toward media populism becomes apparent not only in inputs by Eurosceptic political parties, which are made salient by mainstream media, but also in the many user comments and reactions that give voice to resentments against elites and against political representatives. The dynamics of EU polity contestation are in this sense self-sufficient, expanding the horizon for the self-identification and self-expression of a European collective. Autonomy is thus given back to citizens by new interactive media formats, turning the current crisis into an experimental field for interpreting their collective experiences and asking for political empowerment and the expansion of rights in a European context. Media use is an integral part of citizens' everyday practices and, as such, can help constitute a transnational political and social space as part of the lifeworld experiences of Europeans. Crisis as a moment of society-building is intrinsically related to this unfolding media drama. The different representations of European societies as "being in crisis" that are conveyed by the media become a signifier that potentially unifies Europeans' experiences and allows them to share interpretations of their common destiny.[25]

NOTES

1. On the mainstreaming of Euroscepticism see Leconte (2010) and Ray (2007).

2. This link between EU politicization and democratization is discussed in Statham and Trenz (2014) and Risse (2014a, 2014b). See also my previous thoughts on an inbuilt 'democratic functionalism' in the EU system of governance in Trenz and Eder (2004).

3. As noted by Andrew Glencross: http://blogs.lse.ac.uk/europpblog/2014/03/25/europes-crises-offer-ample-opportunities-for-teachers-to-illustrate-the-importance-of-european-integration-to-students/?fb_action_ids=10152279477159020&fb_action_types=og.likes

4. See, for example, Yanis Varoufakis's thoughts on the need for an enlightened crisis government, a document that was widely distributed through alternative media and within academic circles before the new Syriza government was formed in Greece in January 2015. http://yanisvaroufakis.eu/2014/02/03/germanys-choice-authoritarianism-or-hegemony/ (last accessed on August 8, 2015)

5. As Claus Offe (2013: 603) soberly concludes, the EU in its present form is troubled not only by a lack of power of taxation and an inability to cope with a much-reduced budget but is also composed of member states with governments that are unwilling to support EU solidarity and redistribution and unlikely to take any steps in this direction in the near future.

6. Presidency Conclusions. Lisbon European Council, March 23 and 24, 2000 (available at: http://consilium.europa.eu/ueDocs/cms_Data/docs/pressData/en/ec/00100-r1.en0.htm, last accessed on August 15, 2015)

7. Deep budget cuts are not only reported in the defense sector but also in the field of humanitarian action since member states could not agree on setting priorities in aid policies. See the report of FRIDE, edited by Grevi and Keohane (2013).

8. The new 'disintegration paradigm' in EU studies is discussed controversially by Krastev (2012), Scheller and Eppler (2014), and Schmitter (2012).

9. For an overview of the sociological literature on crisis and its status in modern society see Holten (1987) and, more recently, Vobruba (2014).

10. For the most important contributions on the effects of crisis on the balance of political institutions and its democratic implication see the collections of Piattoni (2015) and Isakhan and Slaughter (2014).

11. See the FP7 *Lifewhat* project: 'Living in Hard Times. Citizens' Resilience in Times of Crisis' (2013–2016) (http://www.livewhat.unige.ch/) and the FP7 *Rescue* project: 'Citizens' Resilience in Times of Crisis' (http://www.rescueproject.eu/our_member.html).

12. For a typology of resilience see Handmer and Dovens (1996), Hearn Morrow (2008: 2–3).

13. See my elaboration in chapter 3 on social transnationalism.

14. According to this critical understanding, the new politics of resilience are seen as an intrinsic element of "neoliberal governance." They individualize responses to collective problems, redistribute responsibilities to individual members of society, and "train" individuals to cope with higher levels of insecurity and risk. For a critical review of this literature and an attempt to formulate an emancipatory account of "resilience" as "adaptive democratic self-government," see J. Schmidt (2014).

15. For a summary of this debate on EU politicization in the context of crisis see Statham and Trenz (2014), Risse (2014a, 2014b).

16. This does not imply that the 'return to protest' necessarily reverses previous trends of incorporating civil society organizations as part of the governance structures of the EU (Jobert and Kohler-Koch 2008). The EU's multilevel architecture, which is reflected in a multilevel European civil society structure, makes it likely for civil society organizations to opt for

cooperative roles while at the same time fundamentally questioning their roles in EU and global governance.

17. For this ambivalence between redistributive and identitarian conflicts as structuring elements of EU politicization see Statham and Trenz (2014) and Risse (2014a).

18. Quoted from Giorgio Agamben: "The 'Latin Empire' should strike back." Originally published in *Libération*, March 26, 2013. An English version can be retrieved at http://www. voxeurop.eu/en/content/article/3593961-latin-empire-should-strike-back; last accessed on December 20, 2014.

19. Quoted in Ancelovici (2015: 193).

20. The collaboration of Asimina Michailidou in drafting this section on the role of the media as an amplifier of EU crisis is gratefully acknowledged. For a full elaboration and documentation of the research findings of our comparative online media survey of crisis-related debates, see Michailidou et al. (2014).

21. On the role of the media in constructing and diffusing European crisis narratives, see Cross and Ma (2015a; 2015b), Picard (2015), and Michailidou and Trenz (2015).

22. The research field of crisis communication and the media is demarcated by Coombs and Holladay (2010) and Raboy and Dagenais (1992). Considering the press coverage of the Eurocrisis and its implications for public understandings and legitimacy of EU institutions, see the contributions in Picard (2015).

23. Our study, part of the ARENA Eurotrans/EuroDiv projects, included the two most popular online news media in France, Germany, Greece, Norway, the Netherlands, Spain, Sweden, and the UK. We focused on news coverage of three specific Eurocrisis events: the agreement on Greece's first 'bail-out' in May 2010; the 2011 announcement by then-Prime Minister George Papandreou of a referendum on whether Greece would accept a second loan agreement; and the ratification by the German parliament of the second loan agreement for Greece in December 2012. For further details see, Michailidou et al. (2014).

24. Recall the shutdown of the Hellenic Broadcasting Corporation in June 2013.

25. See my interpretation of the role of 'mediated repersentative politics' in the EU (Trenz 2014.)

Conclusion

An Overview of the Discursive Field of Europeanization: Unified, Fragmented, or Complementary?

In this book, I have investigated variants of Europeanization as a form of social imagination of the unity and diversity of European society. My sociological account of Europeanization has moved away from a purely 'analytical use' of Europeanization as a one-directional process of change that is measured and quantified in terms of shifting power relations and causal impact. Instead, a discursive approach to Europeanization has been developed, turning the object of analysis (the EU and its potential impact) into the main protagonist of what can be termed the narrative construction of a European society. The field of practices that becomes relevant for the development and promotion of such discourses about Europe's unity and diversity is populated by the various proponents and opponents of European integration: by institutional and governmental actors; by think tanks and other agencies as promoters of ideas and innovation; by the media organizations and infrastructures that help diffuse and frame such ideas and discourses; by citizens in their role as addressees of EU institutions and programs as well as in their role as critical and often creative respondents; by the critical voice of public intellectuals; and ultimately also by Europe's scientific observers, who constitute the influential European studies community and in this role propose explanatory models and causalities about the functioning of the European Union.

Turning the 'science of Europe' into the object of analysis allows four main narratives to be distinguished. These are used to construct Europe as a meaningful social entity and to interpret its historical origins, processes of change, and future trajectories. This saga of Europeanization is at the core of

European studies, yet it is told differently by different disciplines that claim to contribute to the science of Europe. Europeanization differentiates into narratives (or 'sagas' or 'tales,' as I have labeled them in this book), which are ways of constructing causalities about impact and social change attributed to Europe. These differentiated narratives make up the many faces of Europeanization. At the same time, these scientific narratives inform popular culture, are filtered and amplified by the European media, and as such reach a European audience, which interprets and translates them into everyday experiences.

For many of its followers, the saga of Europeanization is virtually a confession of faith in the irreversibility of European integration, for which evidence is collected, narrated, and interpreted. In popular-scientific terms, this is turned into the natural law interpretation of Europeanization as something taken for granted and given, as the background of our everyday interactions, as the template for institution-building and society-building. Such a natural history of Europeanization is, of course, itself a narrative construct, but it has powerful consequences for the imagination of people who 'live' this history, interpret it as part of their everyday lifeworlds, and translate it into collective choices and action.

The Eurocrisis has thrown into doubt the functionalist and natural history account of European integration, which is being replaced by new politicized dynamics through which not only governance (in terms of EU regulation and decision-making) but also government (in terms of the legitimacy of EU polity design) are fundamentally challenged. The austerity regime imposed by the EU is perceived as a form of heteronomy and domination, placing citizens on alert with regard to the state of democracy. At the same time, the policies and institution-building processes that are linked to crisis governance continue the automatism of integration. Based on the idea of the irreversibility of the common currency, the European Central Bank and the governments and institutions supporting it have reinforced the iron cage of Europeanization. EU institutions and governments thus continue the myth of a natural history of Europeanization that becomes common destiny rather than choice. The saga of Europeanization provides the standard solution for resolving integration problems by constantly taking further steps of integration. The same logic is applied in debating the Greek debt crisis: what matters is always the superior rationality of Europe and not the particularity of a member state. The fact that human suffering (as in the case of Greece) is now tolerated to defend the inviolability of the European project (or simply of the monetary union) turns the idea of Europe (and its common currency) into a fetish, which is defended by taboos rather than by arguments.

In confronting the current crisis, the old school of progressive Europeanism finds itself in an increasingly defensive position, which leads to normatively significant changes in the original plot of the story of Europeanization as synonymous with emancipation and democratization. The rationality of Europe is no longer deliberated in light of Europeans' well-being but is instead enshrined in the irrevocable standards of integration, which must be defended even at the price of transforming Europe into an authoritarian hegemon. Progressive Europeanists have begun decoupling economic rationality from the normativity of the European project. Progressive Europeanization without the normative and humanitarian appeal is the ultimate rescue of a disillusioned political elite, who have learned that their ideas were insufficiently spelled out to convince the masses (as in the failed project of EU constitution-making) but who still insist on the project's validity, which no longer passes the test of being synonymous with progress in reality.

A political sociology of European integration is useful for testing the conditions under which such counterfactual assumptions can be upheld and the consequences that this has for the legitimacy of the underlying systems (both national and European).[1] Europeanization is still linked to processes of institutionalization, which are complemented by processes of society-building from below, both with regard to Europeans' shared everyday life experiences and enhanced public contestation and resistance. In this new interpretative context, the acclaimed inescapability and irreversibility of Europeanization is no longer taken as a social law that explains progress toward a more enlightened European society, emancipated from the constraints of the national. It instead becomes the fate of those who are obliged to suffer its negative consequences. Europeanization as fateful history bears in itself, however, the seeds of once again turning into a progressive force, one driven by negative accounts and experiences and the effort to overcome them (not least by grasping the opportunities offered by European integration: citizenship, mobility, resilience, and resistance). Beyond the iron cage, Europeanization remains a social force for formulating new normative horizons and reorganizing social relationships. Such a process is not only necessarily conflictual; it is also intrinsically political. Resistance to Europeanization is not excluded but is expected, and it is not a major rupture but is instead based on a continuity of practices and experiences. Europeans continue to be haunted by the eternal struggle to achieve the vision of unity in diversity.

From this final perspective of continuity in the discursive contestation of Europe, the more recent salience of a new politics of identity can also be interpreted as a response to ongoing Europeanization. This contradicts other scholars' accounts, which cast the new identity politics as a turning point that calls into question the viability of the European integration project. For authors such as Jan Zielonka, these types of deep identitarian conflict disrupt integration beyond remedy. Has European integration, as an effect of politicization and deep identity conflicts, therefore come to a halt (Zielonka 2012)? As I argued in chapter 5, it remains difficult to speak of a failure of Europeanization since the European project of building supranational unity can neither be verified nor falsified. History does not come to an end.

The sociological account of Europeanization as society-building, which I took the opportunity to develop in previous chapters, is meant to de-dramatize particular moments of accelerated change and crisis. The purpose of this book has not been to explain this project's likelihood of success or failure but rather to contextualize it historically and to identify the different social forces that shape it and account for its ongoing contestation. The historicized account of European resistance (like Euroscepticism) and the kind of "deep conflicts" linked to it instead invite us to apply a perspective of long-term constitutionalization of the EU. Constitutionalization is used here in a broad sense, meaning that institutions cannot escape the normativity of the project of European enlightenment and modernity and must accommodate demands for rights and justice that are raised by society in a context of the self-constitution and confinement of a democratic political order (Eriksen 2014). Deep conflicts over European integration, as have been observed in the past years, should in this sense be reinterpreted as long-term constitutional conflicts over the normativity of political and societal order. They are consequential conflicts in the unfinished process of the EU's constitutionalization and simultaneously a continuation of its ongoing (yet equally unfinished) democratization (Trenz and Eder 2004).

The question remains whether there is also a means of overcoming these fragmented tales of Europeanization, of recollecting the different threads of the story and using them to construct a metanarrative, a story about the stories, which allows us to unify our knowledge and experiences. Three solutions are provided to arrive at such a metanarrative of Europeanization. One is intra-scientific, the second is inter-scientific, and the third can be called ideological or critical. The intra-scientific solution is based on measurement of the account's accuracy and its correspondence to what is called 'factual.' The idea of uniting the fictional and the factual underlies the EU studies approach of empiricism and causality. It mainly applies to short-range case studies, for example, concerning the implementation of EU regulation or the transfer of rules and norms within particular policy sectors (Exadaktylos and Radaelli 2009). The inter-scientific solution is based on the magic formula of interdisciplinarity as a means of overcoming the functional differentiation of science, engaging in a parallel reading of the semantics of Europeanization, and testing possible recombinations. The need for interdisciplinarity is emphasized by the broader European studies community and its attempts to establish comparative research programs for middle-range and broad-range surveys of the Europeanization of politics, culture, and society.[2]

The third solution is to enter the competition between the narrative accounts of Europeanization and to critically assess Europeanization in terms of its proclaimed aims and its success or failure. An important element of this

critical agenda is to engage in normative debate as to whether Europeanization is desirable, needed, or appropriate. The debate on Europeanization then
shifts from the attribution of causalities to the validation of norms. Does
Europeanization enhance problem solving? Does it lead to 'good governance' or to better governance? How does Europeanization affect democracy?
Does it constrain or even damage national democracy? Or does it open new
paths to enhancing democracy beyond the nation-state?

My aim has been to study competition within the discursive field of
Europeanization. Different accounts of European society not only compete
with each other but also enter into dispute with parallel accounts of national
society-building. The credo of Europeanization discourses is that the European and national frames of society-building are compatible or even complementary and that the one shall not substitute the other. Yet this claim of
compatibility is itself contested and interpreted differently in different times
and places, resulting in unequal and asynchronous developments. The saga of
Europeanization can thus be linked to the discursive dynamics of legitimacy
contestation between member states and the EU as well as between the
various actors involved in this process. Such a discursive understanding of
Europeanization is highly applicable to the transdisciplinary debate on state
transformation. It assists understanding of the reconfiguration of political
legitimacy in a world in which fully sovereign and independent nation-states
are no longer the sole guarantors of welfare, peace, and security.

This intrinsic relationship between discursive Europeanization and legitimation furthermore enhances our understanding of the responsiveness of
different narratives that compete for salience and attention in the public
sphere. We have seen, for instance, how Euroscepticism can respond to
heroic Europeanism but can equally react to the stalemate of banal Europeanism. To break this stalemate, even European institutions have repeatedly
sought to relaunch the heroic idea of Europe, to constitutionalize or to formulate a new narrative in support of the European integration project. Another
common horizon for critical debate within the European studies community
is controversy over the success or failure of Europeanization. To speak of the
European success story or of failed Europeanization reminds us once again of
the intrinsic normativity of European studies approaches and their accounts
of social integration.

The ongoing competition among these narrations and among their social
carriers confines a social space of dense interactions and close mutual observation that differs significantly from the nationalistic scenario of a fragmented Europe marked by incommensurable cultural frictions and clashes of collective identification. It is unlikely that this constellation of creative cultural
and social interchange will be replaced by the dominance of any of these four
narratives in the near future. Any doomsaying about the imploding fragmented Europe scenario that is sometimes evoked in relation to crisis is thus

misplaced. Narratives of Europeanization do not represent closed and incommensurable worldviews but instead live and are developed through their open confrontation. Neither do they result in mutually exclusive attitudes toward European integration (that is, either pro-European or anti-European) nor in a new people's dissensus on European integration that is sharply demarcated from the heroic discourse of triumph of the past. The four narrations do not suggest such a temporal sequence in the sense of an evolution of European integration from permissive consensus to constraining dissensus and failure even though such a temporal construction is often found as an element of narration.

Sociologists have learned to mistrust evolutionary accounts of society and have emphasized the role of uncertainty, ambiguity, and contingency in their models of societal change and order. In this tradition, I have found ambiguity in the struggle over the legitimacy of a transnational political order, which has been manifested, in particular, in the debates accompanying the constitutionalization process of the EU, dividing European populations into enthusiastic supporters of a postnational Union and fierce defenders of the nation-state. I have also emphasized, however, that there is a degree of consensus surrounding the underlying principles and core values of the modern political order, which drives such contestation and makes narrations mutually understandable. There is a cultural and cognitive repertoire upon which Europeans can draw in their disputes. Narratives of Europeanizations might remain ambiguous, but they are not arbitrary. Ambiguity is even an asset for the proponents and opponents of narration, who can develop flexible strategies and more easily adapt to unexpected events or to the unassertiveness of the EU's fledgling society (Fossum and Trenz 2006a; Schrag Sternberg 2013). The protagonists of Europeanization often engage in multiple narratives or shift between narrations. They tend to be open toward new arguments—either strategically, because they adapt to new discursive constellations, or sometimes even because they learn and are convinced by the argumentative strength of their opponent. Sociology contributes in this sense to our understanding of how narratives relate to each other in a creative way, confining the discursive field of Europeanization.

This ambiguity in interpreting and making sense of Europe is also reflected in public receptions, for instance, in the way in which individuals often consider a political entity such as the EU simultaneously negatively and positively (van Ingelgom 2014). Ambivalence toward the EU is even found to increase with the level of political sophistication since individuals with enhanced levels of knowledge are particularly likely to hold both negative and positive opinions about the EU (Stöckel 2012).[3] A narrative reconstruction of the discursive field of Europeanization is in this sense a good substitute for one-dimensional measurements of political attitudes (as, for instance, in public opinion surveys). As pointed out by Stöckel (2012), ambivalence of attitudes toward the EU should not be interpreted as indifference but instead reflects a growing engagement with the EU. Support for or opposition to the EU matters for ordinary citizens, but even though this question has become more relevant for citizens over time, the available answers have at the same time become less certain. The availability of competing European narratives is no such substitute for certainty. Narratives are not programs for collective action and organization; they are, rather, points of orientation for interpreting European integration and assessing its positive or negative consequences. The narration of European society stands for this growing engagement, not for an increase of certainty about, orientation of, or even support for Europe. For many Europeans, being involved in narration might therefore increase ambivalence yet decrease indifference to Europe.

From our discursive perspective on Europeanization, we can identify the repertoire of knowledge or the underlying cognitive structures of EU opinion formation and their dynamic interlinkage with ongoing political contestation. This delivers an important template for the integration of the multidisciplinary field of EU studies. The four different paths to Europeanization that I followed in the four main chapters of this book provide a shared cognitive and cultural repertoire of knowledge and a normative framework for institution building, public opinion formation, and collective action. They thus link the institutional perspective of European integration studies with the societal perspective, which is at the focus of sociology. There is a continuity of Europeanization as a process that interlinks state and (civil) society through public discourse. Facilitating this interlinkage in Europeans' collective imagination is the major function of narration and of the cognitive and normative apparatus linked to it. I have called this the *narration of European society* without assuming that such a society materializes and arises as a confined place or as an identitarian community. *European society* is a blueprint for democratic contestation. It is a forum for productive conflict in which participants appear like players in a game, who accept some basic rules and know their team members and adversaries (Schrag Sternberg 2013: 227). European society is a game from which some joy is derived and that has some value for its participants. To keep the game going, some kind of motivation is required from its participants, but there is also a shared rule system at their disposal, and there are institutions that establish path dependencies. Interpretative sociology can make an important contribution to our understanding of how EU institution building and EU society building are closely related and are reflexively and communicatively guided by means of cognitive rules, cultural schemes, and norms, which are contained in narration.[4] But this in no way implies that European society will also consolidate in the form of a value- and culture-based community.

The analytical value added by our narrative approach to Europeanization is a clear focus on the dynamics (forms and practices) of meaning-making and interpretation that underlie and drive collective exchanges among the Europeans. The European political order is not only linked to justificatory processes in the negotiation of the validity of norms for application to institution building and the establishment of public authority. The narrations of Europeanization also provide the cognitive foundations of these institution-building and norm-building practices. Such a program of interpretative sociology thus helps connect the normative paradigm of integration alongside the building of democratic institutions and government with the cognitive-communicative processes of the public sphere that enable such institutions to function (O'Mahony 2013). This perspective on narrations as both normatively and cognitively guided interpretations of Europeanization furthermore provides a useful template for historical sociology and the reconstruction of the generation of modern institutions as well as the particular normative rule systems and cultural-cognitive models linked to them. Continuities (in terms of collective learning) and disruptions (in terms of crisis) can thus be traced back from a transnational-European perspective, and cognitive-cultural exchanges across time and space can be rendered comprehensible. Europeanization could ultimately be traced back as a form of collective learning that simultaneously makes visible the potentials for societal change and institutional transformation and thus helps delineate future options for integration and disintegration of the European political and social space.

My proposal of a matrix of four narratives of Europeanization is not intended as a comprehensive and fully instructive how-to guide for a sociological analysis of European society. My distinctions instead represent a research synthesis of my own involvement in interdisciplinary and collaborative projects on selected topics of research. This selection is in part random, which is why I do not claim to deliver here a representative textbook account of a sociology of European integration. Other researchers might wish to further develop this program for an interpretative sociology of Europeanization by emphasizing other useful distinctions of narration. This ongoing revision process of Europe's narrative and ideational inventory is partly informed by new interventions from EU scholars, who creatively reinterpret the 'state of the Union,' the 'nature of the beast,' the 'choices for Europe,' and the trajectory of integration. Research grants and programs funded by the European Union keep this circle of narration going, distribute rewards for persuasive interpretations, and encourage EU scholars to place their interventions in public debates. In the current context (summer 2015), it is, for instance, highly instructive to see how so-called post-crisis accounts of European integration are promoted by public intellectuals and the media, which discuss the rise of the new German hegemony and its rupture with the notion of European solidarity, the European Union of 'equal partners' and 'everyone benefits' scenarios. In response, there is an ongoing shift from institutional accounts of integration and their emphasis on smooth transition and accommodation to political economy accounts of unequal markets and highly divergent economic institutions, practices, and cultures.[5] At the intersection of modern capitalism and social life, a prominent new role is ascribed to the European social substrate, which is searched for in a politicized demos of dual (national and European) identities (Risse 2014a). Such accounts no longer seek to defend EU legitimacy against the template of majoritarian democracy but instead seek pragmatic solutions for reconciling essentially conflictual social relations among the people of Europe in a model of multilevel European democracy or in demoi-cracy.[6] In relation to these event-driven narrative shifts, one must understand the conditions of (often short-term) popularity of such narratives, how they become salient, how media (especially new media) contribute to their diffusion, and how and with what effects institutions adapt to such changes (or, as sometimes suggested, ignore them). Historians could complete this picture by pointing out previous fluctuations in the short-term popularity of these narratives, explain variation across European countries and populations (audiences), and identify factors that condition them. Political scientists could eventually find this matrix useful for analyzing political contention and coalition among political parties (for instance, in the context of European or national election campaigns) and exploring the more direct and often immediate links between narration and legitimation of EU political institutions and governance.

Europeanization ultimately creates a multidisciplinary research field in which we cannot expect to be able to follow a single, straight story line alone. In tracing back the narration of Europeanization, we can learn that European integration is no longer relevant only for bureaucrats and for students who seek to become bureaucrats. Europe has become relevant for sociology, for cultural studies, for media studies, for anthropologists. An upcoming research program will consider how European integration through institutions, norms, and rules shapes the ways in which citizens experience their daily lives as well as their relationships with one another. We call this "Europeanization," and we are aware that this notion and the processes to which it refers remain heavily contested. The tales of Europeanization are not only told by us scientists; they are part of how society interprets itself. As such, they are becoming the story of us all.

NOTES

1. For the following, see also our elaboration upon a political sociology of crisis in Guiraudon et al. (2015).

2. Most universities have established their own interdisciplinary European studies programs, often in collaboration with other programs. Interdisciplinarity also informs the Framework Programmes for collaborative research and the Horizon 2020 calls launched by the European Commission as well as the various research cooperation programs administered by

the European Science Foundation. There is thus an evolving European studies industry that self-referentially promotes its own agenda.

3. My gratitude to an anonymous reviewer of the book manuscript for drawing my attention to these important works on ambivalent EU attitudes, which includes ambiguity in interpretation by academics and by those who commission them.

4. This formulation bears some similarities with our understanding of the dynamics of public communication and the public sphere. Following the classical understanding of the public sphere (Habermas 1989), the latter provides the modes of social integration between the formally organized sphere of the state and the sphere of civil society. But it also fulfils an important function in linking the private sphere of citizens' emotions and everyday encounters with the public complex of culture, knowledge, and procedural rationality. For the reformulation of this Habermasian program in the sense of a cognitive sociology of the public sphere, see O'Mahony (2013: 417–46). For the program of a sociology of knowledge of European integration, see Adler-Nissen and Kropp (2015).

5. As, for instance, manifested in the drama of negotiating the third bailout package in June and July 2015 between the Greek government and the partners of the Eurozone countries. The appearance of a new German hegemon not only horrifies entire populations in the South of Europe. The alarm bells are also sounded by German intellectuals, who accuse the German government of being prepared to "gamble away Germany's postwar reputation" (Jürgen Habermas) or of 'emotional devastation' in the South of Europe (Wolfgang Streeck). See the interview with Jürgen Habermas in *The Guardian* (http://en.protothema.gr/habermas-to-merkel-youre-gambling-away-germany-post-war-reputation/; last accessed on August 17, 2015); his previous intervention, 'Why Angela Merkel is wrong' (http://www.socialeurope.eu/2015/06/why-angela-merkels-is-wrong-on-greece/, last accessed on August 17, 2015); and the article written by Wolfgang Streeck for *Le Monde Diplomatique*: German Hegemony: Unintended and Unwanted (http://wolfgangstreeck.com/2015/05/15/german-hegemony-unintended-and-unwanted/; last accessed on August 17, 2015).

6. For Scharpf (2015), the ground rules for a multilevel European democracy are meant to reduce the domain of EU constitutional law and re-empower national constituencies. Such a substantial reversion of the community method and supremacy of EU law is also contained in the normative program of EU demoi-cracy promoted by political scientists as a normative rule system for a reform of EU governance (Nicolaïdis 2013; Cheneval and Schimmelfennig 2013). A critical reconstruction of this debate in defense of the Habermasian vision of majoritarian democracy at the EU level as a tool of democratic control of EU governance can be found in Gaus (2014), Hurrelmann (2014), and the contributions in Piattoni (2015).

References

Adler-Nissen, R., and Kropp, K. (2015). 'A Sociology of Knowledge Approach to European Integration: Four Analytical Principles.' *Journal of European Integration*, 37(2): 155–173.

Alexander, J. C., Eyerman, R., Giesen, B., Smelser, N. J., and Sztompka, P. (2004). *Cultural Trauma and Collective Identity*. Los Angeles: University of California Press.

Ancelovici, M. (2015). 'Crisis and Contention in Europe: A Political Process.' in H. J. Trenz, C. Ruzza, and V. Guiraudon (eds). *Europe's Prolonged Crisis: The Making or the Unmaking of a Political Union*. (Basingstoke: Palgrave Macmillan), pp. 189–209.

Anderson, P. J. (2004) 'A Flag of Convenience? Discourse and Motivations of the London-Based Eurosceptic Press.' in R. Harmsen and M. Spiering (eds), *Eurscepticism: Party Politics, National Identity and European Integration*. (Amsterdam, NY: Rodopi), pp. 151–170.

Anderson, P. J., Williams, M., and Ogola, G. (2013). *The Future of Quality News Journalism: A Cross-Continental Analysis*. London: Routledge.

Arato, A. (2011). 'Revis(it)ing Civil Society.' in U. Liebert and H. J. Trenz (eds), *The New Politics of European Civil Society*. (London: Routledge), pp. 195–207.

Arditi, B. (2007). *Politics on the Edges of Liberalism: Difference, Populism, Revolution, Agitation*. Edinburgh: Edinburgh University Press.

Ash, T. G. (1993). *In Europe's Name: Germany and the Divided Continent*. New York: Random House.

Bach, M. (2008). *Europa ohne Gesellschaft: Politische Soziologie der Europäischen Integration*. Wiesbaden: VS Verlag.

Bach, M. (2014). 'Paradoxes Europa. Zur (Eigen-)Dynamik der Eurokrise.' *Serie Europa—Europe Series 03-2014*, available at: http://www.uni-leipzig.de/leus/wp-content/uploads/2014-03-Bach-Paradoxes-Europa.pdf (last accessed September 3, 2015).

Balibar, E. (2014). *Equaliberty: Political Essays*. Durham and London: Duke University Press.

Bartolini, S. (2005). *Restructuring Europe: Centre Formation, System Building, and Political Structuring between the Nation State and the European Union*. New York: Oxford University Press.

Bauböck, R. (2007). 'Why European Citizenship? Normative Approaches to Supranational Union.' *Theoretical Inquiries in Law*, 8(2): 453–488.

Bauman, Z. (1998). *Globalization. The Human Consequences*. New York: Columbia University Press.

Bauman, Z. (2004). *Europe: An Unfinished Adventure*. Oxford: Wiley.

Beck, U. (2003). 'Cosmopolitanism as Critique: Toward a New Critical Theory with a Cosmopolitan Intent.' *Constellations*, 10(4): 453–468.

Beck, U. (2005). *The Cosmopolitan Vision*. Cambridge: Polity Press.

Beck, U. (2013). *German Europe*. Cambridge: Polity Press.

Beck, U., Giddens, A., and Lash, S. (1994). *Reflexive Modernization: Politics, Tradition and Aesthetics in the Modern Social Order*. Stanford: Stanford University Press.

Beck, U. and Grande, E. (2007). *Cosmopolitan Europe*. Cambridge: Polity Press.

Bettin, G. and Recchi, E. (2005). *Comparing European Societies: Towards a Sociology of the EU*. Milano: Monduzzi.

Bieler, A. (2011). 'Labour, New Social Moevements and the Resistance to Neoliberal Restructuring in Europe.' *New Political Economy*, 16(2): 163–182.

Billig, M. (1995). *Banal Nationalism*. London: Sage.

Blokker, P. (2009). 'Democracy through the Lens of 1989: Liberal Triumph or Radical Turn?' *International Journal of Politics, Culture, and Society*, 22(3): 273–290.

Bohman, J., and Rehg, W. (1997). *Deliberative Democracy*. Cambridge, MA: Massachusettes Institute for Technology Press.

Boje, T., Steenbergen, V., and Walby, S. (1999) *European Societies: Fusion or Fission?* London: Routledge.

Boltanski, L., and Thévenot, L. (1999). 'The Sociology of Critical Capacity.' *European Journal of Social Theory*, 2(3): 359–378.

Boltanski, L. and Thévenot, L. (2006). *On Justification: Economies of Worth*. Princeton, NJ: Princeton University Press.

Bondebjerg, I., Novrup Redvall, E., and Higson, A., (eds). (2015). *European Cinema and Television. Cultural Policy and Everyday Life*. Basingstoke: Palgrave Macmillan.

Börner, S., and Eigmüller, M. (2015). 'Comparing Processes of Change: How European Integration Can Learn from Past Experiences.' In S. Börner and M. Eigmüller (eds), *European Integration, Processes of Change and the National Experience* (Basingstoke: Palgave Macmillan), pp. 3–25.

Börzel, T. A. (1999) 'Towards Convergence in Europe? Institutional Adaptation to Europeanization in Germany and Spain.' *Journal of Common Market Studies*, 37(4): 573–596.

Börzel, T., and Risse, T. (2003). 'Conceptualising the Domestic Impact of Europe.' in K. Featherstone and C. Radelli (eds), *The Politics of Europeanization* (Oxford: Oxford University Press).

Börzel, T. A., and Risse, T. (2011). 'From Europeanisation to Diffusion: Introduction.' *West European Politics*, 35(1): 1–19.

Bouza Garcia, L. (2015). *Participatory Democracy and Civil Society in the EU. Agenda-Setting and Institutionalisation*. Basingstoke: Palgave Macmillan.

Braun, D., and Tausendpfund, M. (2014). 'The Impact of the Euro Crisis on Citizens' Support for the European Union.' *Journal of European Integration*, 36(3): 231–245.

Bronk, R., and Jacoby, W. (2013). 'Avoiding Monocultures in the European Union: The Case for the Mutual Recognition of Difference in Conditions of Uncertainty.' *LEQS Paper 67, LSE 'Europe in Question' Discussion Paper Series*.

Brüggemann, M. (2010). 'Information Policy and the Public Sphere: EU Communications and the Promises of Dialogue and Transparency.' *Javnost-The Public*, 17(1): 5–22.

Brunkhorst, H. (2004). 'A Polity without a state? European Constitutionalism between Evolution and Revolution.' in E. O. Eriksen, J. E. Fossum, and A. J. Menéndez (eds), *Developing a Constitution for Europe* (London: Routledge), pp. 88–105.

Brunkhorst, H. (2006). 'The Legitimation Crisis of the European Union.' *Constellations*, 13(2): 165–180.

Brunkhorst, H. (2012). 'Kollektiver Bonapartismus? Demokratie in der europäischen Krise.' *Blätter für deutsche und international Politik* 12(4): 83–93.

Brunkhorst, H. (2014). *Das doppelte Gesicht Europas. Zwischen Kapitalismus und Demokratie*. Frankfurt a. M.: Suhrkamp.

Bruter, M. (2004). 'Civic and Cultural Components of a European Identity. A Pilot Model of Measurement of Citizens Levels of European Identity.' In R. Herrmann, Th. Risse, M. B. Brewer (eds), *Transnational Identities: Becoming European in the EU* (Lanham, MD: Rowman and Littlefield), pp. 186–213.

Bruter, M. (2005). *Citizens of Europe? The Emergence of a Mass European Identity*. Basingstoke: Palgrave Macmillan.

Bruter, M. (2008). 'Legitimacy, Euroscepticism and Identity in the European Union: Problems of Measurement, Modelling and Paradoxical Patterns of Influence.' *Journal of Contemporary European Research*, 4(4): 273–285.

Burgi, N. (2014). 'Societies without Citizens: The Anomic Impacts of Labor Market Restructuring and the Erosion of Social Rights in Europe.' *European Journal of Social Theory*, 17(3): 290–306.

Buttler, F., Ingensiep, C., Israel, S., and Reimann, C. (2014). 'Connected Europe(ans)? The Quantitative Measurement of Horizontal Europeanisation.' *Pre-prints of Research Group 'Horizontal Europeanisation' 2014 - 02*, available at: http://www.horizontal-europeanization.eu/downloads/pre-prints/PP_HoEu_2014-02_buttler_etal.pdf (last accessed September 3, 2015).

Byrnes, T. A., and Katzenstein, P. J., (2006) *Religion in an Expanding Europe*. Cambridge: Cambridge University Press.

Calhoun, C. (2002). 'Imagining Solidarity: Cosmopolitanism, Constitutional Patriotism, and the Public Sphere.' *Public Culture* 14(1): 147–171.

Calhoun, C. (2003). 'The Class Consciousness of Frequent Travellers: Towards a Critique of Actually Existing Cosmopolitanism.' In D. Archibugi and M. Koenig-Archibugi (eds), *Debating Cosmopolitics* (New York: Verso), pp. 86–116.

Canovan, M. (2002). 'Taking Politics to the People: Populism as the Ideology of Democracy.' In Y. Mény and Y. Surel (eds), *Democracies and the Populist Challenge* (Basingstoke: Palgrave Macmillan), pp. 25–44.

Cappella, J. N., and Jamieson, K. (1997). *Spiral of Cynicism: The Press and the Public Good*. Oxford: Oxford University Press.

Casanova, J. (2006). 'Religion, European Secular Identities, and European Integration.' In T. A. Byrnes and P. J. Katzenstein (eds), *Religion in an Expanding Europe* (Cambridge: Cambride University Press), pp. 65–92.

Castelli, P., and Froio, G. C. (2014). 'Opposition in the EU and Opposition to the EU: Soft and Hard Euroscepticism in Italy in the Time of Austerity.' *Institute of European Democrats Working Paper*, available at: https://www.academia.edu/5481179/Opposition_in_the_EU_and_opposition_to_the_EU_Soft_and_hard_Euroscepticism_in_Italy_in_the_time_of_austerity (last accessed September 3, 2015).

Castoriadis, C. (1975). *The Imaginary Institution of Society*. Cambridge, MA: MIT Press.

Chalmers, D. (2013). 'Democratic Self-Government in Europe. Domestic Solutions to the EU Legitimacy Crisis.' *Policy Network Paper May 2013*, available at: http://www.policy-network.net/publications/4399/Democratic-Self-Government-in-Europe (last accessed 03.09.2015).

Chambers, S. (2009). 'Rhetoric and the Public Sphere: Has Deliberative Democracy Abandoned Mass Democracy?' *Political Theory*, 37(3): 323–350.

Champeau, S., Closa, C., Innerarity, D., and Maduro, M. P. (2014). *The Future of Europe: Democracy, Legitimacy and Justice after the Euro Crisis*. Lanham: Rowman & Littlefield.

Chandler, D. (2014). *Resilience: The Governance of Complexity*. London: Routledge.

Cheneval, F., and Schimmelfennig, F. (2013). 'The Case for Demoicracy in the European Union.' *Journal of Common Market Studies*, 51(2): 334–350.

Closa, C. (2004). 'Deliberative Constitutional Politics and the Value-Based Constitution.' In C. Closa and J. E. Fossum (eds), *Deliberative Constitutional Politics in the EU* (Oslo: ARENA Report 5/04).

Closa, C. (2010). 'Negotiating the Past: Claims for Recognition and Policies of Memory in the EU.' *Instituto de Políticas y Bienes Públicos(IPP), CCHS-CSIC,Working Paper, Number 8*, available: http://hdl.handle.net/10261/24430 (last accessed September 3, 2015).

Collier, D., Hidalgo, F. D., and Maciuceanu, A. O. (2006). 'Essentially contested concepts: Debates and applications.' *Journal of Political Ideologies*, 11(3): 211–246.

Conill, J., Castells, M., and Cardenas, A. (2011). 'Beyond the Crisis the Emergence of Alternative Economic Practices.' In M. Castells, C. J. and G. Cardoso (eds), *Aftermath: the Cultures of the Economic Crisis*, (Oxford: Oxford University Press), pp. 210–248.

Conti, N., and Memoli, V. (2015). 'The Emergence of a New Party in the Italian Party System: Rise and Fortunes of the Five Star Movement.' *West European Politics*, 38(3): 516–534.

Conway, M., and Patel, K. K. (2010). *Europeanization in the Twentieth Century: Historical Approaches*. Basingstoke: Palgrave Macmillan.

Cooke, M. (2006). *Re-Presenting the Good Society*. Cambridge, MA: MIT Press.

Coombs, W. T., and Holladay, S. J. (2010). *The Handbook of Crisis Communication*. Oxford: Wiley.

Cooper, I. (2008). 'Subsidiarity and Autonomy in the European Union.' In L. W. Pauly and W. D. Coleman (eds), *Global Ordering: Institutions and Autonomy in a Changing World* (Vancouver: UBC Press), pp. 234–254.

Couldry, N. (2012). *Media, Society, World: Social Theory and Digital Media Practice*. Cambridge: Polity Press.

Cram, L. (2001). 'Imagining the Union: A Case of Banal Europeanism.' In H. Wallace (ed.), *Interlocking Dimensions of Integration* (London: Palgrave Macmillan), pp. 231–246.

Cram, L. (2012). 'Does the EU Need a Navel? Implicit and Explicit Identification with the European Union.' *Journal of Common Market Studies*, 50(1): 71–86.

Crespy, A., and Verschueren, N. (2009). 'From Euroscepticism to Resistance to European Integration: An Interdisciplinary Perspective.' *Perspectives on European Politics and Society*, 10(3): 377–393.

Cross, M. K. D., and Ma, X. (2015a). 'EU crises and Integrational Panic: The Role of the Media.' *Journal of European Public Policy* (preprint DOI:10.1080/13501763.2014.984748): 1–18.

Cross, M. K. D., and Ma, X. (2015b). 'A Media Perspective on European Crises.' In H. J. Trenz, C. Ruzza, and V. Guiraudon (eds), *Europe's Prolonged Crisis: The Making or the Unmaking of a Political Union* (Basingstoke: Palgave Macmillan), pp. 210–231.

Crouch, C. (1999). *Social Change in Western Europe*. Oxford: Oxford University Press.

Crum, B. J. J., and Fossum, J. E. (2009). 'The Multilevel Parliamentary Field: A Framework for Theorizing Representative Democracy in the EU.' *European Political Science Review*, 1(2): 249–271.

Daianu, D., D'Adda, C., Basevi, G., and Kumar, R. (2014). *The Eurozone Crisis and the Future of Europe: The Political Economy of Further Integration and Governance*. Basingstoke: Palgrave Macmillan.

de Koster, W., Achterberg, P., and van der Waal, J. (2013). 'The New Right and the Welfare State: The Electoral Relevance of Welfare Chauvinism and Welfare Populism in the Netherlands.' *International Political Science Review*, 34(1): 3–20.

de Smaele, H. (2009). 'The Enlarged Audio-Visual Europe: The Many Faces of Europeanization.' In A. Charles (ed.), *Media in the Enlarged Europe: Politics, Policy and Industry* (Bristol: Intellect), pp. 13–22.

De Vreese, C. H. (2001). ''Europe' in the News: A Cross National Comparative Study of the News Coverage of Key EU Events.' *European Union Politics*, 2(3): 283–307.

De Vreese, C. H. (2004). 'The Effects of Strategic News on Political Cynicism, Issue Evaluations and Policy Support: A Two-Wave Experiment.' *Mass Communication and Society*, 7(2): 191–213.

de Vreese, C. H. (2007). 'A spiral of Euroscepticim: The media's fault?' *Acta Politica*, 42(2-3): 271-286.

De Vreese, C. H., and Kandyla, A. (2009). 'News Framing and Public Support for a Common Foreign and Security Policy.' *Journal of Common Market Studies*, 47(3): 453–481.

de Vries, C. E., and Edwards, E. E., (2009) 'Taking Europe to Its Extremes: Extremist Parties and Public Euroscepticism.' *Party Politics*, 15(1): 5–28.

de Wilde, P. (2011). 'No Polity for Old Politics? A Framework for Analyzing Politicization of European Integration.' *Journal of European Integration*, 33(5): 559–575.

de Wilde, P., Michailidou, A., and Trenz, H. J. (2013). *Contesting Europe. Exploring Euroscepticism in Online Media Coverage*. Colchester: ECPR Press.

de Wilde, P., Michailidou, A., and Trenz, H. J. (2015) 'Euroscepticism in Online Media: Conflictual, Ambiguous, Pervasive.' In S. Usherwood, N. Sitter, and S. Guerra (eds), *New Dimensions in Euroscepticism and Opposition to the EU* (Cheltenham: Edgar Elgar).

de Wilde, P., and Trenz, H. J. (2012). 'Denouncing European Integration: Euroscepticism as Polity Contestation.' *European Journal of Social Theory*, 15(4): 537–554.

de Wilde, P., and Zürn, M. (2012). 'Can the Politicization of European Integration Be Reversed?' *Journal of Common Market Studies*, 50(S1): 137–153.

Delanty, G., (2009). *The Cosmopolitan Imagination*. Cambridge: Cambridge University Press.

Delanty, G., and Rumford, C. (2005). *Rethinking Europe: Social Theory and the Implications of Europeanization*. London: Routledge.

Delhey, J., Deutschmann, E., Graf, T., and Richter, K. (2014). 'Measuring the Europeanization of Everyday Life: Three New Indices and an Empirical Application.' *European Societies*, 16(3): 355–377.

Della Porta, D. (ed). (2009). *Another Europe*. London: Routledge.

Deutsch, K. W. (1966). *International Political Communities*. New York: Anchor Books.

Diez, T. (2001a). 'Europe as a Discursive Battleground: Discourse Analysis and European Integration Studies.' *Cooperation and Conflict*, 36(1): 5–38.

Diez, T. (2001b). 'Speaking "Europe": The Politics of Integration Discourse.' In T. Christiansen, K. E. Jørgensen, and A. Wiener (ed.), *The Social Construction of Europe* (London: Sage), pp. 85–100.

Díez Medrano, J. (2003). *Framing Europe: Attitudes to European Integration in Germany, Spain, and the United Kingdom*. Princeton, NJ: Princeton University Press.

Díez Medrano, J. (2008). 'Social Class and Identity.' In A. Favell and V. Guiraudon (eds), *Sociology of European Integration* (Houndmills: Palgrave Macmillan), pp. 28–49.

Díez Medrano, J. (2015). 'Individual and Collective Responses to Crisis: An Analytical Framework for the Study of Social Resilience.' In H. J. Trenz, C. Ruzza, and V. Guiraudon (eds), *Europe's Prolonged Crisis: The Making or the Unmaking of a Political Union* (Basingstoke: Palgrave Macmillan), pp. 104–123.

Dorf, M., and Sabel, C. (1998). 'A Constitution of Democratic Experimentalism.' *Columbia Law Review*, 98(2).

Douglas, M., and Wildavsky, A. (1982). *Risk and Culture: An Essay on the Selection of Technical and Environmental Dangers*. Berkeley and Los Angeles: University of California Press.

Downs, W. M. (2011). 'A Project 'Doomed to Succeed'? Informational Asymmetries, Euroscepticism, and Threats to the Locomotive of Integration.' *Contemporary Politics*, 17(3): 279–297.

Duchesne, S., Frazer, E., Haegel, F., and Van Ingelgom, V. (2013). *Citizens' Reactions to European Integration Compared: Overlooking Europe*. Basingstoke: Palgrave Macmillan.

Durkheim, É. (1964 [1893]). *The Division of Labor in Society*. New York, NJ: The Free Press.

Durkheim, É. (1982). *The Rules of Sociological Method*. New York: Free Press.

Duru, D. N. (2015). 'From Mosaic to Ebru: Conviviality in Multi-Ethnic, Multi-Faith Burgazadasi, Istanbul.' *South European Society and Politics* 20(2): 43–263.

Duru, D. N., Michailidou, A., and Trenz, H. J. (forthcoming). 'The Multiple Allegiances of European Citizens in the Face of Crisis.' In I. P. Karolewski and V. Kaina (eds), *European Identity Revisited: New Approaches and Recent Empirical Evidence* (London: Routledge).

Easton, D. (1975). 'A Re-assessment of the Concept of Political Support.' *British Journal of Political Science*, 5(4): 435–457.

Eder, K. (2000). 'Integration through Culture? The Paradox of the Search for a European Identity.' In K. Eder and B. Giesen (eds), *European Citizenship: Between National Legacies and Postnational Projects* (Oxford: Oxford University Press), pp. 222–244.

Eder, K. (2006a). 'The Public Sphere.' *Theory, Culture & Society*, 23(2–3): 607–611.

Eder, K. (2006b). 'Europe's Borders: The Narrative Construction of the Boundaries of Europe.' *European Journal of Social Theory*, 9(2): 255–271.

Eder, K. (2011). 'Europe as a Narrative Network: Taking Serious the Social Embeddedness of Identity Constructions.' In S. Lucarelli, F. Cerutti, and V. A. Schmidt (eds), *Debating Political Identity and Legitimacy in the European Union: Interdisciplinary Views* (London: Routledge), pp. 38–54.

Eder, K. (2013). 'Struggling with the Concept of the Public Sphere.' In A. Salvatore, O. Schmidtke, and H. J. Trenz (eds), *Rethinking the Public Sphere through Transnationalizing Processes: Europe and Beyond* (Basingstoke: Palgrave Macmillan), pp. 25–55.

Eder, K. (2015). 'The Crisis of Europe—A Case of Creative Destruction.' In H. J. Trenz, C. Ruzza, and V. Guiraudon (eds), *Europe's Prolonged Crisis: The Making or the Unmaking of a Political Union* (Basingstoke: Palgrave Macmillan), pp. 270–289.

Eder, K., and Giesen, B. (2001). 'Citizenship and the Making of a European Society.' In K. Eder and B. Giesen (eds), *European Citizenship: Between National Legacies and Postnational Projects* (Oxford: Oxford University Press), pp. 245–269.

Egeberg, M., (ed). (2006). *Multilevel Union Administration. The Transformation of Executive Politics in Europe*,.Basingstoke: Palgrave Macmillan.

Egeberg, M. (2012). 'Experiments in Supranational Institution-Building: The European Commission as a Laboratory.' *Journal of European Public Policy*, 19(6): 939–950.

Eichenberg, R. C., and Dalton, R. J. (2007). 'Post-Maastricht Blues: The Transformation of Citizen Support for European Integration, 1973–2004.' *Acta Politica*, 42(2/3): 128–152.

Eigmüller, M., and Mau, S., (eds). (2010). *Gesellschaftstheorie und Europapolitik: Sozialwissenschaftliche Ansätze zur Europaforschung.* Berlin: Springer.

Eising, R., and Kohler-Koch, B. (1999). 'Introduction: Network Governance in the European Union.' In B. Kohler-Koch and R. Eising (eds), *The Transformation of Governance in the European Union* (London: Routledge), pp. 3–13.

Eriksen, E. O. (2006). 'The EU—A Cosmopolitan Polity?' *Journal of European Public Policy*, 13(2): 252–269.

Eriksen , E. O. (2014). *The Normativity of the European Union.* Basingstoke: Palgrave Macmillan.

Eriksen, E. O., and Fossum, J. E., (eds), (2000). *Democracy in the European Union. Integration through Deliberation?* London: Routledge.

Eriksen, E. O., and Fossum, J. E. (2008). 'Reconstituting European Democracy.' *ARENA Working Paper*, 2008/01, ARENA—Centre for European Studies

Eriksen, E. O., and Fossum, J. E., (eds), (2012). *Rethinking Democracy and the European Union.* London: Routledge.

Eriksen, E. O., Fossum, J. E., and Menéndez, A. J., (eds), (2004). *Developing a Constitution for Europe.* London: Routledge.

Eriksen, E. O., and Weigård, J. (2003), *Understanding Habermas. Communicative Action and Deliberative Democracy.* London/New York: Continuum.

Exadaktylos, T., and Radaelli, C. M. (2009), 'Research Design in European Studies: The Case of Europeanization.' *Journal of Common Market Studies*, 47(3): 507–530.

Favell, A. (1998). *Philosophies of Integration: Immigration and the Idea of Citizenship in France and Britain.* Basingstoke: Palgrave Macmillan.

Favell, A. (2006). 'The Sociology of EU Politics.' in K. E. Joergensen, M. Pollack, and B. Rosamond (eds), *The Handbook of EU Politics.* London: Sage.

Favell, A. (2008). *Eurostars and Eurocities: Free Moving Urban Professionals in an Integrating Europe.* Oxford: Blackwell.

Favell, A. (2009). 'Immigration, Migration, and Free Movement in the Making of Europe.' In J. T. Checkel and P. J. Katzenstein (eds), *European Identity* (Cambridge: Cambridge University Press), pp. 167–189.

Favell, A. (2014). 'The Fourth Freedom: Theories of Migration and Mobilities in 'Neo-Liberal' Europe.' *European Journal of Social Theory.*

Favell, A., and Guiraudon, V. (2011). *Sociology of the European Union.* Basingstoke: Palgrave Macmillan.

Favell, A., and Recchi, E. (2011). 'Social Mobility and Spatial Mobility.' In A. Favell and V. Guiraudon (eds), *Sociology of the European Union* (Basingstoke: Palgrave Macmillan), pp. 50–75.

Favell, A., Reimer, D., and Solgaard Jensen, J. (2014). 'Transnationalism and Cosmopolitanism: Europe and the Global in Everyday European Lives.' In EUROCROSS (ed.), *Final Report: The Europeanisation of Everyday Life: Cross-Border Practices and Transnational Identifications among EU and Third-Country Citizens*, pp. 138–168, available at: http://www.eucross.eu/cms/ (last accessed September 3, 2015).

Featherstone, K., and Radelli, C., (eds), (2003). *The Politics of Europeanization.* Oxford: Oxford University Press.

Finlayson, A. (2014). 'Becoming a Democratic Audience.' In S. Rai and J. Reinelt (eds), *The Grammar of Politics and Performance* (London: Routledge), pp. 93–121.

Fishkin, J. (2009). *When the People Speak: Deliberative Democracy and Public Consultation.* Oxford: Oxford University Press.

Fligstein, N. (2002). *The Architecture of Markets: An Economic Sociology of Twenty-first Century Capitalist Societies.* Princeton: Princeton University Press.

Fligstein, N. (2008). *Euro-Clash: The EU, European Identity, and the Future of Europe.* Oxford: Oxford University Press.

Foret, F., and Itçaina, X. (eds), (2013). *Politics of Religion in Western Europe: Modernities in Conflict?* London: Routledge.

Foret, F., and Schlesinger, P. (2007). 'Religion and the European Public Sphere.' In J. E. Fossum and P. Schlesinger (eds), *The European Union and the Public Sphere: A Communicative Space in the Making?* (London: Routledge), pp. 187–205.

Fossum, J. E. (2000). 'Constitution-making in the European Union.' In E. O. Eriksen and J. E. Fossum (eds), *Democracy in the European Union—Integration through Deliberation?* (London: Routledge).

Fossum, J. E. (2003). 'The European Union In Search of an Identity.' *European Journal of Political Theory*, 2(3): 319–340.

Fossum, J. E. (2014a). 'Integration and accommodation in Europe.' *Unpublished paper. University of Oslo, ARENA, Centre for European Studies.*

Fossum, J..E. (2014b). 'The Structure of EU Representation and the Crisis.' In S. Kröger (ed.), *Political Representation in the European Union. Still Democratic in Times of Crisis?* (London: Routledge), pp. 52–68.

Fossum, J. E., and Menéndez, A. J. (2010). *The Constitution's Gift: A Constitutional Theory for a Democratic European Union.* Lanham: Rowman and Littlefield.

Fossum, J. E., and Trenz, H. J. (2006a). 'The EU's Fledgeling Society: From Deafening Silence to Critical Voice in European Constitution Making.' *Jounal of Civil Society*, 2(1): 57–77.

Fossum, J. E., and Trenz, H. J. (2006b). 'When the People Come In: Constitution-Making and the Belated Politicisation of the European Union.' *European Governance Papers*, /No. C-06-03, EUROGOV.

Fuchs, C. (2014). 'Critique of the Political Economy of Informational Capitalism and Social Media.' In C. Fuchs and M. Sandoval (eds), *Critique, Social Media and the Information Society* (London: Routledge), pp. 51–65.

Fuchs, D., Magni-Berton, R., and Roger, A. (eds), (2009). *Euroscepticism: Images of Europe Among Mass Publics and Political Elites.* Opladen: Barbara Budrich Publishers.

Fukuyama, F. (1992). *The End of History and the Last Man.* Chicago: Free Press.

Gaus, D. (2011). 'The Dyamics of Legitimation: Why the Study of Political Legitimacy Needs More Realism.' *RECON Online Working Paper 2011/15, available at:* http://www.reconproject.eu/main.php/RECON_wp_1115.pdf?fileitem=50512026, (last accessed September 2, 2015).

Gaus, D. (2014). 'Demoi-kratie ohne Demos-kratie. Welche Polity braucht eine demokratische EU?' In O. Flügel-Martinsen, D. Gaus, T. Hitzel-Cassagnes, and F. Martinsen (eds), *Deliberative Kritik—Kritik der Deliberation. Festschrift für Rainer Schmalz-Bruns* (Wiesbaden: Springer VS), pp. 297–322.

Giesen, B. (1999). 'Europa als Konstruktion der Intellektuellen.' In R. Viehoff and R. T. Segers (eds), *Kultur, Identität, Europa. Über die Schwierigkeiten und Möglichkeiten einer Konstruktion* (Frankfurt a. M.: Suhrkamp), pp. 130–146.

Giesen, B. (2003). 'The Collective Identity of Europe: Constitutional Practice or Community of Memory.' In A. Triandafyllidou and W. Spohn (eds), *Europeanisation, National Identities and Migration: Changes in Boundary Constructions between Western and Eastern Europe* (London: Routledge), pp. 21–35.

Giesen, B. (2004), *Triumph and Trauma.* Boulder, CO: Paradigm Publishers.

Gill, S. (2003). *Power and Resistance in the New World Order.* Basingstoke: Palgrave Macmillan.

Glick Schiller, N., Basch, L., and Blan, C. S. (1992). *Transnationalism: A New Analytical Framework for Understanding Migration* New York: New York Academy of Sciences.

Goetz, K. H., and Hix, S. (2001). 'Introduction: Europeanised Politics? European Integration and National Political Systems.' In K. H. Goetz and S. Hix (eds), *Europeanised Politics? European Integration and National Political Systems* (London: Frank Cass), pp. 1–26.

Góra, M., Mach, Z., and Trenz, H. J. (2011). 'Reconstituting Democracy in Europe and Constituting the European Demos?' In E. O. Eriksen and J. E. Fossum (eds), *Reconstituting Democracy in Europe: Theory and Practice* (London: Routledge), pp. 159–178

Graham, T., and Hajru, A. (2011). 'Reality TV as a Trigger of Everyday Political Talk in the Net-Based Public Sphere.' *European Journal of Communication*, 26(1): 18–32.

Grant, W., and Wilson, G. K. (2012). *The Consequences of the Global Financial Crisis: The Rhetoric of Reform and Regulation*. Oxford: Oxford University Press.

Grevi, G., and Keohane, D. (eds), (2013). *Challenges for European Foreign Policy in 2013 Renewing the EU's role in the world*. Madrid: Fride, available at: http://fride.org/descarga/ Challenges_for_European_Foreign_Policy_2013.pdf, (last accessed September 2, 2015).

Gripsrud, J. (2007). 'Television and the European Public Sphere.' *European Journal of Communication*, 22(4): 479–492.

Guiraudon, V., Ruzza, C., and Trenz, H. J. (2015). 'Introduction: The European Crisis, Contributions from Political Sociology.' In H. J. Trenz, C. Ruzza, and V. Guiraudon (eds), *Europe's Prolonged Crisis: The Making or the Unmaking of a Political Union* (Basingstoke: Palgave Macmillan), pp. 1–23.

Gutmann, A., and Thompson, D. (2009). *Why Deliberative Democracy?* Princeton: Princeton University Press.

Haas, E. B. (1958). *The Uniting of Europe: Political, Social and Economic Forces 1950–57*. Stanford: Stanford University Press.

Habermas, J. (1974). 'The Public Sphere: An Encyclopedia Article (1964).' *New German Critique*, 3 49–55.

Habermas, J. (1975). *Legitimation Crisis*. Boston: Beacon Press.

Habermas, J. (1989). *The Structural Transformation of the Public Sphere*. Cambridge, MA: MIT Press.

Habermas, J. (1990). *Die Moderne, ein unvollendetes Projekt: Philosophisch-politische Aufsätze 1977–1990*. Stuttgart: Reclam.

Habermas, J. (1995). 'Remarks on Dieter Grimm's "Does Europe need a Constitution?"' *European Law Journal*, 1(3) 303–307.

Habermas, J. (1996). *Between Facts and Norms: Contributions to a Discourse Theory of Law and Democracy*. Cambridge: Polity Press.

Habermas, J. (2001). *The Postnational Constellation: Political Essays*. Cambridge: Polity Press.

Habermas, J. (2012). *The Crisis of the European Union: A Response*. Cambridge: Polity Press.

Habermas, J (2015a). Interview in *The Guardian* July 16, 2015, available at: http://en. protothema.gr/habermas-to-merkel-youre-gambling-away-germany-post-war-reputation/ (last accessed on August 17, 2015).

Habermas, J. (2015b). 'Why Angela Merkel is wrong.' In *Social Europe.eu*, available at: http:// www.socialeurope.eu/2015/06/why-angela-merkels-is-wrong-on-greece/ (last accessed on August 17, 2015).

Hakhverdian, A., van Elsas, E., van der Brug, W., and Kuhn, T. (2013). 'Euroscepticism and Education: A Longitudinal Study of 12 EU Member States, 1973–2010.' *European Union Politics*, 14(4): 522–541.

Hall, P. A. and Lamont, M. (2013). *Social Resilience in the Neoliberal Era*. Cambridge: Cambridge University Press.

Handmer, J. W., and Dovens, S. R. (1996). 'A Typology of Resilience.' *Industrial & Environmental Crisis Quarterly* 9(4): 482–511.

Hannerz, U. (2004). *Foreign News: Exploring the World of Foreign Correspondents*. Chicago: University of Chicago Press.

Haverland, M. (2013). 'Business as Usual? EU Policy-Making Amid the Legitimacy Crisis (Inaugural Lecture) (June 7, 2013).' Raddraaier, Amsterdam, June 2013, available at: http:// ssrn.com/abstract=2380673 (last accessed September 2, 2015).

Hay, C., and Rosamond, B. (2002). 'Globalization, European Integration and the Discursive Construction of Economic Imperatives.' *Journal of European Public Policy*, 9(2): 147–167.

Hearn Marrow, B. (2008). 'Community Resilience: A Social Justice Perspective.' *CARRI Research Report 4*, available at: http://www.resilientus.org/wp-content/uploads/2013/03/ FINAL_MORROW_9-25-08_1223482348.pdf (last accessed September 2, 2015).

Held, D. (2010). 'Principles of Cosmopolitan Order.' In G. W. Brown and D. Held (eds), *The Cosmopolitanism Reader* (Cambridge: Polity Press), pp. 229–247.

Heritier, A. (2007). *Explaining Institutional Change in Europe*. Oxford: Oxford University Press.

Hix, S. (2007) 'Euroscepticism as Anti-Centralization: A rational-choice institutional perspective,' *European Union Politics*, 8(1): 131–150.

Holten, R. J. (1987). 'The Idea of Crisis in Modern Society.' *The British Journal of Sociology* 38(4): 502–520.

Hooghe, L. (2007). 'What Drives Euroskepticism? Party-Public Cueing, Ideology and Strategic Opportunity.' *European Union Politics*, 8(1): 5–12.

Hooghe, L., and Marks, G. (2007). 'Sources of Euroscepticism.' *Acta Politica*, 42(2/3): 119–127.

Hooghe, L., and Marks, G. (2009). 'A Postfunctionalist Theory of European Integration: From Permissive Consensus to Constraining Dissensus.' *British Journal of Political Science*, 39(1): 1–23.

Huntington, S. P. (1991). *The Third Wave: Democratization in the Late Twentieth Century*. Norman: University of Oklahoma Press.

Hurrelmann, A. (2007). 'Multilevel Legitimacy: Conceptualizing Legitimacy Relationships between the EU and National Democracies.' In J. DeBardeleben and A. Hurrelmann (eds), *Democratic Dilemmas of Multilevel Governance: Legitimacy, Representation and Accountability in the European Union* (Basingstoke: Palgrave Macmillan), pp. 17–37.

Hurrelmann, A. (2014). 'Demoi-Cratic Citizenship in Europe: An Impossible ideal?' *Journal of European Public Policy*, 22(1): 19–36.

Hurrelmann, A., Gora, A., and Wagner, A. (2015). 'The Politicization of European Integration: More than an Elite Affair?' *Political Studies*, 63(1): 43–59.

Immerfall, S., and Therborn, G. (2009). *Handbook of European Societies: Social Transformations in the 21st Century*. Berlin: Springer.

Isakhan, B., and Slaughter, S. (2014). *Democracy and Crisis: Democratising Governance in the Twenty-First Century*. Basingstoke: Palgrave Macmillan.

Isin, E. F. and Saward, P. M. (2013). *Enacting European Citizenship*. Cambridge: Cambridge University Press.

Jachtenfuchs, M., and Kohler-Koch, B., (eds). (1996). *Europäische Integration*. Opladen: Leske & Budrich.

Jachtenfuchs, M. (2003). 'Regieren im dynamischen Mehrenbenensystem.' In M. Jachtenfuchs and B. Kohler-Koch (eds), *Europäische Integration* (Opladen: Leske & Budrich), pp. 15–44.

Jentges, E., Trenz, H. J., and Vetters, R. (2007). 'Von der politischen zur sozialen Konstitutionalisierung Europas: Verfassungsgebung als Katalysator europäischer Vergesellschaftung.' *Politische Vierteljahresschrift* 48(4): 705–729.

Jobert, B., and Kohler-Koch, B. (2008). *Changing Images of Civil Society: From Protest to Governance*. London: Routledge.

Jones, E. (2009). 'Output Legitimacy and the Global Financial Crisis: Perceptions Matter.' *Journal of Common Market Studies*, 47(5): 1085–1105.

Jones, E., and Verdun, A. (eds). (2005). *The Political Economy of European Integration: Theory and Analysis*. London: Routledge.

Jones, S., and Subotic, J. (2011). 'Fantasies of Power: Performing Europeanization on the European Periphery.' *European Journal of Cultural Studies*, 14(5): 542–557.

Judt, T. (2005). *Postwar: A History of Europe since 1945*. London: Penguin Books.

Kaelble, H. (1997). 'Europäische Vielfalt und der Weg zu einer europäischen Gesellschaft.' In S. Hradil and S. Immerfall (eds), *Die westeuropäischen Gesellschaften im Vergleich* (Opladen: Leske & Budrich), pp. 27–68.

Kaelble, H. (2004). *The European Way: European Societies During the Nineteenth and Twentieth Centuries*. New York: Berghahn Books.

Kaelble, H. (2013). *A Social History of Europe, 1945–2000: Recovery and Transformation After Two World Wars*. New York: Berghahn Books.

Kaiser, W., Krankenhagen, S., and Poehls, K. (2014). *Exhibiting Europe in Museums: Transnational Networks, Collections, Narratives, and Representations*. New York: Berghahn Books.

Kamen, H. (2005). *Early Modern European Society*. London: Routledge.

Karolewski, I. P. (2010). 'European Nationalism and European Identity.' in I. P. Karolewski and A. M. Suszycki (eds), *Multiplicity of Nationalism in Contemporary Europe* (Lanham: Lexington Books), pp. 59–80.

Kauppi, N. (2014). *A Political Sociology of Transnational Europe*. Colchester: ECPR Press.

Keating, M., and Jones, B. (1995). *The European Union and the Regions*. Oxford: Oxford University Press.

Keohane, D. 'Lessons from EU Peace Operations.' *Journal of International Peacekeeping*, 15(1–2): 200–217.

Kepplinger, H. M., Geiss, S., and Siebert, S. (2012). 'Framing Scandals: Cognitive and Emotional Media Effects.' *Journal of Communication*, 62(4): 659–681.

Kevin, D. (2003). *Europe in the Media. A Comparison of Reporting, Representation and Rhetoric in National Media Systems in Europe*. Mahwah, NJ: Lawrence Erlbaum Associates Publishers.

Kietz, D., and von Ondarza, N. (2014). 'Europaskeptiker im Europäischen Parlament: In Brüssel isoliert und zerstritten, treiben sie die nationale Europapolitik vor sich her.' *Stiftung Wissenschaft und Politik, SWP-Aktuell 7/2014*.

Klausen, J., and Tilly, L. (1997). *European Integration in Social and Historical Perspective: 1850 to the Present*. Lanham: Rowman & Littlefield.

Knudsen, A. C. L., and Gram-Skjoldager, K. (2014). 'Historiography and Narration in Transnational History.' *Journal of Global History*, 9(1): 143–161.

Kohler-Koch, B. (2007). 'The Organization of Interest and Democracy in the European Union.' In B. Kohler-Koch and B. Rittberger (eds), *Debating the Democratic Legitimacy of the European Union* (Lanham: Rowan & Littlefield), pp. 255–271.

Kohler-Koch, B. (2010). 'Civil Society and EU Democracy: 'Astroturf' Representation?' *Journal of European Public Policy*, 17(1): 100–116.

Kohler-Koch, B., and Eising, R. (1999). *The Transformation of Governance in the European Union*, London: Routledge.

Kompridis, N. (2006). *Critique and Disclosure: Critical Theory Between Past and Future*. Cambridge, Ma: MIT Press.

Koopmans, R. (2007). 'Who Inhabits the European Public Sphere? Winners and Losers, Supporters and Opponents in Europeanised Political Debates.' *European Journal of Political Research*, 46(2): 183–210.

Koopmans, R. (2010). 'Winners and Losers, Supporters and Opponents in Europeanized Public Debates.' In R. Koopmans and P. Statham (eds), *The Making of a European Public Sphere. Media Discourse and Political Contention* (Cambridge: Cambridge University Press), pp. 97–121.

Koopmans, R., and Statham, P., (eds), (2010). *The Making of a European Public Sphere: The Europeanisation of Media Discourse and Political Contention*. (Cambridge: Cambridge University Press).

Kopecky, P., and Mudde, C. (2002). 'The Two Sides of Euroscepticism: Party Positions on European Integration in East Central Europe.' *European Union Politics*, 3(3): 297–326.

Krastev, I. (2012). 'European Disintegration? A Fraying Union.' *Journal of Democracy*, 23(4): 23–30.

Kriesi, H., Grande, E., Lachat, R., Dolezal, M., Bornschier, S., and Frey, T. (2008). *West European Politics in the Age of Globalization*. Cambridge: Cambridge University Press.

Krouwel, A., and Abts, K. (2007). 'Varieties of Euroscepticism and Populist Mobilization: Transforming Attitudes from Mild Euroscpeticism to Harsh Eurocynicism.' *Acta Politica*, 42(2–3): 252–270.

Kumm, M. (2005). 'Constitutional Supremacy and the Constitutional Treaty.' *European Law Journal*, 11(3): 262–306.

Laclau, E. (2005). *On Populist Reason*. London: Verso.

Lacroix, J., and Nicolaïdis, K. (2010). *European Stories: Intellectual Debates on Europe in National Contexts*. Oxford: Oxford University Press.

Lahusen, C. (2013). 'Toward Pan-European Contentions? European Integration and its Effects on Political Mobilization.' In A. Salvatore, O. Schmidtke and H. J. Trenz (eds), *Rethinking the Public Sphere Through Transnationalizing Processes: Europe and Beyond* (Basingstoke: Palgrave Macmillan), pp. 152–167.

Lane, J. E., and Ersson, S. (1999). *Politics and Society in Western Europe*. London: Sage.

Leconte, C. (2010). *Understanding Euroscepticism*. Basingstoke: Palgrave Macmillan.

Leggewie, C. (2008). 'A Tour of the Battleground: The Seven Circles of Pan-European Memory.' *Social Research*, 75(1): 217–234.

Liebert, U., and Trenz, H. J. (2008a). 'Mass Media and Contested Meanings: EU Constitutional Politics after Popular Rejection.' *European University Institute: RSCAS Working Papers 2008/28*

Liebert, U., and Trenz, H. J. (2008b). 'Mediating European Democracy: Comparative News Media and EU Treaty Reform in 14 Member States (2004–2007).' RECON ARENA—Center for European Studies, Oslo, available at: http://www.reconproject.eu/projectweb/portalproject/ResearchReportWP5.html (last accessed September 2, 2015).

Liebert, U., and Trenz, H. J., (eds), (2010). *The New Politics of European Civil Society*. London: Routledge.

Lord, C., and Magnette, P. (2004). 'E pluribus unum? Creative disagreement about legitimacy in the EU.' *Journal of Common Market Studies*, 42(1): 183–202.

Lubbers, M., and Scheepers, P. (2010). 'Divergent Trends of Euroscepticism in Countries and Regions of the European Union.' *European Journal of Political Research*, 49(6): 787-817.

Lucarelli, S., Cerutti, F., and Schmidt, V. A. (2011), *Debating Political Identity and Legitimacy in the European Union*. London: Routledge.

Luhmann, N. (1997). *Die Gesellschaft der Gesellschaft*. Frankfurt a. M.: Suhrkamp.

Magnette, P. (2007). 'How Can One Be European? Reflections on the Pillars of European Civic Identity.' *European Law Journal*, 13(5): 664–679.

Mahoney, C. (2004). 'The Power of Institutions: State and Interest Group Activity in the European Union.' *European Union Politics*, 5(4): 441–466.

Majone, G. (1998). 'Europe's 'Democratic Deficit': The Question of Standards.' *European Law Journal*, 4(1): 5–28.

Majone, G. (2013). 'The General Crisis of the European Union: A Genetic Approach.' Paper presented at the conference "Europe in Crisis: Implications for the EU and Norway," Oslo, March 14–15, 2013.

Majone, G. (2014). *Rethinking the Union of Europe Post-Crisis: Has Integration Gone Too Far?* Cambridge: Cambride University Press.

Mann, M. (1998). 'Is there a society called Euro?' In R. Axtmann (ed.), *Globalization and Europe* (London: Bloomsbury Academic), pp. 184–206.

Manners, I. (2011). 'Symbolism in European Integration.' *Comparative European Politics*, 9(3): 243–268.

Marks, G., and McAdam, D. (1996). 'Social Movement and the Changing Structure of Political Opportunity in the European Union.' *West European Politics*, 19(2), 249–277.

Marks, G., Scharpf, F. W., Schmitter, P., and Streeck, W. (1996). *Governance in the European Union*. London: Sage.

Marks, G., and Steenbergen, M. R. (2004). *European Integration and Political Conflict: Citizens, Parties, Groups*. Cambridge: Cambridge University Press.

Mau, S. (2011). *Social Transnationalism: Lifeworlds beyond the Nation-State*. London and New York: Routledge.

Mau, S., Mewes, J., and Zimmermann, A. (2008), 'Cosmopolitan Attitudes Through Transnational Pracitces?' *Global Networks: A Journal of Transnational Affairs*, 8(1): 1–23.

Mau, S., and Verwiebe, R. (2010). *European Societies: Mapping Structure and Change*. Bristol: Policy Press.

Mazzoleni, G. (2003). 'The Media and the Growth of Neo-Populism in Contemporary Democracies.' In G. Mazzoleni, S. Julianne, and B. Horsfield (eds), *The Media and Neo Populism*. Westport, London: Praeger, pp. 1–20.

McLaren, L. (2007). 'Explaining Mass-Level Euroscepticism: Identity, Interests, and Institutional Distrust.' *Acta Politica*, 42(2/3): 233–251.

McLaren, L. M. (2005). *Identity, Interests and Attitudes to European Integration*. Basingstoke: Palgrave Macmillan.

Meijers, M. (2013). 'The Euro-Crisis as a Catalyst of the Europeanization of Public Spheres?: A Cross-Temporal Study of the Netherlands and Germany.' *LSE Europe in Question Discussion Paper Series No. 62/2013*, available at: http://www.lse.ac.uk/europeanInstitute/LEQS/LEQSPaper62.pdf (last accessed September 2, 2015).

Menéndez, A. J. (2005). 'A Christian or a Laïc Europe?: Christian Values and European Identity.' *Ratio Juris*, 18(2): 179–205.

Menéndez, A. J. (2013). 'The Existential Crisis of the European Union.' *German Law Journal*, 14(5): 453–526.

Michailidou, A., and Trenz, H. J. (2013). 'Mediatized Representative Politics in the European Union: Towards Audience Democracy?' *Journal of European Public Policy*, 20(2): 260–277.

Michailidou, A., and Trenz, H. J. (2014). 'The Mediatisation of Politics: From the National to the Transnational.' *Partecipazione e Conflitto. Journal of Sociopolitical Studies.* 7(3), 469–498.

Michailidou, A., and Trenz, H. J. (2015). 'The European Crisis and the Media: Media Autonomy, Public Perceptions and New Forms of Political Engagement.' In H. J. Trenz, C. Ruzza, and V. Guiraudon (eds), *Europe's prolonged crisis: The making or the unmaking of a political Union* (Basingstoke: Palgave Macmillan), pp. 232–250.

Michailidou, A., Trenz, H. J., and de Wilde, P. (2014). *The Internet and European Integration: Pro- and Anti- EU Debates in Online News Media*. Opladen: Barbara Budrich Publisher.

Milward, A. S. (2000). *The European Rescue of the Nation-State*, 2nd Edition. London: Routledge.

Mitchell, J. K. 1995. 'Coping with Natural Hazards and Disasters in Megacities: Perspectives on the Twenty-First Century.' *GeoJournal* 37(3): 303–312

Monnet, J. (1974). *Mémoirs*. Paris: Fayard.

Moravcsik, A. (1998). *The Choice for Europe: Social Purpose and State Power from Messina to Maastricht*. Ithaca, NY: Cornell University Press.

Morgan, G. (2005). *The Idea of a European Superstate: Public Justification and European Integration*. Princeton, NJ: Princeton University Press.

Morgan, G. (2007). 'European Political Integration and the Need for Justification.' *Constellations*, 14(3): 332–346.

Mouffe, C. (2008). 'Which World Order: Cosmopolitan or Multipolar?' *Ethical Perspectives*, 15(4): 453–467.

Mudrov, S. (2011). 'The Christian Churches as Special Participants in European Integration.' *Journal of Contemporary European Research*, 7(3): 363–379.

Müller, J. W. (2009), *Constitutional Patriotism*. Princeton: Princeton University Press.

Münch, R. (2001). *Offene Räume: Soziale Integration diesseits und jenseits des Nationalstaats*. Frankfurt a. M.: Suhrkamp.

Münch, R. (2008). *Die Konstruktion der Europäischen Gesellschaft*. Frankfurt a. M.: Campus.

Mylonas, Y. (2012). 'Media and the Economic Crisis of the EU: The 'Culturalization' of a Systemic Crisis and Bild-Zeitung's Framing of Greece.' *tripleC. Cognition, Communication, Co-ooperation*, 10(2): 646–671.

Nassehi, A. (2002). 'Politik der Staates oder Politik der Gesellschaft. Kollektivität als Problemformel des Politischen.' In K. U. Hellemann and R. Schmalz-Bruns (eds), *Niklas Luhmanns politische Soziologie* (Frankfurt a. M: Suhrkamp), pp. 38–59.

Nassehi, A. (2006). *Der soziologische Diskurs der Moderne*. Frankfurt a. M.: Suhrkamp.

Neyer, J. (2006). 'The Deliberative Turn in Integration Theory.' *Journal of European Public Policy*, 13(5): 779–791.

Nicolaïdis, K. (2013). 'European Demoicracy and Its Crisis.' *Journal of Common Market Studies*, 51(2): 351–369.

O'Mahony, P. (2013). *The Contemporary Theory of the Public Sphere*. Bern: Peter Lang.

Offe, C. (1972). *Strukturprobleme des kapitalistischen Staates: Aufsätze zur politischen Soziologie*. Frankfurt a. M.: Suhrkamp.

Offe, C. (2000). 'The Democratic Welfare State in an Integrating Europe.' In M. Greven and L. Pauly (eds), *Democracy beyond the State?* (Toronto: University of Toronto Press), pp. 63–90.

Offe, C. (2003). 'Is there, or Can There be, a 'European Society'?' In I. Katenhusen and W. Lamping (eds), *Demokratien in Europa: Der Einfluss der europäischen Integration auf Institutionenwandel und neue Konturen des demokratischen Verfassungsstaates* (Berlin: Springer), pp. 71–89.

Offe, C. (2013) 'Europe Entrapped,' *European Law Journal*, 19(5): 595-611.

Olsen, E. D. H. (2012). *Transnational Citizenship in the European Union: Past, Present, and Future*. London: Bloomsbury Academic.

Olsen, E. D. H. (2015). 'Eurocrisis and EU citizenship.' In H. J. Trenz, C. Ruzza, and V. Guiraudon (eds), *Europe's Prolonged Crisis: The Making or the Unmaking of a Political Union* (Basingstoke: Routledge), pp. 85–103.

Olsen, E. D. H., and Trenz, H. J. (2014). 'From Citizens' Deliberation to Popular Will Formation?: Generating Democratic Legitimacy in Transnational Deliberative Polling.' *Political Studies* 62 (1): 117–133.

Olsen, J. P. (2002). 'The Many Faces of Europeanization.' *Journal of Common Market Studies*, 40(5): 921–952.

Olsen, J. P. (2007). *Europe in Search of Political Order: An Institutional Perspective on Unity/Diversity, Citizens/their Helpers, Democratic Design/Historical Drift, and the Co-existence of Orders*. Oxford: Oxford University Press.

Örnebring, H. (2013). 'Questioning European Journalism.' *Journalism Studies*, 10(1): 2–17.

Outhwaite, W. (2013). *European Society*. Oxford: Wiley.

Page, B., and Shapiro, R. Y. (1992). *The Rational Public: Fifty Years of Trends in Americans' Policy Preferences*. Chicago: University of Chicago Press.

Passerin d'Entrèves, M. P., and Benhabib, S. (1997). *Habermas and the Unfinished Project of Modernity: Critical Essays on The Philosophical Discourse of Modernity*. Cambridge, MA: MIT Press.

Parsons, T. (1967). *Sociological Theory and Modern Society*. New York: Free Press.

Patterson, T. E. (2011). *Out of Order: An Incisive and Boldly Original Critique of the News Media's Domination of America's Political Process*. New York: Knopf Doubleday Publishing Group.

Pérez, F. (2013). *Political Communication in Europe: The Cultural and Structural Limits of the European Public Sphere*. Basingstoke: Palgrave Macmillan.

Petersson, B., and Hellström, A. (2003). 'The Return of the Kings: Temporality in the Construction of EU Identity.' *European Societies*, 5(3): 17.

Petithomme, M. (2008). 'Is there a European Identity?: National Attitudes and Social Identification toward the European Union.' *Journal of Identity and Migration Studies*, 2(1): 15–36.

Piattoni, S. (ed). (2015). *The European Union: Democratic Principles and Institutional Architectures in Times of Crisis*. Oxford: Oxford University Press.

Picard, R., (ed). (2015). *The Euro Crisis and the Media: Journalistic Coverage of Economic Crisis and European Institutions*. London and New York: Tauris.

Pickford, S., Steinberg, F., and Otero-Iglesias, M. (2015). *How to Fix the Euro: Strengthening Economic Governance in Europe*. London: Royal Institute for International Affairs.

Polanyi, K. (1957). *The Great Transformation*. Boston: Beacon Press.

Raboy, M., and Dagenais, B. (1992). 'Media, Crisis and Democracy,' *Canadian Journal of Political Science*, 26(3): 581–582.

Ray, L. (2007). 'Mainstream Euroskepticism: Trend or Oxymoron?' *Acta Politica*, 42(2/3): 153–172.

Raykoff, I., and Tobin, R. D. (2007). *A Song for Europe: Popular Music and Politics in the Eurovision Song Contest*. Aldershot: Ashgate.

Recchi, E., and Favell, A., (eds), (2009). *Pioneers of European Integration: Mobility and Citizenship in the EU*. Cheltenham: Elgar.

Recchi, E., and Salamońska, J. (2015). 'Bad Times, Good Times to Move? The Changing Landscape of Intra-EU Migration.' In H. J. Trenz, C. Ruzza, and V. Guiraudon (eds), *Europe's Prolonged Crisis: The Making or the Unmaking of a Political Union* (Basingstoke: Palgrave Macmillan), pp. 124–164.

Risse, T. (2003). 'The Euro Between National and European Identity.' *Journal of European Public Policy*, 10(4): 18.

Risse, T. (2005). 'Neofunctionalism, European Identity, and the Puzzles of European Integration.' *Journal of European Public Policy*, 12(2): 291–309.

Risse, T. (2010). *A Community of Europeans?: Transnational Identities and Public Spheres*. New York: Cornell University Press.

Risse, T. (2014a). 'No Demos? Identities and Public Spheres in the Euro Crisis.' *Journal of Common Market Studies*, 52(6): 1207–1215.

Risse, T. (ed). (2014b). *European Public Spheres: Politics Is Back*. Cambridge: Cambridge University Press.

Rokkan, S. (1999). *State Formation, Nation Building and Mass Politics in Europe*. Oxford: Oxford University Press.

Rosamond, B. (2000). *Theories of European Integration*. Basingstoke: Palgrave Macmillan.

Rother, N., and Nebe, T. M. (2009). 'More Mobile, More European?: Free Movement and EU Identity.' In E. Recchi and A. Favell (eds), *Pioneers of European Integration. Citizenship and Mobility in the EU* (Cheltenham: Edward Elgar), pp. 120–155.

Rucht, D. (2005). 'Europäische Zivilgesellschaft oder zivile Interaktionsformen in und jenseits von Europa.' In M. Knodt and B. Finke (eds), *Europäische Zivilgesellschaft: Konzepte, Akteure, Strategien* (Wiesbaden: Verlag für Sozialwissenschaften), pp. 32–54.

Rumford, C. (2002). *The European Union: A Political Sociology*. Oxford: Blackwell.

Rumford, C. (2003). 'European Civil Society or Transnational Social Space?: Conceptions of Society in Discourses of EU Citizenship, Governance and the Democratic Deficit: an Emerging Agenda.' *European Journal of Social Theory*, 6(1): 25–43.

Ruzza, C. (2004). *Europe and Civil Society: Movement Coalitions and European Governance*. Manchester: Manchester University Press.

Ruzza, C. (2009). 'Populism and Euroscepticism: Towards Uncivil Society?' *Policy & Society*, 28(1): 87–98.

Ruzza, C., and della Sala, V., (eds), (2007). *Governance and Civil Society in the European Union. Volume 1: Normative perspectives*, Manchester: Manchester University Press

Sanchez Salgado, R. (2014). *Europeanizing Civil Society: How the EU shapes civil society organizations*. Basingstoke: Palgave MacMillan.

Sanders, D., Magalhaes, P., and Toka, G. (2012). *Citizens and the European Polity: Mass Attitudes Towards the European and National Polities*. Oxford: Oxford University Press.

Sassatelli, M. (2009). *Becoming Europeans: Cultural Identity and Cultural Policies*. Basingstoke: Palgrave Macmillan.

Sassatelli, M. (2015). 'Narratives of European Identity.' In I. Bondebjerg, E. Novrup Redvall, and A. Higson (eds), *European Cinema and Television: Cultural Policy and Everyday Life* (Basingstoke: Palgrave Macmillan), pp. 25–42.

Saward, M. (2013). 'The Dynamics of European Citizenship: Enactment, Extension and Assertion' *Comparative European Politics*, 11(1): 49–69.

Scalise, G. (2015). 'The Narrative Construction of European Identity: Meanings of Europe "From Below."' *European Societies*, 1–22, early view: DOI:10.1080/14616696.2015.1072227

Scharpf, F. (1999). *Governing in Europe: Effective and Democratic?* Oxford: Oxford University Press.

Scharpf, F. (2012). 'The Double Asymmetry of European Integration.' *MPIfG Working Paper 09/12, Max-Planck Institute for the Study of Societies.*

Scharpf, F. W. (2015). 'After the Crash: A Perspective on Multilevel European Democracy.' *European Law Journal*, 21(3): 384–405.

Scheller, H., and Eppler, A. (2014). 'European Disintegration—Non-Existing Phenomenon or a Blind Spot of European Integration Research?: Preliminary Thoughts for a Research Agenda.' *eif Working Paper No. 02/2014*, available at: http://eif.univie.ac.at/downloads/workingpapers/2014_02_Eppler_Scheller.pdf (last accessed September 3, 2015).

Schiff, B. (2012). 'The Function of Narrative: Toward a Narrative Psychology of Meaning.' *Narrative Works*, 2(1): 33–47 available at: http://journals.hil.unb.ca/index.php/NW/article/view/19497 (last accessed September 2, 2015).

Schimank, U. (2011). 'The Fragile Constitution of Contemporary Welfare Societies: A Derailed Functional Antagonism between Capitalism and Democracy.' *Welfare Societies Working Paper 01/2011*, available at: http://www.welfare-societies.com/uploads/file/WelfareSocietiesWorkingPaper-No1_Schimank.pdf (last accessed September 3, 2015).

Schimmelfennig, F. (2014). 'European Integration in the Euro Crisis: The Limits of Postfunctionalism.' *Journal of European Integration*, 36(3): 321–337.

Schimmelfennig, F., and Sedelmeier, U. (2005). *The Europeanization of Central and Eastern Europe*, Ithaca, NY: Cornell University Press.

Schmidt, J. (2014). 'Intuitively neoliberal?: Towards a Critical Understanding of Resilience Governance.' *European Journal of International Relations*, 21(2), 402–426.

Schmidt, V. A. (2013). 'Democracy and Legitimacy in the European Union Revisited: Input, Output and 'Throughput.'' *Political Studies*, 61(1): 2–22.

Schmitter, P. C. (2004). 'Neo-Neofunctionalism.' In A. Wiener and T. Diez (eds), *European Integration Theory* (Oxford: Oxford University Press), pp. 45–74.

Schmitter, P. C. (2012). 'European Disintegration?: A Way Forward.' *Journal of Democracy*, 23(4): 39–46.

Schrag Sternberg, C. (2013). *The Struggle for EU Legitimacy: Public Contestation, 1950–2005*. Basingstoke: Palgrave Macmillan.

Schulz-Forberg, H., and Stråth, B. (2010). *The Political History of European Integration: The Hypocrisy of Democracy-through-Market*. London and New York: Routledge.

Seeger, M. W., Sellnow, T. L., and Ulmer, R. R. (2003). *Communication and Organizational Crisis*. Westport, CT: Praeger.

Shaw, J. (1999). 'Postnational Constitutionalism in the European Union.' *Journal of European Public Policy*, 6(4): 579–597.

Shaw, J. (2007). *The Transformation of Citizenship in the European Union*. Cambridge: Cambridge University Press.

Shore, C. (2000) *Building Europe: the cultural politics of European integration*, London: Routledge.

Simmel, G. (1908). *Soziologie. Untersuchungen über die Formen der Vergesellschaftung*. Berlin: Duncker und Humblot.

Sitter, N. (2001). 'The politics of Opposition and European Integration in Scandinavia: Is Euroscepticism a Government-Opposition Dynamic?' *West European Politics*, 24(4): 22–239.

Sjursen, H. (2007). 'The EU as a 'Normative' Power: How Can This Be?' In H. Sjursen (ed.), *Civilian or Military Power? European Foreign Policy in Perspective* (London: Routledge), pp. 67–83.

Smith, D. (2015). 'Not Just Singing the Blues: Dynamics of the EU Crisis.' In H. J. Trenz, C. Ruzza, and V. Guiraudon (eds), *Europe's prolonged crisis: The making or the unmaking of a political Union* (Basingstoke: Palgrave Macmillan), pp. 23–43.

Smith, M. P. (2001). *Transnational Urbanism: Locating Globalization*. Oxford: Blackwell.

Somek, A. (2013). 'Europe: From Emancipation to Empowerment.' *LSE 'Europe in Question' Discussion Paper Series*, No. 60/2013 availabe at: http://www.lse.ac.uk/europeanInstitute/LEQS/LEQSPaper60.pdf (last accessed September 3, 2015).

Sonntag, A. (2012). 'Grilles de perception et dynamiques identitaires dans l'espace européen du football » Le projet FREE.' *Politique européenne*, 36(1): 85–192.

Soroka, S. N. (2014). *Negativity in Democratic Politics: Causes and Consequences*, Cambridge: Cambridge University Press.

Soysal, Y., and Schissler, H. (2004). *The Nation, Europe and the World: Textbooks ans Curricula in Transition*. New York: Berghahn.

Splichal, S. (2012). *Transnationalization of the Public Sphere and the Fate of the Public*. New York: Hampton Press.

Statham, P. (2010). 'What Kind of Europeanized Public Politics?' iIn R. Koopmans and P. Statham (eds), *The Making of a European Public Sphere: Media Discourse and Political Contention* (Cambridge: Cambridge University Press), pp. 277–306.

Statham, P., and Trenz, H. J. (2012). *The Politicisation of Europe: Contesting the Constitution in the Mass Media* London: Routledge.

Statham, P., and Trenz, H. J. (2014). 'Understanding the Mechanisms of EU Politicization: Lessons from the Euro-zone crisis.' *Comparative European Politics*, early view: doi:10.1057/cep.2013.30.

Stoeckel, F. (2012). 'Ambivalent or indifferent?: Reconsidering the Structure of EU Public Opinion.' *European Union Politics*, 14(1): 23–45.

Streeck, W. (2014). *Buying Time: The Delayed Crisis of Democratic Capitalism*. London: Verso.

Streeck (2015) German Hegemony: Unintended and Unwanted, availabe at: http://wolfgangstreeck.com/2015/05/15/german-hegemony-unintended-and-unwanted/ (last accessed on Auust 17, 2015.

Swedberg, R. (1994). 'The idea of 'Europe' and the Origin of the European Union—a sociological approach.' *Zeitschrift für Soziologie*, 23(5): 378–387.

Szczerbiak, A., and Taggart, P. (2008). 'Theorizing Party-Based Euroscepticism: Problems of Definition, Measurement, and Causality.' In A. Szczerbiak and P. Taggart (eds), *Opposing Europe? The Comparative Party Politics of Euroscepticism, Volume 2: Comparative and Theoretical Perspectives* (Oxford: Oxford University Press), pp. 238–262.

Sztompka, P. (2000). 'The Ambivalence of Social Change: Triumph or Trauma?' *Papers // WZB, Wissenschaftszentrum Berlin für Sozialforschung, No. P 00–001* available at: http://hdl.handle.net/10419/50259 (last accessed September 3, 2015).

Tarta, A. (2014). *Social Media and the European Public Sphere*. PhD Thesis, Faculty of Humanities: University of Copenhagen.

Taylor, C. (1989). *Sources of the Self: The Making of the Modern Identity*. Cambridge: Cambridge University Press.

Te Brake, H., van de Post, M., and de Ruijter, A. (2008). 'Resilience from Concept to Practice—the Balance Between Awareness and Fear; Citizens and Resilience; Impact, Dutch Knowledge and Advice cCntre for Post-Disaster Psychosocial Care.' available at: http://www.impact-kenniscentrum.nl/download/file_1221486858.pdf (last accessed September 3, 2015).

Telò, M. (2007). *European Union and New Regionalism: Regional Actors and Global Governance in a Post-hegemonic Era*. Aldershot: Ashgate.

Thatcher, M. (2004). 'Winners and losers in Europeanisation: Reforming the national regulation of telecommunications.' *West European Politics* 27(2): 284–309.

Therborn, G. (1995). *European Modernity and Beyond: The Trajectory of European Societies 1945–2000*. London: Sage.

Tilly, C. (1990). *Coercion, Capital and European States, 990–1990*. London Sage.

Tönnies, F. (1988). *Community and Society*. New Brunswick: Transaction Publishers.

Topaloff, L. K. (2012). *Political Parties and Euroscepticism*. Basingstoke: Palgrave Macmillan.

Trenz, H. J. (2005a). *Europa in den Medien: Das Europäische Integrationsprojekt im Spiegel nationaler Öffentlichkeit*. Frankfurt a. M.; New York: Campus.

Trenz, H. J. (2005b). 'Öffentlichkeit und Zivilgesellschaft in der EU. Zwischen Organisation und spontaner Selbstkonstitution.' In M. Knodt and B. Finke (eds), *Europäische Zivilgesellschaft: Konzepte, Akteure, Strategien* (Wiesbaden: Verlag für Sozialwissenschaften), pp. 55–78.

Trenz, H. J. (2006a). '"Banaler Europäismus." Eine latente Kategorie der Europäisierung politischer Kommmunikation.' In W. R. Langenbucher and M. Latzer (eds), *Europäische Öffentlichkeit und medialer Wandel* (Wiesbaden: VS Verlag).

Trenz, H. J. (2006b). 'Europäische Öffentlichkeit als Selbstbeschreibungshorizont der europäischen Gesellschaft.' In R. Hettlage and H. P. Müller (eds), *Die Europäische Gesellschaft* (Konstanz: UVK), pp. 273–298.

Trenz, H. J. (2007a). "*Quo Vadis* Europe?' Quality Newspapers Struggling for European Unity.' In J. E. Fossum and P. Schlesinger (eds), *The European Union and the Public Sphere: A Communicative Space in the Making?* (Abingdon: Routledge), pp. 89–109.

Trenz, H. J. (2007b). 'A Transnational Space of Contention? Patterns of Europeanisation of Civil Society in Germany.' In V. dell sala and C. Ruzza (eds), *Governance and Civil Society in the European Union: Normative Perspectives* (Manchester: Manchester University Press), pp. 89–112.

Trenz, H. J. (2008). 'Measuring the Europeanisation of Public Communication.' *European Political Science*, 7(3): 273–284.

Trenz, H. J. (2010). 'In Search of the Popular Subject: Identity Formation, Constitution-making and the Democratic Consolidation of the EU.' *European Review* 18(1): 93–115.

Trenz, H. J. (2011). 'Social Theory and European Integration.' In A. Favell and V. Guiraudon (eds), *Sociology of the European Union* (Basingstoke: Palgrave Macmillan), pp. 193–214.

Trenz, H. J. (2013). 'New media dynamics and European Integration.' *Revista Científica de Información y Comunicación*, 10: 35–51.

Trenz, H. J. (2014). 'Mediated Representative Politics: The Euro-Crisis and the Politicization of the EU.' In S. Kröger (ed.), *Political Representation in the European Union: Still Democratic in Times of Crisis?* (London: Routledge), pp. 181–196.

Trenz, H. J., and Eder, K. (2004). 'The Democratizing Dynamics of a European Public Sphere: Towards a Theory of Democratic Functionalism.' *European Journal of Social Theory*, 7(1): 5–25.

Trenz, H. J., Menéndez, A. J., and Losada, F., (eds). (2009). *Y por fin somos Europeos?: La comunicación política en el debate constituyente Europeo*. Madrid: Dykinson.

Trenz, H. J., Ruzza, C., and Guiraudon, V. (eds). *Europe's Prolonged Crisis: The Making or the Unmaking of a Political Union*. Basingstoke: Palgrave Macmillan

Usherwood (2014). Euroscepticism as a lever: Contesting European integration with ulterior motives. Paper prepared for the workshop "Europe's social substrate," Arena, University of Oslo, 5–6.11.2014. available at: http://epubs.surrey.ac.uk/808607/1/Euroscepticism%20as%20a%20lever%20%28Usherwood%29.pdf last accessed November 18, 2015.

Usherwood, S., and Startin, N. (2013). 'Euroscepticism as a Persistent Phenomenon.' *Journal of Common Market Studies*, 51(1): 1–16.

Van Ingelgom, V. (2014). *Integrating Indifference: A Comparative, Qualitative and Quantitative Approach to the Legitimacy of European Integration*. Colchester: ECPR Press.

Vasilopoulou, S. (2013). 'Continuity and Change in the Study of Euroscepticism: Plus ça Change?' *Journal of Common Market Studies*, 5(1): 153–168.

Vetters, R., Jentgens, E., and Trenz, H. J. (2009). 'Whose Project is it?: Media Debates on the Ratification of the EU Constitutional Treaty.' *Journal of European Public Policy*, 16(3): 412–430.

Vink, M. (2003). 'What is Europeanization?: And Other Questions on a New Research Agenda.' *European Political Science Review*, 3(1): 63–74.

Vobruba, G. (2013). 'Gesellschaftsbildung in der Eurokrise.' *Serie Europa—Europe Series* 03(2013): availabe at: http://www.uni-leipzig.de/leus/wp-content/uploads/2013-2003-Vobruba-Gesellschaftsbildung-in-der-Eurokrise.pdf (last accessed September 3, 2015).

Vobruba, G. (2014). 'Währung und Konflikt. Ambivalenzen der Eurokrise.' *Serie Europa—Europe Series,* available at: http://www.uni-leipzig.de/leus/wp-content/uploads/2014-02-Vobruba-W%C3%A4hrung-und-Konflikt.pdf. (Last accessed on August 4, 2015).

Warner, M. (2002). *Publics and Counterpublics*. New York: Zone Books.

Weber, M. (1978). *Economy and Society: An Outline of Interpretive Sociology* [eds G. Roth and C. Wittich]. Berkeley, CA: University of California Press.

Weiler, J. H. H. (2003). *Un'Europa cristiana: Un saggio esplorativo*. Milano: Rizzoli.

Werts, H., Scheepers, P., and Lubbers, M. (2013). 'Euro-Scepticism and Radical Right-Wing Voting in Europe, 2002–2008: Social Cleavages, Socio-Political Attitudes and Contextual

Characteristics Determining Voting for the Radical Right.' *European Union Politics*, 14(2): 183–205.

White, J. (2010). 'Europe in the Political Imagination.' *Journal of Common Market Studies*, 48(4): 1015–1038.

Wiener, A. (1998). *European Citizenship Practice: Building Institutions of a Non-State*. Boulder: Westview.

Wiener, A., and Diez, T. (2003). *European Integration Theory*. Oxford: Oxford University Press.

Wimmer, A., and Glick Schiller, N. (2002). 'Methodological Nationalism and Beyond: Nation–State Building, Migration and the Social Sciences.' *Global Networks*, 2(4): 301–334.

Wodak, R., Mral, B., and KhosraviNik, M. (2013). *Right-Wing Populism in Europe: Politics and Discourse*. London: Bloomsbury Publishing.

Zielinska, K. (2011). 'Localising Secularisation Thesis?: The View from Poland.' *Religion and Society in Central and Eastern Europe*, 4(1): 79–91.

Zielonka, J. (2012). *Is the EU doomed?* Camnridge: Polity Press.

Zimmermann, A., and Favell, A. (2011). 'Governmentality, Political Field or Public Sphere?: Theoretical Alternatives in the Political Sociology of the EU.' *European Journal of Social Theory*, 14(4): 489–515.

Zürn, M. (1998). *Regieren jenseits des Nationalstaates*. Frankfurt a. M.: Suhrkamp.

Index

accountability, xv, 84, 104

acquis communautaire, 127

affirmation, xiv, xx, xxi, 3, 25, 28, 35, 56, 80, 82

affirmation of ordinary life, 56

Agamben, Giorgio, 140

agenda, broader European studies, 58

alternative Europe, 144

ambiguity, 154, 158n3

anomie, 86, 87, 87–88, 90

Anthropology of European Integration, 58

audiences, xviii–xix, xxiin3, 23–24, 26, 64–66, 101–102, 106, 142, 144, 157; European, 106

austerity, 70, 84, 119, 121–122, 125, 144, 150; anti-, 139, 141

autonomy, xv, xvi, 11, 18, 26, 50, 82, 83, 85, 131, 145

Bach, Maurizio, 29n10, 29n16

Balibar, Étienne, xiii

Bartolini, Stefano, 89

Bauman, Zygmunt, 44, 70

Beck, Ulrich, 39, 40–41, 42, 58–59, 66, 118

Belgium, 44

Billig, Michael, 57

Brunkhorst, Hauke, 53n12, 118

bureaucracy, 2, 3, 74, 76, 80, 84, 129

Calhoun, Craig, 44

capitalism, 9, 39, 47, 91–92, 118, 119, 121, 125, 127, 129, 141, 145, 157

Castoriadis, Cornelius, 23

Christian Democratic parties, 47

Christianity, xii, 45, 47, 48–49, 51

churches, 44–47, 51; Catholic and Protestant, 46

citizenry, 76n9, 91; deceived European, 107

citizens, vii, xiii, xv, xviii–xix, xxi, 2, 6, 8, 10, 14, 15, 17, 21, 23, 26–27, 33–36, 39, 40, 42–43, 45, 49, 50, 55–58, 58, 60–61, 66, 69, 70, 72, 74, 76, 76n9, 80, 86, 87, 90, 91, 92, 100, 101, 104–105, 107, 108, 110n4, 115, 119, 122, 124–125, 129, 131, 132, 133–136, 137, 138, 140, 141, 142, 143, 145, 146n11, 149, 150, 151, 155, 157, 158n4; groups of, xix, 72; ordinary, 26–27, 39, 66, 70, 80, 107, 122, 129, 134, 155; vulnerable, 136, 145. *See also* European citizens

citizenship, vii, xv, xviii, xxi, 6–7, 10, 16, 38, 42–43, 49, 52, 61–62, 70–71, 72–73, 76, 85, 98, 122, 132, 134, 135–136, 151; national, 49, 135–136

citizenship enactment, 72

citizenship rights. *See* rights

civic engagement, 89

civil society, 10, 29n12, 35, 39, 40, 41–43, 49, 53n7, 56, 100, 101, 102, 132, 134, 137–138, 141, 145, 146n16, 155,

158n4; new politics of, 132, 141. *See also* European civil society
civil society actors, 48, 56
civil society organizations, 39, 138, 146n16
civilization, xi, xiii, 32, 37, 46, 51; European, xi, 32
class, 15, 36, 44, 70–72, 73–74, 81, 87, 88, 90, 91, 94, 138–139, 141; social, 71, 87, 88
class politics, 138–139, 141
cognition, 58, 59, 64, 68, 99, 100, 106–107, 130
cognitive frames, 8, 98, 106, 108, 109
cognitive structures, 24, 97–98, 100, 129, 130, 155; Cold War xiv, 35, 123
collective action, 90, 119, 127–128, 135–136, 137
collective identities, 9, 19, 25, 40, 145
Collier, David, 98
common currency, 36, 60–61, 124, 125, 131, 150
common market, xviii–xix, 3, 6, 11, 14, 16, 19, 21, 24, 26, 55, 67, 70, 73, 122, 125, 129, 139, 140
communism, xiv–xv, 45, 46–47
conflicts, xiii, xv, xvi, 9, 17, 19, 69, 79, 80, 81, 84, 87, 95–96, 99–100, 126, 132, 138–139, 141, 145, 147n17, 151–152
constituencies, 17, 142, 158n6; national, 158n6
constitutional order, 59, 99
constitutional patriotism, 38, 48, 52, 53n16, 74
constitutional politics, 48, 53n12, 102
Constitutional Treaty, 23, 49, 62
constitutionalism, 37
constitutionalization, xiii, 16, 20, 38, 152, 154
constraining dissensus, 21, 81, 83, 83–84, 105–106, 154
contestation, xii, xiii, xv, xvi, xx, xxi, 7, 9, 12, 13, 23–24, 27–28, 37, 49, 80, 82, 85–86, 89, 92, 94, 95, 95–97, 98, 98–100, 101, 106, 108–109, 110n5–110n6, 110n10, 110n13, 115, 125, 129, 131, 132, 138, 142, 145, 151–152, 153, 154, 155; public, 13, 37, 49, 108, 138, 142, 145, 151

context, institutional, 134
conviviality, 39
coping practices, 135–136
cosmopolitan Europe, 27, 37–38, 42, 52
cosmopolitanism, 32, 38, 40–42, 43–44, 45, 47, 49, 51–52, 53n9, 58–59, 59, 66; methodological, 66
cosmopolitanization, 39, 40, 58, 59, 74
Cram, Laura, 28, 57, 60, 76n6
crisis, vii–viii, xx–xxi, xxi, 25, 27–28, 36, 69–70, 73, 76, 77n17, 82, 83–84, 85–86, 88, 90, 92, 104, 107, 108, 110, 110n3, 113–117, 118–132, 133–135, 136–139, 140–146, 146n4, 146n9–146n11, 146n15, 147n20–147n23, 150, 152, 153, 156, 157n1; consequences of, 114, 120, 125; context of, 28, 104, 133, 138, 140, 141; economic, 82, 130, 143; financial, 114, 121, 124; global, 132, 143; monetary, 83–84, 92, 107–108, 115, 117, 119; political sociology of crisis. *See* political sociology of crisis; post-, 115, 156; symptoms of, 116, 118; system, 128, 129, 130
crisis governance, 83–84, 114, 116, 120, 125, 131, 137–138, 139, 140, 143, 150
crisis-induced societal learning, 128

de Gaulle, Charles, 34
De Wilde, Pieter, 28, 30n23, 110n7, 110n9–110n10, 111n15
Delanty, Gerard, 40, 41
Delhey, Jan, 67–68
democracy, xv, xvi, xxiin3, 9, 10–11, 28, 30n22, 33, 34–36, 37–39, 41, 42, 43, 45, 51–52, 53n9, 57, 59, 70, 76, 81, 92, 93, 96, 97, 98, 99–100, 103, 106–107, 118, 123–124, 129, 131, 137–138, 139, 140–141, 145, 150, 153, 157, 158n6
democratic deficit, xv, 31, 35, 37, 43, 84, 100, 104, 114, 123–124
democratic deficit of the European Union, 31, 123
democratization, xix, 35–36, 38, 85, 98–99, 105, 108, 115, 123–124, 151, 152
demoi-cracy, 157, 158n6

demos, 38, 43, 48, 92, 157; European, 43, 48, 92
denationalization, 36, 74
Denmark, 21, 61, 70, 73, 77n17
destiny, xvi–xvii, 4, 53, 57, 70, 114, 117, 124, 146, 150
destruction, 85, 120, 126, 128, 140
Deutsch, Karl, 67
Díez Medrano, Juan, 133
differentiated integration, 122
differentiation, xix, 1–2, 3, 5, 7, 13, 18, 19, 23, 41, 52, 67, 126, 152
discourse-analytical approaches, 22
disintegration, 12, 18, 38, 117, 122, 125–126, 127–128, 146n8, 156
diversity, xii–xiv, xvi, xviii, xxi, 1, 2, 3, 5, 8, 11, 12–13, 17, 18, 19, 23, 24, 39–40, 40–41, 47, 50, 61, 63, 149–151; European, 11, 13
Douglas, Mary, 133
drama, xix–xx, 20, 21, 22, 55, 64, 79–80, 81, 82, 85, 102, 113, 116–117, 118–119, 123, 141, 146, 158n5
drama of Europeanization, xix, 116, 119
dramatization, 20, 113
Durkheim, Emile, 3, 4–5, 14, 41. *See also* Durkheimian
Durkheimian, 5, 20, 40, 67, 86–87, 87, 107, 133
Dutceac Segesten, Anamaria, 61

Easton, David, 86, 87, 98, 108
ECB. *See* European Central Bank (ECB)
Eder, Klaus, 128
education, xvi, 6, 15, 28n3, 34–35, 45, 51, 62, 70–71, 72–74, 87, 88, 89, 97
EFSF. *See* European Financial Stability Facility (EFSF)
égaliberté, xiii, xiv–xv, 37, 120
elites, 25, 26, 34, 35, 37, 64, 73–74, 76, 80, 91, 93, 100, 107, 117–118, 121, 122, 134, 139, 142–143, 144, 145
emancipation, 80, 85, 86, 90, 91, 118, 151
Enlightenment, xii, 32, 37, 47, 50, 51, 89, 109, 118, 120; anti-, 52; counter-, 80
entry, 76, 135
EPP. *See* European Peoples' Party (EPP)
equal living conditions, xv, 73, 76, 79, 94, 110, 121, 140

Eriksen, Erik Odvar, ix, 30n22, 42, 53n5, 53n12, 110n11
Erlander, Tage, 45
ESA. *See* European Sociological Association (ESA)
ESF. *See* European Science Foundation (ESF)
ESM. *See* European Stability Mechanism
EU citizens. *See* European citizens
EU citizenship, vii, xxi, 43, 52, 61, 72–73, 76, 122, 132, 134, 135–136
EU governance, 29n7, 53n7, 81, 84, 85, 103, 104, 108, 110n3, 110n11, 114, 116, 117, 125, 131, 143, 158n6
EU politicization. *See* politicization
EU polity contestation, 86, 92, 94, 95, 95–96, 97, 98, 99, 101, 106, 109, 110n10, 125, 145
EU studies community, viii, 29n7, 33, 116, 118, 127
Euroclash, 89, 141
Europe of equal living conditions, 73, 121
Europe of free movement, 70, 133, 136
Europe of nation-states, xiii–xiv, 99
European Audiovisual Policies, 24
European Central Bank (ECB), 107, 114, 121, 131, 139, 143, 150
European cinema, 64
European citizens, vii, xxi, 16, 21, 26, 35, 39, 43, 45, 50, 57, 58, 69, 87, 108, 134, 137, 145
European civil society, 10, 35, 39, 138, 146n16
European Commission, 30n23, 39, 46, 64, 89, 103, 114, 131, 132, 143, 157n2
European communities, 5, 14, 33, 37, 55
European constitution, 36, 38, 44, 47–48
European film production, 24
European Financial Stability Facility (EFSF), 121
European identity, vii, xxi, 21, 34, 47, 49, 51–52, 57, 60–61, 64, 76n5, 108
European integration, vii–ix, x, xiii–xv, xvi–xvii, xviii, xxi, 1, 2–3, 4, 5–7, 9, 11–12, 12–13, 14–18, 21–22, 23–25, 27, 28n1, 29n6–29n7, 29n9–29n10, 31–32, 33–34, 36, 37, 39, 43, 44–45, 47, 48, 50–51, 53n1, 55–58, 61, 62, 67, 70, 73, 74, 76, 76n10, 79, 80, 81,

82–84, 85, 86, 87–88, 89–90, 91, 92, 94, 95, 96, 99–100, 101, 105, 107, 109, 113–114, 115, 116–120, 123–124, 127–128, 138, 149, 150, 151–152, 153–155, 156–157, 158n4; attitudinal research on, 87; authoritative account of, 24, 31; beneficiaries of, 90; constrained, 83; narrations of, 61–62; progressive, 128; promoters of, 33, 44, 89; protagonists of, viii, xvi, 12, 31, 33; sociology of, vii, ix, xxi, 7, 9, 14, 16, 24–25, 29n10, 67, 100, 151, 156; success story of, 37, 80, 113

European integration project, xiv–xv, 6–7, 29n7, 34, 43, 50, 58, 118, 123, 127, 151, 153

European Parliament, 28, 48, 64, 66, 104, 105, 111n17, 139

European Peoples' Party (EPP), 48

European political society, xiii, 7, 8, 15

European political space, 89, 127

European public sphere. *See* public sphere

European Science Foundation (ESF), 30n22, 158n3

European social model, 6, 11

European social space, 68, 69, 72, 73, 74, 79, 110, 136

European society, vii, viii–ix, x, xvi, xviii–xx, xx, xxi, 1–3, 4, 4–6, 6–13, 15–17, 18, 23–24, 26, 27, 28n2, 29n11, 67, 74, 110, 126, 134, 149, 151, 153, 155, 156; accounts of, 13, 153; early modern, 2; emerging, xx, 15, 18; enlightened, 151; modern, 2, 10; narration of, xviii, 24, 155

European society-building. *See* society-building

European Sociological Association (ESA), viii–ix, 2, 28

European Stability Mechanism (ESM), 121

European Studies, vii, viii–ix, 13, 19, 24, 58, 150, 153, 157n2–158n3

European Studies community, vii, viii, xvi, xvii, 1, 22, 53n3, 117, 149, 152, 153

European Studies scholars, 24, 33, 69, 120

European unification, xiii, xiv–xv, xvi–xvii, 2, 13, 37, 45

Europeanism, vii, xx, xxi, 21, 25, 28, 34, 39, 51, 57–58, 64, 64–65, 67, 70,

74–75, 76n6, 93, 96, 135, 153; banal, vii, xx, xxi, 21, 25, 28, 39, 57–58, 64, 64–65, 67, 74–75, 76n6, 135, 153; progressive, 93; triumphant, xx, 25, 34, 51, 96

Europeanization: account of, xvi, 14, 31, 81, 87, 93, 109–110, 117, 118, 139, 149, 152; as adaptation, 76; as cosmopolitanization, 40–44; banal, 55, 58, 59, 60–62, 69, 109, 134; bottom-up, 58–59, 132, 134; crisis of, 36, 113–117, 118; discursive field of, viii, xviii, xx, 15, 37, 149, 152–153, 154; enhanced, 37, 114; everyday, 27, 58, 59, 66, 74, 75, 110; failed, 114, 117, 153; horizontal, 29n15, 58, 71; institutional perspective, viii, 20; narratives of, 24–26; natural history of, 150; political science approach to, 1–2; processes of, vii, xv, xxi, 11, 19–21, 38; progressive, 31–37, 50, 51, 85, 91, 120, 151; relative, 68, 69; resistance to. *See* resistance; saga of, 25, 31, 57, 80, 82, 95, 109, 117, 149–150; scientific account of, xviii, 22–23, 27, 149–150; society perspective of, viii, 13, 18; socio-geographic map of, 72, 73; sociological account of, 149, 152; sociology of, 8, 11–12, 14, 23, 29n9, 29n13, 29n15, 37, 156; subjective, 69, 70; success story of, 80–81; tales of, xvi, xvii–xxi, 2, 23–24, 50, 74, 80, 107, 109, 139, 152, 157; triumphant, 37, 59; vertical, 14, 20–21

Europeans: new generation of, 45, 47; ordinary, 32, 70; young, 45, 110n4, 141

Eurovision Song Contest, 63, 64

everyday life, xx–xxi, 20, 25, 28, 58–61, 66, 70, 74, 82, 118, 150, 151

exclusion, xii, 34, 45, 52, 94, 127, 135

experts, 17, 83, 84, 131, 138, 139, 140, 142

Facebook, 66, 111n17

Favell, Adrian, 29n9, 44, 70, 71, 73, 77n15, 77n18

federation, 5–6

Ferguson, Niall, 35, 53n4

finalité, xi, 7, 36–37

Finlayson, Alan, xix

Fligstein, Neil, 73, 89
Fossum, John Erik, ix, 30n22, 42, 53n5,
    53n12, 110n11, 115
France, xiv, 32, 45, 48–49, 64, 71, 131,
    142, 144, 147n23
free movement, xviii, 6, 11, 44, 66, 70,
    72–73, 75–76, 90, 122, 133–134,
    135–136
French referendum debate, 49
French Revolution, xii–xiii, xv, 32, 37, 45,
    49

Gaus, Daniel, 158n6
Gemeinschaft, 3, 13. *See also*
    Vergemeinschaftung
gender, 71, 72, 73, 138
German unification, 35
Germany, xiv, 21, 29n15, 32, 34, 44, 45,
    49, 64, 73, 111n15, 121, 132, 139–140,
    142, 144, 147n23, 158n5
Gesellschaft, 3, 13. *See also*
    Vergesellschaftung
global justice, 28, 35, 38–40, 43, 141
Goetz, Klaus, 22
Grande, Edgar, 39, 41
Greece, 132, 142–143, 144, 146n4,
    147n23, 150, 158n5
Gripsrud, Jostein, 64
Guiraudon, Virginie, ix, 28, 29n9, 29n13,
    157n1

Haas, Ernst, 4, 5, 34
Habermas, Jürgen, xxiin1, xxiin3, 38, 48,
    110n3, 118, 130, 158n4–158n6
Hegemony, 91–92, 140, 142–143, 156
high culture, 24–25, 57
historical sociology. *See* sociology
historiography, 9, 33, 58
Hix, Simon, 22, 110n5
Holocaust, 82
Hooghe, Lisbeth, 29n8, 110n2, 110n5,
    110n7
human rights. *See* rights

identity politics, 21, 81, 83, 84, 89,
    138–139, 144, 151; new, 21, 81, 83,
    151
ideologies, 94, 108, 130, 133

IGC. *See* Intergovernmental Conferences
    (IGC)
imagination, xiii–xiv, xix, 2, 9, 23, 40, 61,
    74, 125, 126, 150, 155; narratives as
    collective. *See* narratives; social, xiv,
    xviii, 22, 23, 74, 126, 127, 149
IMF. *See* International Monetary Fund
    (IMF)
inclusion, xii, xiv, 39, 52, 117, 135
Indignados, 141
institution-building, 15, 128, 138, 150,
    155–156
institutionalization, xiii, 20, 55–56, 66,
    68–69, 127, 151
institutions: reflexive, 40; supplementary,
    128; supranational, 5–6
integration: functional, 85, 109, 124;
    horizontal, 20–21; political, 4, 11, 67,
    117; positive, 17; social, xviii, 1–2,
    3–4, 4, 5–6, 7, 12, 14, 31, 67, 70, 117,
    127, 130, 153, 158n4; system, 3;
    vertical, 20
integration paradigm, 115, 118, 124–125
Intergovernmental Conferences (IGC), 48
International Monetary Fund (IMF), 107,
    114, 131, 139, 143
International Relations, 6
Islam, xii, 51, 81
Italy, 44, 61, 64, 88, 95, 132, 141, 144

journalism, 28, 101–103, 105, 110n12,
    143–144
justification, xviii, 15, 23, 31, 43, 57, 82,
    84, 94, 95, 97, 99, 101

Kohl, Helmut, 45
Kriesi, Hanspeter, 90

Latin Europe, 140
legitimacy: crisis of, 131, 141; democratic,
    108, 125, 129, 139, 141; input, 6, 29n7;
    output, 6, 29n7, 86, 124, 130; political,
    86, 100, 101, 102, 106, 108, 153
legitimacy contestations, 95, 99, 129, 131
legitimation, 6, 16, 29n7, 42, 43, 93, 94,
    95, 96–98, 99, 106, 124, 130, 138, 142,
    153, 157. *See also* legitimation crisis
    and legitimation practices

legitimation crisis, vii, xxi, 85, 110n3, 113, 127–129, 130, 134, 141
legitimation practices, 97, 99
Lisbon strategy, 122
Luhmann, Niklas, xv

Maastricht Treaty, xv
Majone, Giandomenico, 29n7, 117
Mann, Michael, 9
Manners, Ian, 62
market Europe, 19, 35, 75, 120, 125, 134
market integration, 34, 115, 117, 131, 139
Marks, Gary, 29n8, 30n18, 76n1, 76n4, 110n2, 110n7
mass media, 96, 97, 100–101, 106, 142–143, 145
mass politics, 83, 89
Mau, Steffen, 29n9, 29n15, 71, 77n15, 77n18
media discourse, 43, 64, 94, 106, 143, 144
media frames, 106
media narratives. *See* narratives
media negativity bias, 96, 101, 102–103, 104, 105, 106–107. *See also* negativity
media spheres, 141, 142
Michailidou, Asimina, ix, 28, 30n23, 76n9, 147n20–147n23
Milward, Alan, 28n4, 32
mobility, 11, 18, 20, 66, 70–71, 72–74, 77n18, 134, 138, 151; intra-EU, 70, 77n18
modern society, xii, xv, 1, 3, 5, 14, 22, 87, 146n9
modernity, xiii, xiv, 13, 19, 38, 40, 41, 42, 46–47, 80, 152; European, xii, xiv, 12–13, 31, 37, 38, 40, 46, 51, 80–81, 123, 152
modernization, 19, 42, 71, 87, 122; reflexive, 38, 42
Monnet, Jean, 3, 4, 28n4, 33; Monnet Programme, 33
Morgan, Glyn, 94, 99
Mylonas, Yiannis, 143

narrations, xv–xvi; carriers of, xix, 24, 154; function of, xviii–xx, 155
narrations of European integration. *See* European integration

narratives: identity, 59; intellectual, xviii; media, 27; national, xx
narratives as collective imaginations, xviii
Nassehi, Armin, 41
national identity, 34, 49, 51, 56, 59, 83, 88, 89, 142
national societies, xviii, 1–2, 3, 4, 7–8, 15, 17, 18, 41, 153
nationalism, 7–8, 17, 32, 33–34, 41–42, 53n10, 57, 59, 74–75, 80, 82, 94, 110n8; European nationalism, xvii, 5. *See also* supranationalism
negativity, 96, 101, 102, 104, 116, 118. *See also* media negativity bias
neofunctionalism, 4, 6
Netherlands, 45, 88, 142, 147n23
networks, 10, 21, 39, 61, 67, 70, 74, 76n1; research, viii–ix, 28; docial, 9, 12, 20, 26, 65, 70, 133, 136; transnational, 56, 59, 66
network funds, 60
normative power, 123
normativity, viii, 11–12, 130, 151, 152, 153
normlessness, 87–88
North-South divide, 73, 145
Northern Europe/European, 142

Occupy movement, 141
Offe, Claus, 8, 10, 146n5
Olsen, Johan P., ix, 19, 21
O'Mahony, Patrick, 59, 158n4
online media, 94, 106
online media sphere, 144
online media survey, 28, 147n20
ordinary European life histories, 58
Örnebring, Henrik, 102
Outhwaite, William, 10

paradigm loss, 121, 126, 127
paradigm shift, 116, 120
Parsons, Talcott, 4, 5
participation, 6, 16, 39, 61, 69, 70, 91, 102, 124, 129, 135–136, 141
peace, xvii, 32, 33, 36, 45–47, 51, 55, 94, 114, 122–123, 153
permissive consensus, 21, 57, 81, 83, 89, 110n2, 154
Poland, 45, 47

Polanyi, Karl, xxi
political economy approaches to European integration, 79, 90
political parties, 43, 51, 56, 83, 86, 89–90, 99, 101, 104, 105, 132, 140–141, 145, 157
political rights. *See* rights
political society. *See* European political society
political sociology, viii–ix, 11, 14, 15, 28, 29n9, 29n16, 127
political sociology of crisis, vii, xxi, 28, 157n1
political sociology of Europeanization/ European integration, 11, 12, 14, 29n10, 29n13, 151
political space, viii, xiii, xx, 19, 89, 127, 129
politicization, 21, 29n8, 61, 75, 81, 83–84, 89, 115, 138, 143, 144, 151; de-, 41, 76, 92, 115, 137; EU, 137, 138–139; re-, 63, 66, 92, 125, 128, 129, 137, 138, 139, 144
politics,: agonistic, 91, 92; displacement of, 115, 131
polity contestation. *See* EU polity contestation
polity legitimacy. *See* legitimacy
popular culture, 63, 150
popular sovereignty, 45, 81, 95–96, 98, 109, 145
populism, 81, 90, 93–94, 106, 110n8, 139, 140, 144, 145
Portugal, 45, 144
post-crisis. *See* crisis
public opinion, 83–84, 87, 101, 102, 104–105, 105, 122, 141, 154–155
public sphere, 19, 30n20, 128, 130, 153, 156, 158n4; European, 26, 30n20
publicity, 104, 106, 143, 144

reconciliation, 45, 51, 94
redistribution, xv, 74, 138, 140–141, 145, 146n5
referendum, 64, 117. *See also* French referendum debate
reflexivity, 41; higher, 38, 40–41
regionalism, xiv
regionalization, xiv

religion, 40, 45, 47, 50, 51, 63
representation, xiii, 13, 30n22, 56, 62, 93–94, 102, 103, 106, 108, 115, 124, 130, 131, 136, 139, 146
resilience, 129, 132–137, 146n11–146n12, 146n14, 151; citizens', 129, 132, 134, 136, 146n11; social, 27–28, 132–133, 137
resistance, vii, viii, xxi, 28, 47, 59, 61, 63, 64, 70, 81, 83, 86, 90, 91, 94, 107, 109, 110, 118, 119, 129, 132, 136–137, 141, 151; European/Europeanization, 25, 61, 76, 79, 80, 83, 88, 90, 93–94, 107, 109, 110, 118, 119, 129, 136–137, 138, 139–140, 141, 144, 151, 152; Popular, 63–64, 90–92
resources, 132, 134, 135
responsibilities, 143, 145, 146n14
rights, xiii, xv, xviii, xxi, 6–7, 13, 17, 26, 34, 38–39, 41–43, 53, 53n9, 55, 59, 60, 61, 69, 70, 72–73, 76, 85, 92, 95, 98, 122, 124, 129, 132, 133–134, 135–136, 137, 138, 145, 152; citizenship, 38, 136; constitutional, 53, 124; human, 39, 41–42, 53n9, 59; political rights, 76, 135–136, 138; social, xiii, 6, 73, 136; transnational, xv, 135–136; universal, 43, 98
risk, xxi, 74, 104, 116, 127, 131, 133, 146n14
Risse, Thomas, 30n21, 53n6, 76n2–76n3, 110n2, 146n2, 146n15, 147n17
Rokkan, Stein, 89. *See also* Rokkanian
Rokkanian, 86, 89, 107
Roman Empire, xii
Rumford, Chris, 10, 29n16, 41, 76n5
Russia, 123
Ruzza, Carlo, ix, 28, 29n12, 39, 53n7–53n8

saga. *See* saga of Europeanization
Scalise, Gemma, 61
Schuman, Robert, 3, 28n3, 33, 53n10
secularization, 45, 47
security, 6, 33, 114, 115, 123, 131, 153
semantics, 152
Simmel, Georg, 12, 14
Single European Act, 6
social bonds, xvii–xviii, xx, 25

social cohesion, 17, 19, 87, 121–122, 134, 136
social evolution, 126, 128, 132
social integration. *See* integration
social media, 26, 28, 65–66, 71, 106, 111n17, 142, 144
social order, 4, 11, 13, 17, 18, 40
social relationships, 5, 13–14, 15–16, 71, 74, 127, 129, 132, 133, 151
social resilience. *See* resilience
social rights. *See* rights
social security. *See* security
social transnationalism. *See* transnationalism
socialization (of European Citizens), xi, xvi, xxi, 11, 15, 20–21, 26, 34–35, 45, 55, 57, 66, 67, 102, 108
societal change, 4, 19, 137, 154, 156
societal self-organization, 10, 128
societal transformation, 59, 126
society: European. *See* European society: good, 6, 12; national container, 15; theory of, xxi, 7, 9, 13, 17, 29n10; world, xviii, 8, 39, 41
society-building, xviii, xx, 126, 128, 132, 134, 145, 150, 151, 152, 153
sociology: historical, 9, 10, 27, 156; interpretative, 12, 155, 156; political. *See* political sociology
sociology of European integration. *See* European integration
sociology of knowledge, 22, 31, 158n4
solidarity, 8, 10, 11–12, 16, 17, 17–18, 29n7, 40, 45, 46, 47, 50, 66, 74, 107, 128, 132, 136, 137, 140, 145; European, 11–12, 29n7, 40, 43, 47, 50, 73, 107, 110n4, 122, 128–129, 132, 136, 140, 145, 146n5, 156; mechanical, 2, 3, 5; organic, 2, 3, 5, 40–41
Southern Europe/European, 77n17, 131, 142
Spain, 45, 64, 95, 141, 144, 147n23
Stability Pact, 145
Sweden, 21, 61, 147n23
support,: diffuse, 86, 87, 108, 141; public, 84
supranationalism, xiv, 36, 47. *See also* nationalism
symbolic space, 26–27

symbolic taboos, 62

Taylor, Charles, 28, 56
technocracy, 84, 93, 114, 139
transition, xii, 5, 6, 41, 42, 55, 79, 156
transnational practices, 61, 66, 68, 70, 71, 74
transnational rights. *See* rights
transnationalism, 25, 40, 59, 66, 69, 70, 73; everyday, 66, 70; social, vii, xxi, 21, 25, 27–28, 39, 44, 46, 59, 66, 67, 68, 69, 71, 77n15, 146n13
transnationalization, 74, 75, 95
trauma, viii, xvii, xx, xxi, 22, 25, 27, 32, 79, 81–82, 118–120, 128, 130
triumph: of Europe, xx–xxi, 3, 31–37, 50, 51, 79–80
Troika, 9, 114, 125, 131, 139, 143, 143–144
Turkey, 47, 64

UK (United Kingdom), 64, 70, 73, 88, 95, 111n15, 122, 131, 147n23
unification, xii, xiii, xiv–xv, xvi–xvii, 1, 2–3, 5, 13, 19, 23, 33, 35, 36–37, 45, 50
unity, xii, xiii, xvi, xviii, xxiin2, 3, 13, 18, 38, 63, 149, 152; cultural, xii; political, xii, xiv, xv; societal, xiv, xv, 3; spiritual, xii, xiii
unity in diversity, xii, xiii, xiv, xvi, xviii, 2, 5, 8, 11, 12, 18, 19, 23, 24, 40, 50, 63, 151
unity in diversity of Europe, xvi, 11, 19, 23, 24, 149, 151
unity of Europe, xv, xviii, xxi, 2, 4, 18, 36, 40, 149
unity of society, xv–xvi, 5, 12
universalism, 32, 47, 51, 53n9; European, 47, 50–52
United States of America, xiii, 123

Vergemeinschaftung, 13–14, 29n14. *See also* Gemeinschaft
Vergesellschaftung, 11, 13–14, 29n14. *See also* Gesellschaft
Verwiebe, Roland, 29n15, 71
Vobruba, Georg, 139, 146n9
vulnerability, 72, 119, 133

Weber, Max, 13–14, 16, 29n14. *See also* Weberian
Weberian, 3, 28n3, 125, 133
Weiler, Joseph, 50, 53n15
Western democracies, 36, 108
Western Europe, 33, 45, 47, 123
Western Germany, 44
Western societies, 32, 45
Wildavsky, Aaron, 133
White, Jonathan, 61
world of nation-states, 59, 66